Eyes deep with unfathomable histories

Studies in Literature in English

Edited by Liliana Sikorska

Assistant to the editor:
Marta Frątczak

Editorial Board

This is a publication
of the University of Social Sciences (Warsaw)

Volume 4

PETER LANG

Frankfurt am Main · Berlin · Bern · Bruxelles · New York · Oxford · Warszawa · Wien

Liliana Sikorska / Agnieszka Rzepa (eds.)

Eyes deep with unfathomable histories

The Poetics and Politics
of Magic Realism Today and in the Past

PETER LANG
Internationaler Verlag der Wissenschaften

Bibliographic Information published by the Deutsche Nationalbibliothek
The Deutsche Nationalbibliothek lists this publication in the Deutsche Nationalbibliografie; detailed bibliographic data is available in the internet at http://dnb.d-nb.de.

This Publication was financially supported
by the University of Social Sciences.

UNIVERSITY OF SOCIAL SCIENCES
WARSAW

Cover Design:
© Olaf Glöckler, Atelier Platen, Friedberg

ISSN 1868-906X
ISBN 978-3-631-60786-2

© Peter Lang GmbH
Internationaler Verlag der Wissenschaften
Frankfurt am Main 2012
All rights reserved.

www.peterlang.de

Contents

Editorial

Studies in Literature in English (SILIE) is a series published by Peter Lang Verlag which focuses on literature in English.

Literature in English is a relatively new term coined recently to include both English literature in the traditional sense of the word and all the newly emerging literatures written and published in English whose authors may represent various ethnic and cultural backgrounds. New books and journals devoted specifically to this area and other related areas of research have begun to appear and regular annual or bi-annual conferences have also been launched. This series, as well as our yearly Literature in English Symposium (LIES) respond to this growing interest, the latter is organized by the Department of English Literature and Literary Linguistics, at the School of English, Adam Mickiewicz University, Poznań, Poland. Each year the symposium hosts an eminent contemporary writer and an eminent contemporary scholar; the topic of the conference is based on the presenter's literary interests. In previous years our guest speakers included Leland Bardwell, Lindsay Clarke, Anthony Cronin, Paul Durcan, Anne Haverty, Kevin Lavin, Andrew Miller, Adam Thorpe and David Dabydeen, while our plenary speakers included Prof. Leszek Drong, Prof. Sabine Heinz, Prof. Jerzy Jarniewicz, Prof. Wiesław Krajka and Prof. Jerzy Limon, among others.

This year's *Studies in Literature in English* contains selected papers delivered at LIES 2011, as well as papers written by scholars interested in the topic. Like the previous volumes, its title carries a quotation from a literary text, this one reads: "Eyes deep with unfathomable histories. The poetics and politics of magic realism today and in the past". The first part of the title is taken from the poem by Pauline Melville entitled "Homeland".[1] The present volume of papers, unlike all earlier ones was inspired by two areas: the first one was the writings of Pauline Melville, a British novelist, a poet and an actress with Wapisiana (South American Indian) ancestry, and the second by Canadian magic realism. Consequently, the two areas have two editors, with Prof. Agnieszka Rzepa acting as our guest editor responsible for the North American (predominantly Canadian) part of the articles. Since the present volume is the fourth one in the series, we decided to maintain the usual organization and offer a short introduction to the work of our guest of honour Pauline Melville at the beginning and an interview with her friend and colleague, David Dabydeen at the end.

The two contributions provide a frame for a series of articles devoted to North American, primarily Canadian, magic realism. After blooming spectacularly in the English-Canadian literary scene of the late 1970s, magic

---

1 Melville, Pauline. 2001. "Homeland", in: Dabydeen, David (ed.). 2001. *Rented rooms.* Coventry: Dangaroo Press, 47-44.

realism was declared by Geoff Hancock to be a quintessentially Canadian genre,[2] and—later—described as a "sub-genre" of Canadian literature by Jennifer Andrews[3]. While the literary mode has flourished in a variety of literatures all around the world, it has been indeed amply represented in English-Canadian prose throughout the last forty years or so. As the mode lends itself flexibly to a variety of uses, it has been employed by writers working in different genres, and for a variety of purposes. A far-ranging review of different manifestations of the mode in Canadian literature in English is provided for the reader of the present volume by Jeanne Delbaere-Garant. In her article, the eminent critic foregrounds the "third space" hinted at, or created, by authors of many magic realist texts. Her remark that many critics would be happy to discard magic realism as too diffuse a generic label, and her defense of magic realism as "a strategy to break the polarizations of oppression and more generally to serve as an antidote against an excessive domination of the mind", introduce a theme related to critical approaches to magic realism, which reappears—albeit often tangentially—in the articles that follow.

The term "magic realism" has quite often been perceived as burdened with a post-enlightenment and Eurocentric bias, and in effect as one that promotes the exoticisation of non-European (in particular indigenous) subjects and cultures. Therefore, its use in relation to texts by non-white writers, in Canada and beyond, has often been questioned. Hartmut Lutz starts his discussion on "(post-)modern adaptations of the Icelandic 'Vinland' Sagas of North American discovery" in texts by Joan Clark and two aboriginal authors—Bernard Assiniwi and Rachel A. Quitsualik—by voicing his unease with the term for exactly that reason. Ewa Bodal, on the other hand, after comparing the use of elements of Native Canadian beliefs and mythologies as a source of magic in texts by Native and white Canadian authors, concludes her article with a reflection on the acts of cultural appropriation that the white authors might be seen as committing in their texts. Her article is followed by Alanna F. Bondar's re-examination of one of the foundation texts of Canadian magic realism—Robert Kroetsch's *What the crow said*—from a fresh, ecological perspective. Bondar expresses, among others, an optimistic view that "the incorporation of magic realism with aboriginal philosophies and Indigenous 'ways of knowing' provides opportunity for genuine understandings of the complex and oftentimes contentious Native and non-Native political and social dynamic". Specificities of Canadian postcoloniality she points

---

2   Cf. Hancock, Geoff. 1980. "Magic realism", in: Geoff Hancock (ed.). *Magic realism: An anthology*. Toronto: Aya Press, 7-15; and Hancock, Geoff. 1986. "Magic or realism: The marvellous in Canadian fiction", in: Peter Hinchcliffe – Ed Jewinski (eds.). *Magic realism and Canadian literature: Essays and stories*. Ontario: University of Waterloo Press, 30-48.

3   Andrews, Jennifer. 1999. "Rethinking the relevance of magic realism for English-Canadian literature: Reading Ann-Marie Macdonald's *Fall on your knees*", *Studies in Canadian Literature/Études en littérature canadienne* 24, 1: 7.

to, and in particular the impossible desire of the settler to become an indigene, are also pivotal for Agnieszka Rzepa's discussion of the alliance of the utopian and magic realist discourses in Margaret Sweatman's *When Alice lay down with Peter*. The intricacies of the Canadian nation-making project, central to her discussion, are also tangentially present in Nelly Strehlau's contribution, the primary focus of which is the subversive potential of the mode of magic realism, which in the novels she discusses promotes the empowerment of marginalised female subjects. Dagmara Drewniak and Monika Włudzik, in their discussions of aspects of magic realism in novels by Lilian Nattel and Rawi Hage respectively, leave behind the Canadian context to focus on a Jewish shetl and war-torn Lebanon. Finally, Jacob Juntunen examines manifestations of magic realism in the 20th century drama of the United States. We hope that the present volume will prove a valuable contribution to the study of magic realism in literatures in English.

In closing, the editors of the volume would like to take this opportunity to express their profound gratitude to Professor Katarzyna Dziubalska-Kołaczyk, Head of the School of English, Adam Mickiewicz University, as of September 1, 2012, Dean of the Faculty of English, Adam Mickiewicz University; and to Dr Zdzisław Szymański, Dean of the Warsaw Faculty of the Academy of Management. Our words of thanks are also to Dr Katarzyna Bronk, Joanna Jarząb and Marta Frątczak, whose efforts in correcting all the little details of the manuscript are highly appreciated, and to Krystyna Potoczna for her contribution to the organisation of the 2012 LIES. Last but not least, we would like to thank our husbands and friends, Professor Jacek Fisiak and Professor Robert Lew for their unfailing support in the venture.

Liliana Sikorska and Agnieszka Rzepa
Poznań, March 2012

Pauline Melville's marvels of reality

Liliana Sikorska, Adam Mickiewicz University, Poznań / University of Social Sciences, Warsaw

Born in Guyana of an English mother and Guyanese (part South American Indian, African and Scottish) father, Pauline Melville now lives in London but travels all over the world, and frequently to faraway parts with no Internet connection. Writing, as she herself says, gives her an opportunity to understand her mixed parentage, especially her father's side. In her fiction, her English as well as her Guyanese heritage is of paramount importance. In "Mixed" she wrote: "Sometimes, I think/My mother with her blue eyes/And flowered apron/Was exasperated/At having such a sallow child/And my mulatto dadee/Silenced/By having such an English-looking one" (2001: 45).[1] Her Guyanese Indian legacy proved to be the most ample resource of stories, in which the magical and the real come into contact. In contemporary critical works, she is most frequently praised for her innovative use of "lo realismo maravilloso".

No wonder her texts are often evoked in connection with magic realism theory. In a recent work on magic(al) realism, Mary Ann Bower notes that "...Pauline Melville, has written three very different fictional works using the same [as Wilson Harris] magical realist techniques. Her first novel *The ventriloquist's tale* (1997 [1998]) is based in the same geographical terrain of the Caribbean coast as Garcia Marquez, this time in Guyana, where she was born, rather than Colombia, and has the same exuberant narrative and richness of detail" (Bowers 2005. 60). *The ventriloquist's tale* is a text that highlights Guyana's multi-cultural and multi-lingual traditions.[2] Melville is very conscious of the Eurocentric ways of "reading Guyana". She disagrees with the common European claim that Walter Raleigh (c.1552-1618), while looking for El Dorado (1595), discovered the country which was to become British Guiana. She constantly makes us aware that works such as Walter Edmund Roth's (1861-1933) *An inquiry into the animism and folk-lore of the Guiana Indians* (1915) or Evelyn Waugh's (1903-1966) *Ninety-two days* (1932) do not give justice to the land and its people. Writing from the perspective of Wapisiana Indians, Melville is able to circumvent European traditions of the representation of Native Americans. Waugh's Rupununi Savannah is full of flies and heat, has no roads and is a hell to

---

1   The poem is taken from a collection edited by David Dabydeen (2001).
2   Melville uses some of her family history in the novel. Her predecessor, Mr. Melville is still quite a famous figure in Guiana, the family was mentioned by Waugh and perhaps more surprisingly by a Polish traveler and writer Arkady Fiedler (2010: CXCII - CXCV). The book was first suggested to me by Natalia Brzozowska during our Ph.D. seminar (2011) and then given to me as a farewell present by my MA students, the class of 2011.

the Europeans used to certain comforts. Melville's Rupununi Savannah, 5000 square miles of grasslands, swamp lands, and rain forested mountains, is full of wonders of nature and indeed could be treated as "an Eco-Tourist's Dream", the phrase frequently used by the Tourism Association of Guyana[3]. While describing a project of preparing a Wapisiana dictionary, Melville talks about all the drawbacks of such an enterprise, recognizing the legitimacy of the Indian mentality according to which "innovation is not necessarily improvement. Something is always lost for whatever is gained" (Melville, Jan. 21, 2007).[4]

Bearing in mind her Native American birthright, Melville's "Prologue" to *The ventriloquist's tale*[5] is written "in a style imitating oral storytelling and provides an introduction to the narrator's carnivalesque excessive character, who even before his own birth was endowed with extraordinary gifts that allowed him to give guidance to his mother" (Bowers 2005: 60). Melville herself notices that "[i]n *Ninety-two days* Waugh mentions hearing the story of a certain Mr. Melville, a parson's son from Jamaica, who in an unsuccessful attempt at gold-washing in the interior "was found dying of fever by some Wapisiana Indians in the Upper Essequibo". He married two Wapisiana/Atorad sisters and stayed to live with the Wapisiana people – the Wapichannao – and had ten children. To this day there are numerous Melville descendants living throughout that region. It is not too fanciful to imagine that the character of sinister half-Indian Mr. Todd in 'A handful of dust' [inverted commas in original, LS], who captures the ill-fated Englishman and forces him to read Dickens *ad aeternum*, is based on one of them" (Afterword, Pauline Melville, Jan 3, 2007).[6] Melville's novel received Whitbread First Novel Award and was awarded Whitbread Prize for Best First Novel and was shortlisted for the Orange Prize for Fiction. Her stories *Shape-shifter: Stories* (1990), which won the Commonwealth Writers' Prize and the Guardian Fiction Prize and the MacMillan Silver Pen award[7] and *The migration of ghosts* [1998] (1999), which was chosen by the New York Public Library as one of the twenty five Best Books published that year, though are not restricted to Guyana and Britain, still explore the marvellous which occurs in everyday life. Maya Jaggi, in an interview on Jan 2, 2010, claims that Melville is weaves myth with reality in a style reminiscent of an earlier Guyanese writer, Wilson Harris (*Guardian* interview, Jan 2, 2010). To quote Melville's eponymous narrator: "Now, alas,

---

3   Inhabitants: around 15,000 Wapisiana, Macushi and Wai-Wai Amerindians. The Rupununi savannahs are divided north from south, by the Kanuku Mountains.
4   The quotation comes from a paper entitled "The Wapichan Dictionary" which was sent by Pauline Melville (e-mail message, March 10, 2011).
5   Henceforth indicated as *VT* followed by page number. All quotations are from Melville, Pauline. 1997. *The ventriloquist's tale*. London: Bloomsbury.
6   I am using both the "Afterword" to Waugh's *92 Days* as well as the article about Wapichan dictionary from original Pauline Melville's files (e-mail message, March 10, 2011).
7   I am using original Pauline Melville's spelling, from an email message of May, 4th 2012.

fiction had to disguise itself as fact and I must bow to the trend and become a realist" (*VT*, 9).

Melville's most recent novel is *Eating air* (2009), which reworks the myth of Dionysius and the Bacchae, pays homage to Euripides and classical literature. It is both a political novel with some references to political terrorist activity, and a literary one, a true "novel of ideas" in the Huxleyan sense, in the manner of "realismo polifonico". In "polyphonic realism", after all, the "real" is just a matter of perception. At the British Council Contemporary Writers site, Salman Rushdie argues that "Pauline Melville writes with an unusually dispassionate lushness that is both intellectual and sensual ... I believe her to be one of the few genuinely original writers to emerge in recent years" (date of access 8 April 2011).

As an actress Pauline Melville claims that "there is almost nobody in the world I can't imagine myself being" (*Guardian* interview, Jan 02. 2010) and portrays, for example, Mrs. Tall in *Far from the madding crowd* (1967, directed by John Schlesinger). She also appeared as Mrs Wallace in *How to get ahead in advertising* (1989, directed by Bruce Robinson) and as Dawn in *Mona Lisa* (1986, directed by Neil Jordan). She has an episodic part in the new adaptation of Graham Green's novel *Brighton Rock* (2010, directed by Rowan Joffee).

We all remember Pauline Melville in different ways. During LIES 2011 Pauline Melville was so kind as to spend some time with the students who, inspired by her magnificent stories, wanted to get to know the writer and actress better, not only through her storytelling. As Marta Frątczak remembers, "... we expected the author to be a person with rich imagination, sensitivity towards other people and new cultures – and our intuition did not fail us". Excited by being given a chance to speak to her in person during breaks at the conference as well as when sightseeing around Poznan, the students fell under her spell immediately.

Katarzyna Bronk, who as the conference secretary assisted her during the conference, admits to being surprised that the award winning writer and amazingly talented actress turned out to be a very humble and kind person, genuinely interested in other people's lives. Wanting to be almost invisible to the outside world, Melville prefers to be anonymous so as to observe people, and life in general, and allow herself to be inspired by the magic of the everyday. And magic does happen to Melville. It is enough to mention, Bronk says, a talented violin player staying at the same hotel as the writer. Curious and appreciative of the beauty of the music that was flowing out of his room, she could not resist meeting the musician in person. Melville indeed *feels and sees* people and sometimes, as Joanna Jarząb recounts, she notes down conversations or ideas that she hears in the street, on the train or the bus.

Katarzyna Burzyńska adds that Melville, who is "a brilliant author of fiction, turned out to be also an electrifying personality full of appreciation for Polish culture and curious about Polish people. ... For her Poland emerged as a country with an extremely rich peasant culture and a huge body of legends and folk stories". Frątczak also remembers that Melville admitted to being a devoted admirer of the late Wisława Szymborska, who, according to her, "possessed the unique ability to express the inexpressible through simple images and words".

Reminiscing on Melville's visit, Joanna Ludwikowska-Leniec recounts a conversation about maps and travelling. It seems that the Wapisiana not only do well without maps, but have no need at all to use them. They memorize details of terrain and describe any journey according to the sites which need to be passed by, never drawing them on anything, trusting in their topographic memory. Jarząb remembers Melville's personal story of getting lost while visiting her family's neighbours on foot. The Guyanese quite often travel more than one day so no one is afraid when he or she does not get back home by night, even though this means spending the night on the savannahs or in the forest. Scary as it may sound, such scenes are then magically woven into Melville's poetry and prose.

During the conference lecture – even though Melville always stresses that she is not an academic – the writer started with a statement that she never wore a watch for fear of having "time strapped to her body". This initial comment imparted a sense of mystery, which prevailed throughout her whole lecture. Melville also commented on the double meaning of the abbreviation of the conference's name – LIES. In her opinion the name perfectly fit the topic of the symposium as "it reflected the shifting borders between reality and its representation encapsulated in language or in literature". She then presented her stance on the possible sources of magic realism as well as the presence of magic in the Guyanese consciousness. According to Melville, history proper starts with the written word. However, before the written word comes into being it is oral history, belonging to the illiterate, that prevails. As it seems, ordinary people in Guyana would tend to trust the orally-transmitted word much more.

When commenting on magic realism, Melville said that the presence of mystery, magic and myth is also reflected in the native language of indigenous Wapsiana people. The lyric quality of the language is seen already in its basic phrases; for instance "good morning" in Wapsiana can be rendered in English as "Are you awake?" while a cobweb is a "spider's hammock". To give one more example, the word for "snack" in Wapsiana is "liar", because a snack is something that pretends to be a real meal, something that only deceives our stomachs. So it seems that already on the level of language Guyanese Amerindians are particularly sensitive to the intrusion of magical lyricism into the dimensions of time and space.

In her presentation Melville also addressed the use of mythology as characteristic of magic(al) realism which are ever present in her own fiction. She referred to the Amerindian beliefs in the magic qualities of solar eclipses. She also reminded the audience of the "kanaima" myth of the spirit of revenge, and with that she attempted to contrast the opposing outlooks on life in North America and among the indigenous peoples of South America. Western culture as epitomized by the USA is all about "reinventing" oneself, while the Amerindians do not believe in progress or change. Melville highlighted the fact that along with the spread of the European Enlightenment and rationalism, the world – although richer with the ideas of secular humanism – lost part of its spiritual element, which is still present in the culture of Amerindians. Guyanese native inhabitants seem inactive and passive because for them the idea of progress is just an illusion. As a result, their culture is still infused with richness of myth and magic, which make it such a potent material for magic realist authors.

However, as Melville's *Eating air* proves, myth can be also used to make a political statement. In the last part of her talk Melville addressed the use and function of myth in her seemingly political novel about the phenomenon of terrorism. Although at a first glance the novel seems to have little in common with magic realism, references to myths play quite an important role in it. As Melville outlined it, the mysterious Baron S., an intriguing and slightly funny narrator of the story, is indeed a classic voodoo character from Haiti. Baron S. or Baron Somedi ("Somedi" means Saturday) is one of the Loa – Haitian voodoo spirits of fertility and death. He is known for his inclinations towards strong drinks and tobacco. In the novel he is dressed in a top hat and elegant clothes of an English gentleman. Surprisingly enough, Melville's depiction is not far from the original, traditional rendering of the spirit. Being the master of life and death, Baron S. seems to be a metaphorical rendition of "god-like" qualities of the narrator in the novel. As Melville put it, he is the "magical narrator" in the novel.

Apart from Haitian myths, Melville also pointed out allusions to classical mythology present in *Eating air*. In her presentation Melville acknowledged a passing reference to the myth of Venus and Adonis, as well as a loose re-working of *The Bacchae* by Euripides. In her opinion, one of her protagonists, Donny, is an anarchic force standing for the Dionysian force, while Ella is one of the wild maenads. For Donny what is most important is the euphoria of action. Ella, being a ballet dancer, is like a wild maenad following Dionysus. These characters are, according to Melville, people belonging to "the Dionysian explosion" – larger than themselves. Thus, even in this seemingly political novel, the mythic and the magical emerges from the rich web of characters and events.

Marta Frątczak summarises Melville's LIES lecture: "She told us how two distant traditions, English and Guyanese, affected her as a writer. From the former, she claims to have drawn her love for the written word. From the latter, sensitivity to myth, the world of nature and orally transmitted stories". And even though she claims that Guyanese Indians do not really need her as a writer, anyone interested in venturing into the world of magic and myth, while having one foot still fixed on the solid ground, will look into Melville's "eyes deep with unfathomable stories" with pleasure.

In *The ventriloquist's tale*, Melville says that "[a]ll stories are told for revenge or tribute" (*VT*, 9). Ours is certainly written as a tribute to a great writer, who helped us to re-discover the marvellous Guyana and the marvellous in Guyana and so much more.

References

Bowers, Maggie Ann. 2005. *Magic(al) realism*. London: Routledge.
Dabydeen, David (ed.). 2001. *Rented rooms*. Coventry: Dangaroo Press.
Fiedler, Arkady. 2010 [1968]. *Gujana. Spotkałem szczęsliwych Indian* [Guiana. I met happy Indians]. Pelplin: Biblioteka Poznaj Świat.
Melville, Pauline. 2009. *Eating air*. London: Telegram.
Melville, Pauline. 1998. *The migration of ghosts*. London: Bloomsbury.
Melville, Pauline. 1997. *The ventriloquist's tale*. London: Bloomsbury.
Melville, Pauline. 1990. *Shapeshifter*. London: Picador.
Raleigh, Walter. 2008. *The discovery of Guiana with related documents*. (Edited with an Introduction by Benjamin Schmidt.) Boston, New York: Bedford/St. Martins.
Roth, Walter Edmund. 2008. *An inquiry into the animism and folk-lore of the Guiana Indians*. Forgotten Books.
Waugh, Evelyn. 2007. *92 Days*. (Afterword by Pauline Melville.) London: Serif.

Towards a "third space": Magic realism in English Canadian literature

Jeanne Delbaere-Garant, Université Libre, Brussels

ABSTRACT

Drawing on Homi Bhabba's concept of the "third space" the essay draws attention to such notions as *overlapping, remembering and healing* which keep recurring in many magic realist texts. It argues that instead of reconciling opposites within a single subject as in modernist novels, or substituting one side for the other as in mainstream postcolonial fiction, magic realism opens a new interstitial third space of ongoing negotiation in which potentially antagonistic individuals or cultures interact with each other and become ultimately transformed into something not only different but more genuine. This is illustrated in English Canadian texts written by white settlers, First-Nations writers and non-Caucasian migrants.

> On the far side of the subjective, on this side of the objective, on the narrow ridge where I and Thou meet, there is the realm of 'between'. This reality, whose disclosure has begun in our time, shows the way, leading beyond individualism and collectivism, for the life of future generations. Here the genuine third alternative is indicated, the knowledge of which will help to bring about the genuine person again and to establish genuine community   (Martin Buber).

My personal connection with magic realism dates back to the 1980s when Jean Weisgerber, a colleague of mine at the University of Brussels, planning to edit a book on magic realism in different geographical areas as well as in a diversity of fields, asked me if I would like to contribute the chapter on magic realism in English literature. I accepted at once but found myself awfully embarrassed when it came to writing the first line of my essay. For me the strange oxymoron conjured up something like a childhood memory when, scratching the frost flowers on the windowpane of my bedroom, I had seen our garden magically transformed by the snow. But magic realism *in English literature*?

A few days later I came by chance upon an article which used the term in connection with Canadian artists. In no time I contacted Bill New at the University of British Columbia, who advised me to read Jack Hodgins's *The invention of the world* and to get in touch with Geoff Hancock, the editor-in-chief of *Canadian fiction magazine*. My German colleague Walter Pache sent me his copy of Hodgins's novel, my very first contact with English Canadian literature. Not long after that, on my first visit to Canada, I invited Geoff Hancock to meet me in my hotel in Toronto to talk about magic realism. As soon as he arrived, he immediately embarked on his favourite subject. Hancock was a formidable talent scout but he was a little carried away by his enthusiasm. It was not magic realism that put Canadian literature on the world map (though it was for me!) but the enormous financial effort of the Canadian government in all cultural fields since

1967, the year of the Centennial. And when Canadian literature did reach European universities the names of Margaret Atwood, Margaret Laurence and Alice Munro fared better than those of Jack Hodgins or Robert Kroetsch. "I wish I were called Alice or Margaret", Jack Hodgins jokingly remarked when we met a few years later. The 1970s was indeed the decade when the search of the country for its cultural identity was closely paralleled with that of its female writers for a distinctive gender identity.

Hodgins and Kroetsch were male, and they were not in the mainstream. They were less concerned with nation-building than with the need to give voice and visibility to their respective hinterlands. They looked towards Latin America (Marquez) and the rural American South (Faulkner, Flannery O'Connor) for their literary sources. In so doing they introduced a variety of magic realism in Canada which combined the characteristics of the aesthetic and psychic orientation of its European progenitor with the more mythic and politically oriented Latin American *real maravilloso*. They shared with the latter a close geographical anchorage which gives Canadian magic realism its specificity. As a resistance tool against the hegemonic centre their magic realism was also in tune with the decentring agenda of postcolonialism and its foregrounding of marginality as a valid ideological and aesthetic alternative to the master-narratives.

Since the 1970s, Canadian magic realism has been enriched by the trickster stories and the ecological concerns of First Nations writers, and it has evolved to include other margins and other centres in a complex network of multi-ethnic and multi-racial interconnectedness. For clarity's sake, I have chosen to deal separately with magic realism in works by White settlers, First Nations writers and non-Caucasian migrants.

White Settlers

The Latin American influence is what made Canadian magic realism "visible" in the first place: Robert Kroetch's *What the crow said*[1] with the Rabelaisian loudness of its rural tellers, the epic proportions of their hunting parties, the "magic" pregnancy by a swarm of bees of its female protagonist; Hodgins's invasions of all kinds: hordes of dishevelled hippies in search of hallucinatory mushrooms in *The Barclay family theatre* or tidal waves in *The resurrection of Joseph Bourne* bringing on their crests all sorts of "magical" gifts and creatures like the blue whale which turns into the fat woman after whom the town of Port Annie is named, or Raimey the "seabird" emerging from a Peruvian freighter and causing a series of miracles to happen before the town is wiped off the map by a giant mudslide. This was definitely something new in the puritanical

---

1   Henceforth indicated as *WCS* followed by page number. All quotations come from Kroetch, Robert. 1983 [1978] *What the crow said*. Toronto: General.

Canadian literary landscape. But when you exist only on the margin of a society the only way to draw attention to yourself is by being outsized or extravagant enough. The crazy disguises of Mayor Weins and the exaggerated proportions of Fat Annie, Big Glad Littlestone, Mr Pernouski, surely made these grotesque characters as "visible" as the giants, clownish figures on stilts, or distorted masks in carnival parades. At the same time they introduced a new way of writing about reality.

But Canada is not Latin America. Canada is a no-nonsense country in which miracles, when they occur, often have a clear moral meaning. For all its contamination of the real by these crazy "invasions", the magic realism of the white settlers seems to me to have remained closer to the European psychological realism than to the Latin American *real maravilloso*, achieving, in typical Canadian fashion, a "quiet revolution" from modernism to postmodernism. Indeed thematically magic realism often appears in novels of initiation. It is, in Wilson Harris's definition of the concept, "an alchemical pilgrimage, a ceaseless adventure within the self and without the self in nature and beings that are undervalued or that have been eclipsed or imprisoned by models of conquest" (Maes-Jelinek 1991: 48).

This is beautifully conveyed in "Kingsmere", the three-page central section of Gwendolyn MacEwen's *Noman*. In this estate where MacKenzie King, the former Prime Minister of Canada, was living half way between the present and the past, between the living and the dead, a large classic arch separates his collection of stone ruins, "these broken bits of history" (MacEwen 1985: 52), from the awe-inspiring reality of the wilderness: *"There, beyond the arch, is the forest. There is the naked, ancient door. You have only to pass under the arch to be free, to be away from this place, but you watch the arch and grow afraid, for the arch is watching you. The little King and the Fairy Queen are watching you. And all the trees are silently screaming"* (MacEwen 1985: 54, italics in the original, J. D-G). On the last page of the novel Noman removes his clothes and, inviting his female companion Kali to join him, passes through the archway into a future of his own. Like Noman the white settler is prisoner of a "synthetic history", not necessarily his own, artificially transplanted into the new country. To build his own future he must leave behind "the unreal Grecian columns" and confront the "silently screaming" trees, for what is seen through the arch is "not Athens, nor Rome nor even Palmyra, but the green Gatineau hills of Kanada" (MacEwen 1985: 53).

Unlike its vague and often unspecified counterpart in Europe the site of initiation in Canadian magic realism is indeed closely connected with the local topography: the Vancouver Island of Keith Maillard, Jack Hodgins or Gail Anderson-Dargatz; the Prairie of Robert Kroetsch; the Maritimes of Jane Urquhart, Susan Kerslake or Ann-Marie MacDonald. Here the edge of consciousness is also the edge of a continent or that of the characters' everyday environment—an in-between zone where the shoreline meets the Ocean or where the familiar borders on the unknown. The south end of Kroetsch's Big Indian "faded into bald prairie and a Hutterite colony" while its north end "vanished into the bush country and an Indian reserve" (*WCS*, 36); Urquhart's *Away* is set "on the extreme edge of the country called Canada" (Urquhart 1993: 5); Morgan's house in *Middlewatch* is "right ... at the edge of the sea" (Kerslake 1976: 115), its back door opening out into untamed nature; the street in the little mining town where Ann-Marie MacDonald's characters used to live in *Fall on your knees* "leads out past the edge of town to where the wide, keeling graveyard overlooks the ocean" (MacDonald 1997: 1).

The configuration of the landscape or such cataclysmic events as earthquakes, landslides, giant waves are objective correlatives of the characters' inner disturbances. Thus the "green" rain of Vancouver Island blurring the line between earth and sky in Keith Maillard's *Two strand river* is also the physical equivalent of the still undefined zone of Alan and Leslie's gender orientation while the tectonic plates off its west coast which the young swimmer in Hodgins's "Separating" refers to when he tells Spit about the "crack that runs all around the ocean floor ... squeezing lava out like toothpaste ... pushing the continents farther and farther apart" (Hodgins 1976: 18), is the topographical projection of the "dividing line" that is currently opening a crack in the protagonist's psychic life.

For the white settlers the Jungian *Shadow* is the unexplored and specifically Canadian space beyond the familiar environment, a space often haunted by the eclipsed populations that once occupied the territory they now claim as their own. In *Two strand river* Leslie is constantly aware of hidden connections, of something that is always there "like a reflection on the edge of a dream—memory—of where we've been together, where we've come from. For whether we walked or came by boat, we come from the same place. And for us, it's the Indians who stand at the edge of a dream, behind them, the bush, were we all began" (Maillard 1982: 229). For their initiation to take place she and Alan will have to make the dangerous trip to the bush and to the sacred Indian places. The Pacific beach where Spit Delaney first hears the troubling question about the "dividing line" in "Separating" is teeming with disturbing Indian legends and transformation myths like that of Kanikiluk, who sometimes steps out of the ocean to turn people into fish. In "Spit Delaney's island" he does indeed feel like a legless old seal stranded on the beach and repeatedly dreams that he is turned into a fish. When he gives a lift to Phemie Porter and briefly "overlaps" with her emotionally, she sends him a poem whose title "The man without legs" scares him because of its weird correspondence with his own dream. He feels that though he does not understand the poem, it must contain another reality full of unsuspected possibilities.

Sometimes the white settlers carry with them the memory of a traumatic past of their own in which they remain trapped and which continues to imprison them psychologically in their new country. This is the case with the Irish past in Hodgins's *The invention of world* and in Jane Urquhart's *Away*. In their different ways Hodgins's down-to-earth Maggie and Urquhart's writer Esther set off on a real or an imaginative pilgrimage to retrieve it. In so doing they free themselves and their community from a ghost-ridden present and pave the way for the construction of the future. However if total absence of memory leads to an amnesia that blocks the future, an excessive cult of memory can also be a dangerous weapon in the hands of tyrannical masters who appropriate the mythology of those they want to enslave. Only through a selfless and creative use of memory can the past be correctly deciphered and transformed. True, Maggie does not have Esther's gift for words but she is endowed with what Wilson Harris calls the "literate imagination" which has little to do with intellectual literacy but is rather a capacity to "read the world" imaginatively (Harris 1989: 21).

Because it telescopes into one powerful moment the entire meaning of a novel, the magic realist initiation shares some of the characteristics of the modernist epiphany though it also differs from it in a significant way. Let me give three examples, starting with James Joyce since he is the one who coined the term. Stephen Dedalus' epiphany in *Portrait of the artist as a young man* takes place when his vision of a bird-like creature on the seashore, half angel, half sensual female, helps him reconcile the former dichotomies of his self. The location between land and sea as well as the hybrid nature of the bird are also typical ingredients of magic realism but here the epiphany spells closure, as is usually the case in modernist texts. The circle of the self is closed, the bird-like creature left out and forgotten. Stephen is free to produce his work away from ordinary reality in the ivory tower of his mind. In 1971, the first year of a decade in which nationalism and feminism became closely interwoven in Canada, Alice Munro revisited Joyce's novel in her own *Lives of girls and women*. Here the epiphanic moment is also connected with baptism and water but the girl in the water is the protagonist Del Jordan, a creature of flesh and blood refusing to let her boyfriend baptize her by force: no symbolic reconciliation of opposites here but a clear assertion of female resistance and separateness.

In *The invention of the world* the epiphany takes place on a hill top in Ireland where the fake prophet Keneally was allegedly born. Maggie and Wade, accompanied by Becker, have come there on a pilgrimage to get rid of Keneally's ashes. It falls to Becker, the artist, to articulate what the other two can only intuit: "Myth", he declares while scattering the ashes, "like all the past, real or imaginary, must be acknowledged ... Even if it's not believed. In fact, especially when it's not believed. When you begin to disbelieve in Keneally you can begin to believe in yourself" (Hodgins 1977: 314). The mist before Maggie's eyes is indeed suddenly lifted as she acknowledges the reality of Wade, epitomized in his shoe magically transformed by her love: "For a moment she wanted to touch it, to put her face down, to feel the childlike shape of it in her hands. She was tempted to brush the mud away, with her fingertips" (Hodgins 1977: 315). In the last pages of the novel she and Wade, the "new woman" and the "new man", are on their way to the House of Revelation, Keneally's former dwelling with its painful history of suffering and exploitation, which they intend to turn into a new "colony" based on love and solidarity. The "perfect circle" of the tyrant is replaced by the "broken arcs" of everyday reality.[2]

We see clearly that Maggie's magic realist epiphany is neither a reconciliation of opposites within a single identity as was the case in the modernist texts nor a substitution of one side for the other as in mainstream postcolonial fiction but an inter-personal process in which each side acknowledges the reality of the Other before *both* change into something else, allowing for an open space of ongoing negotiation not only between them but also between them and others. Only interaction with the Other can open the closed circle of the self and induce metamorphosis.

My title refers to Homi Bhabba's theoretical notion of hybridity and the "third space" which is metonymically illustrated here. Though she recognizes that she will not be able to heal them all, Maggie will nevertheless do her best to open her door to the worst assorted sorts of boarders and to *create,* not *invent* as Keneally had done, a tentative "third space" in which every single person will be taken into consideration. Her initiation also foregrounds the three main notions of *overlapping,*[3] *remembering* and *healing* which keep recurring in many magic realist texts not only in Canada but also across other postcolonial cultures.[4]

First Nations Writers

In his *Transgressive itineraries: Postcolonial hybridizations of dramatic realism* Marc Maufort, considering magic realism as a valid framework for reading

---

2   Wade mentions the "broken arcs" in his wedding speech when he quotes two lines from Robert Browning's "Abt Vogler", a poem he has found in one of Lily Hayworth's books: "What was good shall be good, with, for evil, so much good more: On the earth the broken arcs; in heaven, a perfect round" (Hodgins 1977: 361).

3   Rather than "overlapping" Mary Louise Pratt speaks of "contact zones" for the intersecting trajectories of subjects previously separated geographically and historically: "By using the term 'contact' I aim to foreground the interactive, improvisational dimensions of   colonial encounters so easily ignored or suppressed by diffusionist accounts of conquest and domination. A "contact" perspective emphasizes how subjects are constituted in and by their relations among colonizers and colonized ... not in terms of separateness and apartheid,   but in terms of co-presence, interaction, interlocking understandings and practices, often within asymmetrical relations of power" (Pratt 1992: 7).

4   In *Feats and defeats of memory* Agnieszka Rzepa also considers that magic realism "lends itself particularly fruitfully to explorations of different aspects of memory" (Rzepa 2009: 22). She studies the process of "retrieving, narrativising and articulating suppressed traumatic memories" in Tomson Highway's *Kiss of the Fur Queen* and Ann-Marie McDonald's *Fall on your knees*, two novels which, she writes, "create potentially hybrid, fluctuating cultural spaces that influence individual identity formation" (Rzepa 2009: 156). On the uses and abuses of memory see also Todorov 1995 and Delbaere 2000.

Aboriginal texts across the postcolonial cultures of Canada, New Zealand and Australia shows that Native Canadian playwrights like Tomson Highway, Daniel David Moses and Drew Hayden Taylor currently hybridize the codes of Western dramatic realism by combining them with the tradition of native ritual performance. In *Feats and defeats of memory* Agnieszka Rzepa analyses Lee Maracle's *Ravensong* and Tomson Highway's *Kiss of the Fur Queen* as texts which explicitly address "the specific and troubled context of the First Nations interactions with the non-Native population" (Rzepa 2009: 145) and rightly argues that it is within the boundaries of the white culture that indigenous writers can reclaim their own mythic past and give it legitimacy in the present.

If the white settlers must sometimes come to terms with a colonial past of their own, the First Nations people, who have been without exceptions forcibly assimilated and dispossessed by the European colonizers, must always, not only confront their collective victimization in the past—a victimization that often continues in the present—but also reclaim and re-appropriate their eclipsed mythic culture. For them *remembering* has a double and even a threefold meaning: that of Toni Morrison's "re-memory", which highlights the organic presence of the past in the present; that of Homi Bhabha's "re-member" as "a putting together of the dismembered past to make sense of the trauma of the present" (Bhabha 1994: 63) and that of "re-member" in the sense of re-integrating their Indian community as its scattered members. They must indeed reconstruct what has been dismantled: their roots, their language, and their link with nature on which the traditional life of their ancestors was based.

The two texts I am going to examine are about the return of the Trickster in the contemporary world of the First Nations people. This magic realist collision belongs to the category of "mythic realism" since here the magic is literal and not projected from the characters' psyches as in the initiation novels discussed above.

In her short text "This is a story" Jeanette Armstrong uses the Trickster to wake up an Okanagan community assimilated by the Whites. She denounces both their passivity and the ecological damage caused by the non-natives' commercial and technological exploitation of nature. Armstrong's story is told by a woman responsible for keeping the fire alive during the three days and nights of a traditional pow-wow. After "an unusually short nap" Kyoti the Trickster decides to visit the Okanagan People to whom he used to bring salmon. When he reaches the river he no longer recognizes the familiar environment: the People and their villages have gone, a lot of "Swallow people" are now living along the bank and at two different places a "huge thing" stretches way up and across the river. The few People he encounters do not understand him: they speak in "Swallow talk", live in "Swallow houses" and eat "Swallow food". The only person who still speaks the native language is the great-grandson of the Salmon chief. Like his father and grandfather the young Native has been watching the river every day during salmon-run time but like them he has been waiting in vain. On hearing this,

Kyoti asks the Elder to get the People together and to tell them that Kyoti is back and is going to break the dam. He takes out the shining rainbow ribbons, hangs them on his staff and shows how he can make the ground shake by shaking the staff. "Sometimes", the storyteller concludes "I think of that story and that morning at Owl Rock, when I see rainbow colours in the oil slicks along the river, during salmon-run time in the Okanagan, and I feel the ground shake ever so little" (Armstrong 1990: 135).

Kyoti the Trickster enters the realistic narrative frame as yet another character in the story. He jokingly apologizes for oversleeping a little when the old woman blames him for having been away so long. "Actually," she comments, "Kyoti was well known for oversleeping all the time. And actually Kyoti always used that as an excuse for being too late for something important" (Armstrong 1990: 132). Again and again she insists on the truth of what she is reporting. But Kyoti's time scale belongs to another plane: living simultaneously in various juxtapositions of time and space, he challenges by his presence the western conception of these categories as monolithic. When he hangs the rainbow ribbons on his staff he challenges not just the literary conventions of mimetic representation but the very rational basis of the western conception of reality. And yet the destruction of the dam he prophesies can occur through any real enough natural disaster from lightning to earthquake to landslide, as was indeed the case since the story was written with the collapse, on June 13, 2010, of the Testalinden Lake dam near Oliver in the Okanagan.

In Drew Hayden Taylor's recently published first novel *Motorcycles & sweetgrass*[5] the trickster also returns to a modern-day Reserve, this time riding a 1953 red Chief Indian motorcycle with white old-fashioned headlights, an elongated Indian headdress on the gas tank, a black solo seat with black leather fringes and larger than normal wheel fenders. Sweetgrass is a native plant of North America supposed to attract positive energies. It is lit and burned in braided form in Native rituals. Like Jeanette Armstrong's text the novel opens in the oral tradition of aboriginal storytelling: "Hey, wanna hear a good story? Supposedly it's a true one. It's a long story but it goes something like this ..." (*MS*, 1). What we are told is at once hilarious and at times extremely moving. Lillian, a grandmother in her seventies, summons to her deathbed the boyfriend with whom, in the Prologue, she is seen swimming in Otter Lake on the eve of her departure for residential school. This boyfriend is in fact the Trickster Nanabush. Though as a girl she turned her back on him to follow Jesus instead, he has never ceased loving her. He therefore answers her call, changes his shape into that of a blond white guy and creates a sensation in the Ojibway community of Otter Lake Reserve, Ontario, when he appears on his vintage motorcycle. The novel is about

---

5   Henceforth indicated as *MS* followed by page number. All quotations come from Taylor, Drew Hayden. 2011. *Motorcycles and sweetgrass*, Toronto: Vintage Canada.

the magic but also the mayhem which John-Nanabush's arrival introduces in the lives of Lillian's dear ones: her widowed daughter Maggie; her teenage grandson Virgil; her youngest and favourite son Wayne. Her death leaves these three characters even more cut off from each other than before: as Chief of the community, Maggie is hassled by the competing opinions of the natives about what must be done with a new government-granted piece of land; Virgil, neglected by his mother, has taken to missing school and risks having to repeat his year; Wayne lives as a recluse on a small island on the other side of the lake where he invents a native martial art.

Magic realism permeates the novel because of the presence of the ubiquitous shapeshifter in the Reserve. Maggie has a good time when he beds her, but Virgil, who had already surprised the stranger kissing his grandmother Hollywood fashion on her deathbed at the time of his arrival, notices a series of other anomalies that give him an eerie feeling and launch him on a personal quest: though a non-native, the stranger speaks the Ojibway language perfectly; the colour of his eyes keeps changing; he introduces himself as John but each time with a different last name. Fearing mischief Virgil recruits his uncle Wayne to get rid of the unwelcome motorcyclist. An epic battle ensues between John-Nanabush and Wayne. The former comes off with a few cuts but Wayne must be taken to hospital: "Boy, something magic can really hurt" (*MS*, 321), he tells the nurse who cleans his wounds. After the fight the thirteen-year old Virgil is more confused than ever: "Part of him wanted to walk right up to the man and hit him as hard as he could. Another part wanted to run away and hide, and hope that the man would just disappear. Still another part wanted to ask why the man had decided to torment Virgil and his mother. Having so many questions paralyzed him" (*MS*, 321-322). His long conversation with the trickster in the last but one chapter completes the boy's initiation. He and Nanabush part as good friends, each with a gift from the other: Virgil with a sentence to ponder on and the Trickster with a braided strand of local sweetgrass which he attaches to the mirror on the left handlebar of his motorcycle as do the natives for good luck.

Another memorable encounter in the novel is the confrontation, in each other's dream, of the two "tricksters" of the Christian and Indian belief systems, Jesus and Nanabush. Taylor puts them on exactly the same level: same size, same age, same long hair. They engage in casual conversation in which their different priorities come to the fore; this does not lead to a reconciliation between their antagonistic views nor to the supremacy of the one over the other but to a third space of literal negotiation and sharing of "tricks", a space where they manage to "overlap" thanks to Lillian's love for both: "if a woman like Lillian can hold both of us in her heart, we can't be that far apart" (*MS*, 269), Jesus remarks. Before taking his leave Nanabush asks Jesus to teach him a trick which would make his own travelling a lot easier. Though we guess what it is, we do not hear Jesus' answer but we may assume that John's request has been granted for he is seen smiling in his sleep. Besides, in the epilogue an old man on his deathbed remembers the day when he was fishing in the lake and a large red-and-white motorcycle passed his boat at full speed before disappearing in the distance. Whenever the old man told the story nobody in the Reserve believed him except the three main characters of the book.

At the end of the novel these three characters are happier than they were before the arrival of Nanabush. They are now reunited like the three bunches of a sweetgrass braid: Maggie devotes more time to her son, having now adopted a more Zen approach to her political activities; Wayne's bruises are healing and he plans not only to reintegrate the community but also to date the young nurse he met in hospital; Virgil is happily playing outside on the grass with his cousin Dakota. His initiation has passed through a necessary confrontation with his mythic past embodied in the Trickster: "He's a hero, a fool, a teacher, someone silly, someone clever—my grandmother would say he's us" (*MS*, 325). He feels that Nanabush's last words before he left will make a great title for the essay assigned to him as a condition for his admission in the next class. He also treasures them as a guideline for the years ahead: "*There are no such things as dead ends. Only people who find dead ends*" (*MS*, 337, italics in the original, J. D-G).

For all his iconoclastic and farcical humour Drew Hayden Taylor also addresses serious issues. He does not ignore the damage done on the First Nations People by the "People in Black" in residential schools (Lillian's rebellious cousin, now an old drunk, has never been able to overcome the trauma of their sexual and mental abuse) but he knows that the past, painful though it is, must be confronted and transcended if dead ends are to be avoided in the future. Jesus must be accepted by the First Nations people as part of their traumatic past but he must be downgraded to the same status as Nanabush. Despite their antagonistic doctrines the two tricksters can co-exist in the minds of the people as they did in the dead Lillian's heart: ".. a walking contradiction … Sweetgrass and holy water. That was my mother" (*MS*, 181), Maggie comments. Like Maracle's *Ravensong* and Highway's *Kiss of the Fur Queen* Drew Hayden Taylor's novel suggests that contemporary Native identity can hardly be built "without a recognition of the inescapable presence of the white culture, which has had most tragic and destructive influence on Native communities and cultures, but at the same time in the contemporary context offers spaces that can be meaningfully explored also by First Nations people" (Rzepa 2009 158-9).

What the old woman had asked Nanabush on her deathbed was to re-inject a little magic in the alienated lives of her three dear ones. Likewise Drew Hayden Taylor also attempts to re-inject magic and contradiction in the rationality and materialism of an alienated modern Native community. In so doing he clearly paves the way for what Homi Bhabha calls "that productive space of the construction of culture as difference, in the spirit of alterity or otherness" (Rutherford 1990a: 209).

Non-Caucasian Migrants

The experience of exile, migration, displacement, which turns migrants into what Salman Rushdie has called "translated" human beings, requires an appropriate mode of literary expression to accommodate their hybrid identities, not only in Canada but anywhere in the world. Here again magic realism can help writers throw bridges between these displaced communities and the host country so that new spaces of negotiation can be created in which their different and sometimes potentially antagonistic sets of cultural values can co-exist with those of their new geographical and human environment.

In one of the chapters of *Le Rideau* entitled "Le pont argenté" Milan Kundera remembers his exile in Paris and his conversations with Carlos Fuentes, who was at the time ambassador of Mexico in the French capital: "Nous causions et un pont argenté, léger, tremblotant, scintillant, s'érigeait comme un arc-en-ciel au-dessus du siècle entre ma petite Europe centrale et l'immense Amérique latine; un pont qui reliait les statues extatiques de Matyas Braun à Prague et les églises en folie du Mexique (Kundera 2005: 101).[6] Though miles apart, two neglected countries, Mexico and Czechoslovakia, are shown here to share a common experience of political and religious oppression epitomized in their baroque statues and churches.

In her analysis of Lee Maracle's *Ravensong* Agnieszka Rzepa shows that Stacey, the native girl who crosses every day the bridge between the "white town" and the village of her Salish community to go to school, also has "to negotiate the cultural and social rift between the two" (Rzepa 2009: 118). Bridges can indeed *connect* like Kundera's "silvery bridge" or *separate* like the bridge in *Ravensong*. One of the Canadian writers who knows the importance of bridges, real or metaphorical, connecting or keeping apart, is Michael Ondaatje. It is on a bridge of *In the skin of a lion* that a famous magic realist collision occurs between a Macedonian immigrant worker and a flying nun falling from the unfinished Bloor Street Viaduct, a collision which eventually changes them both: the solitary and silent Temelcoff begins to tell stories to his wife while the nun metamorphoses into Alice, an actress and the mother of the nurse in *The English patient*[7]. *In the skin of a lion*, of which *The English patient* is partly a sequel, ends with the protagonist enjoining Hana to switch on the headlights of the car as he and the girl prepare to join Clara in a "third place" of reconstruction after Alice's accidental death by the bomb she was transporting. The last word "Lights!" hints at some

---

6 "We were talking, and a silvery bridge, light, flickering, scintillating, stretched like a rainbow over the century between my little central Europe and the immensity of Latin America, a bridge connecting the ecstatic statues of Matyas Braun in Prague with the mad churches of Mexico" [translation mine, J. D-G].

7 Henceforth indicated as *EP* followed by page number. All quotations are from Ondaatje, Michael. 1992. *The English patient*. Toronto: Vintage Canada.

hope for the future but, as often in Ondaatje's fiction, healing is at best temporary: in *The English patient* Hana hears that Patrick has been burned to death in a French dove cot during the war while she herself is nursing a burned man in a ruined Tuscan villa.

The English patient is, in its author's own words, "a book about very tentative healing among a group of people" (Wachtel 1994: 255-56). Brought together by the war, the Canadian nurse, the faceless patient, the Indian sapper and Caravaggio, who had been a friend of Hana's father in Canada, form a sort of planetary family cutting across race, gender, religion and even ordinary morality (the English patient is a traitor, Caravaggio a thief); the villa San Girolamo is yet another provisional third place, where they tentatively recreate some sort of coherence among the ruins of the world and of themselves. Invisible threads hold the four characters together, counterpointing the equally invisible though real enough wires attached to unexploded bombs all over the place.

Kirpal Singh, "some kind of loose star on the edge of their system" (*EP*, 75), is responsible for clearing the place of its mines. Nicknamed Kip, the young Sikh sticks to his own cultural and religious habits but the otherness of western mythology is forced upon him in a series of magic realist "visions" through his rifle telescope. The first of these occurs in the church of Arezzo where he is confronted with the beautiful face of Piero della Francesca's Queen of Sheba. The fresco shows the queen on her arrival in Jerusalem, kneeling in adoration before a bridge over the Cedron made of the tree on which Christ would be later crucified. This bridge connecting the foreign Queen with the sacred wood is also a metaphorical bridge between Kip's Sikhism and the western Biblical legend. In the Sistine chapel in Rome Kip comes face to face through his telescope with another Biblical figure, that of Isaiah whose prophetic words the English patient will eventually sing to him. Like the villa, the Arezzo church and the Sistine chapel are sites of overlapping and transformation where healing can begin even if only provisionally. On another occasion Kip is observing the enemy's movements on the east coast of Italy when some darker outline in his rifle sights suddenly turns into an illuminated halo around the head of the Virgin Mary. Though the latter occurrence is quite factual (it happens during a marine Festival of the Virgin) and though the Virgin is a mere plaster figure held by two men while two others are rowing the boat to the coast, the magic realist apparition of the haloed face in Kip's telescope has a strong mythic resonance.

In each of these epiphanic moments, the young Sikh's picking up of a target through his military implements does not lead to the expected sniping at an enemy but to an overlapping between himself and western Biblical figures which strike him as familiar because they belong to the collective experience of mankind: a beloved, a father, a mother, sister or daughter. What is stressed here is the possibility for Kip to hold in his mind the contradictory mythologies of East and West disencumbered of their ideological and political connections.

Towards the end of the book Ondaatje devotes a few pages to the day in Naples when Kip and some other sappers are assigned the delicate task of clearing thousands of mines assumed to be wired to the dormant electric system of the city. In the last hour just before one of the soldiers is going to turn on the city's electricity Kip enters the church of San Giovanni a Carbonara where he remembers having seen a few days earlier a painting with two large human figures: an angel and a woman in a bedroom. Exhausted after working all night, he stretches out beside the painting, reflecting that if he is going to explode he will at least do so in the company of these two parental figures. This is a moment of great tension when the fate of the young Sikh hangs by a thread and when the angel of the Annunciation, the harbinger of life, can easily turn into a harbinger of death:

> The tableau now, with Kip at the feet of the two figures, suggests a debate over his fate. The raised terra-cotta arm a stay of execution, a promise of some great future for this sleeper, childlike, foreign-born. The three of them almost at the point of decision, agreement. Under the thin layer of dust the angel's face has a powerful joy. Attached to its back are the six light bulbs, two of which are defunct. But in spite of that the wonder of electricity suddenly lights his wings from underneath, so that their blood-red and blue and goldness the colour of mustard fields shine animated in the late afternoon
>
> (*EP*, 281).

On the next page and without transition Kip hears about the bombing of Hiroshima. By juxtaposing these two moments Ondaatje shows that healing is indeed provisional and its victory short-lived. History catches up with the young Sikh, dragging him away from his little oasis of timelessness into a whirlpool of conflicting forces that, as an individual, he is powerless to control. "From now on, the personal will forever be at war with the public" (*EP*, 292), Hana writes to Clara in Canada, thereby echoing Patrick's remark to her own mother years before: "The trouble with ideology, Alice, is that it hates the private. You must make it human" (Ondaatje 1988: 135). This antagonism between the public and the private is aptly conveyed by the juxtaposition of the atomic Bomb and the little light bulbs on the angel's wings brought to life again through the individual efforts of a few healers.

Turning his back on the "third space" that his foreign friends have managed to create in the Tuscan villa, the young Sikh hardens back into cultural and religious assertion, turning them into an abstract idea of the West and the white race. Yet what has been gained is not completely lost. On his flight "home" he carries in his mind the memory of the Other's burned body and of his songs about Isaiah's vision of the recovered garden where the wolf dwells with the lamb and the leopard with the kid. The last paragraph also suggests that though they have gone their separate ways on separate continents he and Hana have remained as mysteriously connected as Professor Godbole and Mrs. Moore in E. M. Forster's *Passage to India*.

On an even larger scale the English patient had himself gone far beyond national, religious or cultural divisions in search of the lost oasis of Zerzura in the Lybian desert, an oasis which had become for a whole decade a "third place" of connection and solidarity between individuals of different nationalities before it was turned into one of the theatres of war and those who had been close friends had re-donned the separate clothing of their respective countries.

Conclusion

That I should have found my first anglophone magic realist writers in Canada, Mac Luhan's "borderline" place, is hardly surprising. Even less surprising is that these writers should have lived in remote places like Vancouver Island, the Prairies or the Maritimes, margins of the margin from where they wanted their voices and those of their characters to be heard at the time when nation-building was taking place at the centre on the basis of two founding nations or at the best on that of a mosaic. It seems clear today that the Canadian identity can no longer be constructed from a double nor for that matter from a multicultural viewpoint decided by the hegemonic centre, but by the creation of a number of hybridized third spaces of ever-changing white, aboriginal and ethnic formations. My trip on the track of magic realism in Canada has taken me from an illiterate Vancouver Islander in whose mind Phemie Porter's poem shimmers as a magic key that might open the door to a richer reality were he only able to understand it, to, at the other extreme, the hyper sophisticated English patient, familiar with the communal book of mankind in which human beings and stories are linked across time and space. When personal or planetary disaster strikes, the coarse-minded Spit and the erudite burned man, distant though they are in all respects, both cling like Janet Frame's protagonist in *The Carpathians* to the "Memory Flower," i.e. to the world of imagination.

With other cosmopolitan writers from diverse origins—David Malouf, Salman Rushdie, Janet Frame, Wilson Harris and others—Michael Ondaatje situates the human subject in a framework of global connectedness. These writers have sometimes been blamed for a universalism that fails to fit the national agenda of their native places. Though they cannot be grouped as a "school" they share a holistic approach to life and a common faith in the role of the creative imagination as a potential factor of evolution towards a better world. They throw bridges between past and present, liberating stories, legends, myths or works of art from their rigid frames in a particular historical period so that, like seeds, they can germinate elsewhere in a ceaseless organic recreation of the imagination which alone can counteract the inorganic domination of modern technology. One thinks of the poppy which has mysteriously found its way in the wasteland where the poet Ovid is exiled in David Malouf's *An imaginary life*. Interestingly all these writers occasionally resort to magic realism when they have something particularly important to convey.

Because of its sporadic occurrences and because it does not have a precise literary or critical foundation, some critics would rather give up using the term magic realism altogether. Let them do so. The more the concept escapes being pinned down by theory the better. Magic realism is not a literary genre, it is a strategy to break the polarizations of oppression and more generally to serve as an antidote against an excessive domination of the mind. It is a useful weapon when totalizing ideologies—whether in politics, religion or science—threaten to endanger the integrity and the survival of the human being. A shapeshifter sharing the elusiveness of the Aboriginal Trickster, magic realism may also, like Him/Her, oversleep for a while, but it is sure to re-emerge when and where the world needs healing. It will always be there because it posits a "suspension of disbelief" that is the definition of poetry itself, poetry which, in Robert Bringhurst's words, is *"the language of being"*. The breath, the voice, the song of being. It does not need us. We are the ones in need of it" (Bringhurst 1999: 147, italics in the original, J. D-G).

References

Armstrong, Jeanette C. 1990. "This is a story", in: Thomas King (ed.), 129-135.

Bhabha, Homi. 1994. *The location of culture*. London: Routledge.

Bringhurst, Robert. 1999. "Coterminous worlds", in: Elsa Linguanti – Francesco Casotti – Carmen Concilio (eds.), 139-149.

D'Aguiar, Fred. 2003. "Interview with Wilson Harris", *Bomb*, 82: 74-80.

Delbaere, Jeanne. 2000. "Memory as healing: Transcending the Irish past in Jack Hodgins's *The invention of the world* and Jane Urquhart's *Away*", *English Studies*, 9: 81-98.

Delbaere, Jeanne. 1996. "'Only re-connect': Temporary pacts in Michael Ondaatje's *The English patient*", in: Marc Delrez – Bénédicte Ledent (ed.), 45-56.

Delrez, Marc – Bénédicte Ledent (ed.). 1996. *The contact and the culmination. Essays in honour of Hena Maes-Jelinek*. Liège: L³.

Gilkes, Michael (ed.). 1989. *The literate imagination: Essays on the novels of Wilson Harris*. London: Macmillan Caribbean.

Hannan, Annika (ed.). 2010. *Jack Hodgins: Essays on his works*. Toronto: Guernica.

Hannan, Annika. 2010a. "New world myth and feminine creation: Magic realism in Jack Hodgins' *The invention of the world*", in Annika Hannan (ed.), 48-76.

Harris, Wilson. 1989. "Literacy and the imagination: A talk", in: Michael Gilkes (ed.), 13-30.

Hodgins, Jack. 1976. *Spit Delaney's island*. Toronto: Macmillan.

Hodgins, Jack. 1977. *The invention of the world*. Toronto: Macmillan.

Hodgins, Jack. 1979. *The resurrection of Joseph Bourne; or, A word or two on those Port Annie miracles.* Toronto: Macmillan.

Kerslake, Susan. 1976. *Middlewatch.* Ottawa: Oberon Press.

King, Thomas (ed.). 1990. *All my relations. An anthology of contemporary Canadian native fiction.* Toronto: McClelland & Stewart.

Kroetch, Robert. 1983 [1978] *What the crow said.* Toronto: General.

Kundera, Milan. 2005. *Le Rideau.* Paris: Gallimard.

Linguanti, Elsa – Francesco Casotti – Carmen Concilio (eds.). 1999. *Coterminous worlds. Magic realism and contemporary post-colonial literature in English.* Amsterdam: Rodopi.

MacDonald, Ann-Marie. 1997 [1996]. *Fall on your knees.* London: Vintage.

MacEwen, Gwendolyn. 1985 [1972]. *Noman.* Toronto: General.

Maes-Jelinek, Hena (ed.). 1991. *Wilson Harris: The uncompromising imagination.* Mundelstrup/Sydney: Dangaroo Press.

Maillard, Keith. 1982 [1978] *Two strand river.* Toronto: General.

Maufort, Marc. 2003. *Transgressive itineraries. Postcolonial hybridizations of dramatic realism.* Peter Lang.

Ondaatje, Michael. 1988 [1987]. *In the skin of a lion.* London: Picador.

Ondaatje, Michael. 1992. *The English patient.* Toronto: Vintage Canada.

Pratt, Mary Louise. 1992. *Studies in travel writing and transculturation.* London: Routledge.

Rutherford, Jonathan (ed.). 1990. *Identity: Community, culture, difference.* London: Lawrence & Wishart.

Rutherford, Jonathan. 1990a. "The third space. Interview with Homi Bhabha", in: Jonathan Rutherford (ed.), 207-221.

Rzepa, Agnieszka. 2009. *Feats and defeats of memory: Exploring spaces of Canadian magic realism,* Poznań: Wydawnictwo Naukowe UAM.

Taylor, Drew Hayden. 2011. *Motorcycles and sweetgrass,* Toronto: Vintage Canada.

Todorov, Tzvetan, 1995. *Les abus de la mémoire.* Paris: Arléa.

Urquhart, Jane. 1993. *Away.* Toronto: McClelland & Stewart.

Wachtel, Eleanor. 1994. "An Interview with Michael Ondaatje", *Essays in Canadian Writing,* 53: 250-61.

Weisgerber, Jean. 1987. *Le réalisme magique. Roman. Peinture. Cinéma.* Lausanne: L'Age d'Homme.

Sagas of Northern contacts and magic realism: From historical conflicts to fictional conciliations

Hartmut Lutz, University of Szczecin

ABSTRACT

Depicted in the Norse *Grœnlandiga saga* and *Eirik's saga*, the so-called "Vinland-Sagas", the first recorded contacts between Northern Europeans and Indigenous North Americans a thousand years ago foreshadow the conflicts which began in earnest five hundred years later: from welcome and peaceful trade to armed violence, manslaughter, kidnapping and enforced acculturation of Indigenous children. Fictional narratives of historical relations between "Skrælings" and Vikings tended to either celebrate European supremacy or later served to criticize European materialism. Most recently, individual Aboriginal and non-Aboriginal authors in Canada have begun to create and publish narratives which tend to meta-fictionally or "magically" conciliate the conflicts depicted in the sagas.

Starting with two novels by Newfoundland author Joan Clark, i.e. her historiographic metafiction *Eiriksdottir* (1994) and her magic realist juvenile fiction *The dream carvers* (1995), this paper explores depictions of Native—non-Native relations in historical novels about Vinland written by non-Aboriginal authors. It then compares such narratives with revisionist historiography by Aboriginal authors. In the first part of his historical novel *La saga des Béothuks* (1996), set in pre-Columbian Newfoundland, the francophone Cree author Bernard Assiniwi fictionalizes a Norse-Beothuk encounter around the year 1,000 A.D., whereas Inuit writer Rachel A. Quitsualik in her short story "Skraeling" (2004) depicts a tragic misunderstanding between Norse and Inuit and reads it against other European encounters with non-European others. Given the colonial legacy of Native—non-Native relations the conciliatory stance of the Aboriginal texts may come as a surprise.

An introductory caveat

The following paper deals with an intercultural encounter as narrated in texts stemming from three very different cultural contexts. A meeting between Europeans and Aboriginal people in what is today Canada was first described in mediaeval sagas from Iceland. That description was re-visited and fictionalized in several 20th century novels in Canada (Salvarson, Mowatt, Clark), and most recently that encounter was again revised by two Aboriginal Franco- and Anglophone authors from Canada, Bernard Assiniwi and Rachel Quitsualik. While the sagas at first sight seem staunchly realistic, the postmodern historiographic metafictions by Joan Clark easily transcend the boundaries between historical realism and fictional fantasy. But what about the texts by Aboriginal authors—one from a First Nation and one an Inuit—who come from cultural backgrounds that traditionally are oral and therefore not originally part of Western categories of literature, nor do they share the heuristic conventions of the European enlightenment, which we have learned to be so proud of?

Be it admitted right from the start, that the author of this essay is neither fully comfortable with the term "magic realism", nor can he claim any scholarly authority with regards to magic realism's theoretical ramifications. The term itself seems to be a very elusive and complexly arbitrary one that covers a variety of cultural meanings and artistic expressions. By pairing two semantic opposites which western enlightenment has constructed as irreconcilable, the magic and the real, it presents a semantic oxymoron. While this oxymoronic reading only sees it as a paradox, there is also another more political reading of the term within a postcolonial context, because, a priori the term "magic realism" assumes the discursive authority to distinguish between that which is "real"—a conviction which postmodernist constructivism no longer seems to uphold—and that which is "not-real", and which is even 'othered' as being "magic". Thus the term semantically upholds the Eurocentric hegemony of enlightenment logic. In its contradictory semantics, by implication, the very term claims heuristic authority vis-a-vis cultures which, very likely, do not subscribe to western notions of reality, or cultures for which reality extends far into realms which the enlightenment discards as not-real or denounces as superstitious or magic. Therefore, this author, until now, has been more than reluctant to use "magic realism" when speaking or writing about Native American or First Nations literatures, because all too often we as western readers may classify actions in Aboriginal texts as "magic realist", which in terms of Aboriginal cultural traditions are likely to be perceived as being just as "real" as day and night. If such phenomena are defined as "magic", the immediate reaction is to ask: "Says who?" Should we, as children of the enlightenment, really assume the authority to define as "magic" what for traditional peoples is very "real"? Isn't that just as colonialist a gesture as the appropriation of Indigenous artefacts by European museums or oral traditions by non-Aboriginal authors? Does enlightenment rationalism authorize us to define as "magic" those parts of Indigenous philosophies or *weltanschauungen,* which rest on the experience that the departed have the power to be present visually, vocally and at times even physically (as some Icelandic sagas suggest), or that animals have the ability to speak to us (as First Nations narratives indicate), or that words have the "magic" power to create and shape material reality (as *Genesis* and Aboriginal philosophies demonstrate)? Is the enlightenment Manichaeism between the real and the magic still tenable at a time, when "magic realist" literature from Latin America has imploded that very dichotomy, and at a time when constructivism and new historicism have seriously questioned the existence of a reality beyond or outside its narrative emplotment? In the past this author has shunned these—Eurocentric?—ontological questions, leaving the definition of what is "real(ist)" to Western philosophers, and leaving the definition of (the extension of that) realism (into what western Manichaeism defines as magic) to those peoples who experience as real what the enlightenment has taught us to externalize as magic.

In preparation for this conference on the poetics and politics of magic realism, however, a very brief terminological check was conducted by looking up "magic realism" in the two most canonical 30 volume encyclopaedias the author has access to: the *Encyclopaedia Britannica* and the *Brockhaus*. Surprisingly, the 15th edition of the *Britannica* (2005), with micro-, macro- and propaedia, has no entry under "magic realism" at all, but refers the reader to the German term "Neue Sachlichkeit" (vol. 8, 619), i.e. a phenomenon in 1920s expressionist painting, leading to so-called "hyperrealism" in the visual arts, where the exaggeratedly realist portrayal of "reality" evokes the sense that there is a "reality beyond" (Thiersch 2002: 187f. et passim)—a reality, which is emotionally imminent but not visually evident, uncanny perhaps and often gothic, but of course not on the surface of the canvas but in the psyche of the beholder. This is a definition for the visual arts which is also put forth in the 19th edition of *Brockhaus Enzyklopädie*. There, we also find an entry for "Magischer Realismus" in literature, as the post World War II development towards a literature where reality becomes a metaphor for another, i.e. magic reality, and it refers us to the fantastic in Latin American literature (vol. 14, 18). By these "definitions" some of the texts discussed in the following seem clearly to fall into the category "realism" in the most conventional sense, while some of the contemporary fictions may indeed be read as magic realist. A more fitting category, however, would be to read them as "historiographic metafictions". According to Linda Hutcheon, historiographic metafictions are narratives that are set in, or that consciously reflect, historical occurrences, but that take certain fictional liberties in their treatments of history (Hutcheon 1988: 60-77). Such texts foreshadow or take for granted the new historicist notion of the narrative constructedness of all historiography, and they consciously transcend and blur the boundaries between historical fact and mimetic fiction, between material reality and the non-tangible "beyond." In this postmodern sense, some of the texts discussed in the following, may also be understood as magic realist.

Talking about Margaret Atwood's feminist fiction, Wolfgang Klooss described the (post-)modern emancipatory project of moving the marginalized from their positions at the rim into the centre, as a process of 'relocation' and re-placing. But Klooss also says that "The idea of replacing is equally important for those writers who either deal with particular ethnic and cultural groups or present outstanding historical figures in their writings" (Klooss 1994: 58). In the following this thought is taken up by looking at (post-)modern adaptations of the Icelandic "Vinland" Sagas of North American discovery. One focus rests in the presentation of "ethnic or cultural groups," i.e. the indigenous inhabitants of what is today Newfoundland and Labrador, the Skrælings, and an additional focus will be trimmed on one "outstanding historical figure", i.e. the remarkable female character Freydis, the illegitimate daughter of Eirik the Red, who was the founder of the Norse colony in Greenland and also father of Leif the Lucky, the "discoverer" of North America. After having briefly introduced these characters from the mediaeval Norse Sagas, attention will then be turned to the revisionist readings the Newfoundland novelist Joan Clark gives Saga-Freydis in her historiographic metafiction *Eiriksdottir* (1994) and its juvenile fiction sequel *The dream carvers* (1995). In a third step, two texts by the aforementioned Aboriginal authors will be discussed, which also deal with this encounter.

The Sagas

Two Sagas deal with the Norse (Greenlandic & Icelandic) discovery, exploration and settlement of North America from Helluland (Baffin Island) to Markland (Labrador) to Vinland (Newfoundland and South): "The saga of the Greenlanders" and "Eirik the Red's saga".[1] These brief and concise narratives are well-known enough, but suffice it to say that the historical encounter they mention took place around the year 1000 AD, that the sagas were written down two centuries later, and that the truth of the sagas was not corroborated until 1960 by the Norwegian couple Helge and Anne Stine Ingstad, who discovered and excavated the Viking settlement "Leifsbudir" at L'Anse aux Meadows on the northern tip of Newfoundland, from where, on a clear day, you can look across the Strait of Belle Isle to the wooded coast of Labrador.

The mediaeval sagas are staunchly realist, based on oral tradition and written in a terse, concise and often minimalist prose. At times they blend realism with the "magic" or fantastic. In *Greenlanders saga*, there are descriptions of "magical" occurrences related to the Christian character Gudrid (*GS*, 647), and in *Eirik the Red's saga* that same Gudrid even takes part in pagan sorcery (*ERS*, 659). Some characters can communicate with the spirits of the dead, who sometimes refuse to let go of their beloved in life—but this type of "magic" is certainly not the product of a magic realist literary strategy but part of a reality as it was perceived and acted upon by pagan and early Christian Vikings a thousand years ago. We find similar occurrences in other sagas of the times.

Most encounters between the Greenlanders and the Aboriginals, whom the Vikings called "Skrælings", are rather brief. They either trade with each other or they kill each other. Ethnocentrically, the sagas depict the Skrælings in terms which make them look inferior to the Norse: "They were short in height with threatening features and tangled hair on their heads. Their eyes were large and their cheeks broad" (*ERS*, 669).[2] Being so short and dark, the Skrælings did not

---

1 Henceforth referred to as *GS* and *ERS* respectively, both followed by page number. All quotations are from *The sagas of Icelanders: A selection*. 2000. (Preface by Jane Smiley. Introduction by Robert Kellogg. Translated by Keneva Kunz.) Harmondsworth, Middlesex: Penguin.

2 Other translations are equally negative: "They were small [or: "dark- coloured", as explained in a footnote, HL] and evil looking, and their hair was coarse; they had large eyes and broad

amount to much by Viking (proto-Aryan?) standards of beauty, and the Norse treated them in precisely the same fashion as did white men after Columbus: they cheated them in trade, they killed them wantonly, and they kidnapped their children and sought to civilize them.[3]

If there is a female protagonist in the two sagas, it would be the devout Christian Gudrid, who gave birth to the first European child in North America, who outlived several husbands, who later undertook a pilgrimage to Rome and became a nun, and whose offspring became prominent clergymen in Iceland (*GS,* 651f.; *ERS,* 674).[4] Gudrid is truly a remarkable character—wise, beautiful, pious and entrepreneurial—but some of the most outrageous occurrences in the Sagas are related to Freydis, a mediaeval *femme fatale,* who plots and schemes to increase her wealth and power. In the *Greenlander saga* Freydis single-handedly kills five women of the competing Icelandic crew with an axe (*GS,* 650f.), and in the *Saga of Eirik the Red* she frightens off an attacking group of Skrælings, who have already put the Viking men to flight , by bearing one of her breasts and slapping it with a sword (*ERS,* 670f.). Clearly, when seen from a Christian perspective, Freydis is portrayed as an altogether unsympathetic figure. According to the Swiss scholar of Scandinavian philology, Walter Baumgartner, the mediaeval Christian epic contrasts the eventual bad luck of the ill-fated pagan Freydis with the success of the devout Christian Gudrid, who finally prevails

---

cheekbones" (*The Vinland sagas*, 98), and another: "They were dark, ugly men who wore their hair in an unpleasant fashion. They had big eyes and were broad in the cheeks" (Gwyn Jones' 1961 translation in the Oxford UP edition, quoted in Mead 1976: 19).

3   The following quotations may substantiate this general statement:
Uneven Trade:
They [...] began trading with the visitors, who mostly wished to trade for red cloth.. They also wanted to purchase swards and spears, but Karlsefni and Snorri forbade this. They traded dark pelts for the cloth, and for each pelt they took cloth a hand in length, which they bound about their heads. This went on for some time, until there was little cloth left. They then cut the cloth into smaller pieces, each no wider than a finger's width, but the natives gave just as much for it or more" (*ERS*, 670).
Wanton killing of sleeping First Nations people (with pemmican supply):
Sailing north along the shore, they discovered five natives sleeping in skin sacks near the shore. Beside them they had vessels filled with deer marrow blended with blood. They assumed these men to be outlaws and killed them" (*ERS*, 671);
Kidnapping boys to 'civilize' them:
They had southerly winds and reached Markland, where they met five natives. One was bearded, two were women and two of them children. Karlsefni and his men caught the boys but the others escaped and disappeared into the earth. They took the boys with them and taught them their language and had them baptized" (*ERS*, 672).

4   For a feminist celebration of Gudrid's achievements see Nancy Marie Brown's *The far traveler: Voyages of a Viking woman* (2007), which combines the sagas with historiography, anthropology, archaeological evidence, linguistics, fiction and the author's own accounts of the research voyages she undertook to write the book.

(Baumgartner 1998: 392-396). 1000 AD was the year when the Icelanders in their annual Allthing assembly officially adopted Christianity as their religion, but the old belief in the Nordic gods lingered on, and many sagas, written down by Christian scribes two centuries later, bear witness to the struggle between the old religion and the new.

There is a crucial and exemplary scene in which the Greenlander Freydis manages to instigate her husband and his men to kill all members of the competing Icelandic crew, with whom they travelled together, and with whom they share the buildings, Leifsbudir,[5] erected earlier by her brother Leif. It is given below in full:

> Early one morning Freydis got up and dressed, but did not put on any footwear. The weather had left thick dew on the grass. She took her husband's cape and placed it over her shoulders and went to the brothers' longhouse and came to the doorway. A man had gone out a short while earlier and had left the door half-open. She opened the door and stood silently in the door awhile. Finnbogi lay awake at the inner end of the house.
> He spoke: 'What do you want here, Freydis?'
> She answered, 'I want you to get up and come outside. I have to speak to you.'
> He did as she said. They went over to a tree trunk lying near the wall of the house and sat down there.
> 'How do you like it here?' she asked.
> 'I think the land has much to offer, but I don't like the ill-feeling between us, as I don't think there is reason for it.'
> 'What you say is true,' she said, 'and I agree. But my purpose in coming to see you was that I want to exchange ships with the two of you, as you have a larger ship than I do and I want to leave this place.'
> 'I suppose I can agree to that,' he said, 'if that will please you.'
> After this they parted. She returned home and Finnbogi went back to his bed. When she climbed back into her bed her cold feet woke Thorvard, who asked why she was so cold and wet.
> She answered vehemently, 'I went to the brothers, to ask to purchase their ship, as I wanted a larger ship. They reacted so angrily; they struck me and treated me very badly, but you're such a coward that you will repay neither dishonour done to me nor to yourself. I am now paying the price of being so far from my home in Greenland, and unless you avenge this, I will divorce you!'
> Not being able to ignore her upbraiding any longer, he told the men to get up as quickly as they could and arm themselves. Having done so, they went at once to the longhouse of the brothers, entered while those inside were still asleep and took them, tied them up, and once bound, led them outside. Freydis, however, had each one of the men who was brought out killed.
> Soon all the men had been killed and only the women were left, as no one would kill them.
> Freydis then spoke: 'Hand me an axe.'

---

5   The "Leifsbudir" (Leif's huts) have been located, archaeologically excavated, and partly reconstructed at L'Anse aux Meadows, on the northernmost tip of Newfoundland. They are now a UNESCO world heritage site.

This was done, and she then attacked the five women there and killed them all.
They returned to their house after this wicked deed, and it was clear that Freydis was
highly pleased with what she had accomplished

(GS, 649f).

Historiographic (meta-)fictions

Talking about "historiographic metafiction" Linda Hutcheon wrote: "this kind of
metafiction thematizes its own interaction with the historical past and with the
historically conditioned expectations of its readers" (Hutcheon 1988: 65). Joan
Clark's postmodern novel *Eiriksdottir* (1994)[6] does exactly that. On the one hand
it very closely follows parts of the sagas, at times even verbatim, and on the other,
her text enters into a lively and often contradictory dialogue with them. This is
most obvious in the crucial scene in which Freydis instigates the Greenlanders'
massacre of the Icelandic crew. The novel engages deeply with this passage, but
Clark fictionalizes the incident in a revisionist way, which exculpates novel-
Freydis, who throughout the narrative comes across as a strong, shrewd,
courageous and self-determined woman. In Clark's rendering novel-Freydis
wakes up after a bloody dream in which she sees herself as a valkyrie, who cleans
up a battlefield but cleaves the heads of wounded survivors. A sympathetic reason
is given for her remaining barefooted—her shoes "were too far under the bench to
reach without disturbing Thorvard" (*Eiriksdottir*, 349). The Icelander who had
gone out earlier and left the door ajar has a name: Gudlaug. He has gone out for
an early fishing venture before breakfast. When novel-Freydis talks to Finnbogi,
sitting on a driftwood log on the beach, the Icelander at first verbally agrees to
lend her his boat, but then the early fisherman, Gudlaug, returns and asks:

'What's this? Some sort of joke?' He had been with Finnbogi for years and knew the
Icelander would never give up his ship.
'Indeed it is.' Finnbogi laughed. 'But as you know, Greenlanders are so gullible they'll
fall for anything'

(Eiriksdottir, 351).

After this insult, and outraged by his betrayal, novel-Freydis attacks Finnbogi, but
she is held back by Gudlaug, and has to endure Finnbogi's taunts. She then returns
to the sleeping Thorvard. When novel-Thorvard asks his wife why her feet are so
cold, she starts "weeping and snuffling" and tells him how she was humiliated by
the Icelanders. And here Joan Clark's omniscient narrator makes a direct intertextual reference to the saga texts, refuting it by concluding: "Freydis aroused
Thorvard's anger so well that there was no need to threaten him with divorce if he
refused to avenge Finnbogi's wrongdoing" (*Eiriksdottir*, 352). Both novel-

---

6   Henceforth indicated as *Eiriksdottir* followed by page number. All quotations are from Clark,
     Joan. 1995 [1994]. *Eiriksdottir: A tale of dreams and luck*. Toronto: Penguin Books Canada.

Thorvard and novel-Freydis are drawn as more positive characters than their saga-"forbears." Even Freydis' killing of two—instead of five—women appears in a more positive light in the novel: she first kills in self-defence and after that in a trancelike stupor (*Eiriksdottir*, 355f.).

In their historiographic metafictional and revisionist reading of history postmodern novels, according to Klooss (1994: 58), often re-place the marginalized into the centre. This is certainly true in a feminist sense when we look at the character of Joan Clark's novel-Freydis and compare her to saga-Freydis. Clark revises and re-invents the *femme fatale* of the sagas by constructing her as an "outstanding historical figure" (*Eiriksdottir*, 58) matching Klooss' model. While in the sagas this character is only known for her misdeeds and has no plot function beyond that, Freydis in Clark's novel is the one who actually plans and organizes the Greenlander's voyage to Vinland, and who as the protagonist, gives the novel *Eiriksdottir* its title. As a postmodern text the novel employs at least three different narrative voices—omniscient narrator, Ulfar's vellums and the voice of Groa's ghost—as well as at least thirteen different types of texts, ranging from the novel's narrator to "found" parchments, inset tales, skaldic verses, songs in Gaelic, maps, lists of characters as well as mottoes taken from Sagas, from Victorian poetry and from runic inscriptions.

In the final two chapters, *Eiriksdottir* abandons historiographic realism altogether. Having accompanied Freydis and her crew back to Greenland, the narrative then returns to the other Icelandic group in Vinland who had left Leifsbudir under Finbogi's brother, Helgi Egilsson, before the massacre, and who had sailed south in a third longship, "Paradise Seeker", to explore Vinland the Good. There they partake so much of the proverbial wine that their plans of returning to Leifsbudir and "civilization" become more and more unrealistic, and they fall victim to the never ending supply of wine, which is miraculously provided by the hidden folk, and to the temptations of their own flesh. Here, the novel moves into the fantastic. The survivors do indeed find paradise: "It was the nature of Vinland that no sooner did someone express a desire for some kind of food than the wish was granted" (*Eiriksdottir*, 395f.). Gradually, they shed their Icelandic work ethic, their will to return, their boat and their clothes, and Finna, Helgi's wife, is last seen riding away on a white unicorn (*Eiriksdottir*, 416). This fantastic ending may be read as magic realism. The narrative abandons even the conventions of historiographic metafiction. Anything is possible in the new found Vinland paradise. Helgi and Finna can grow fins to swim like fish, and there are no Indigenous inhabitants besides hidden folk and elvish beings. In such a narrative, there is no room to give Viking-Skræling relations a revisionist reading or to re-place Aboriginals as "ethnic or cultural group" from margin to centre.

This changes fundamentally, however, in Joan Clark's second novel about the Vikings in Vinland. *The dream carvers*, a book for young readers, was published a year after *Eiriksdottir*. Its plot structure follows classical Indian Captivity

Narratives: attack and capture by Natives—abduction and remove from "civilized" European society—integration and adoption into Native American civilization; albeit, without the moment of return into European culture.[7] In *The dream carvers,* 14 year old Thrand from Gardar in Greenland, gradually integrates into a Beothuk extended family and eventually gives up his initial plans of returning to his Viking kin but decides to stay Beothuk. *The dream carvers* is much more conventionally told than *Eiriksdottir.* It is a very accessible realist historical novel, told in the first person voice of the central character, whose observations provide the readers with a reliable view of the "other" culture. In the process, Clark portrays the Beothuk as the more humane, peace-loving and ecologically superior culture, thus using the conventional image of the Noble Savage for a (conservative) critique of European aggressive greed and expansionist imperialism.[8] While the Icelandic Sagas tend to celebrate European supremacy, thus establishing a norm which still persists into modernism, Clark's fictional narratives of historical relations between Skrælings and Vikings adopt a postcolonial stance and serve to criticize European materialism.

Aboriginal responses

Bernard Assiniwi (1939-2000) is a well-known and widely published Francophone Algonquin-Cree non-status First Nation writer from Québec, while Anglophone Inuit author, Rachel A. Quitsualik, is a (yet) less widely published author from Nunavut. Assiniwi's text, *La saga des Béothuks,* published in French in 1996, and appearing only four years after in an English translation by Wayne Grady,[9] is a 515 pp. historical revisionist novel about the Beothuk, a First Nation

---

7　This pattern, i.e. the remove from and the return to Euro-colonial civilization was followed by all autobiographical and most fictional captivity narratives, but it was not necessarily the most common sequence of events as enacted in real history, where many European captives preferred to stay in Native communities rather than return to military service or to the armed conflicts between the European colonial powers. Such stories, however, were generally not recorded in autobiographical or even in fictional captivities, the overall function of which was propagandistic.

8　Joan Clark follows a similar ideological convention in her earlier novel *The victory of Geraldine Gull* (1988), set in contemporary Canada.

9　Grady won a Governor General's award as a translator, but unfortunately one needs to be suspicious of Grady's translation of Assiniwi's novel. When first reading the English translation in 2004, this author came across passages which contained such logical inconsistencies, that they warranted a check on the French original. In all three cases checked, the original had been mistranslated into English. To wit, when the protagonist finds green grass early in the year and asks himself (in the translation): "Or perhaps the grass had never dried out in these parts? Had it been an exceptionally cold [sic !] season here, too, with little snow and only short periods of intense cold? Was it perhaps always this warm [sic!]?" (*The Beothuk Saga,* 54f.). Assiniwi's original is quite logical: "À moins que cette herbe n'ait jamais séché? Était-ce un hiver exceptionellement chaud? Ce pays-ci était-il toujours aussi

who were exterminated during their colonial contact with European Newfoundlanders. Similarly, Quitsualik's text is also a revisionist historiographic metafictional text, a 29 pp. short story about first contact of Thule and Dorset Inuit with Vikings, contextualized within colonial contacts world-wide, and aware of historical millennia. It was published in 2004 in *Our story*, a prestigious collection of "Aboriginal voices on Canada's past" (subtitle), with a foreword by Adrienne Clarkson. To the author's knowledge, these two texts are the first Aboriginal fictionalizations of the Skræling-Viking encounter, and they are the first narratives which tend to meta-fictionally or "magically" conciliate the conflict depicted in the sagas.

Bernard Asiniwi was a prolific writer, who published more than a dozen expository books, seven works of juvenile fiction, a drama, a novella and three novels. *The Beothuk saga* is his last. In three parts it follows the history of the Beothuk people from their first encounters with Norse and Inuit around 1000 AD (Part I: "The Initiate", 1-133), to their early post-Columbian contacts half a millennium later (Part II: "The Invaders", 135-216), to the life of the last survivors in the eighteenth and nineteenth century and the death of Shanawdithit on June 6th, 1829 (Part III: "Genocide", 217-322). A map, a historical "Chronology of events", "A Beothuk lexicon" and a "Bibliography" complete this fictional historiographic homage to a people who were wiped out by European colonialism's genocidal tactics. *The Beothuk saga*[10] in itself may be read as an honouring song for the members of a nation who were made to disappear. It is written by a contemporary First Nations author against forgetting that the Beothuk once existed as the Aboriginal inhabitants of what is today Newfoundland. The first part of the novel, "The Initiate" follows the last stages of the protagonist Anin's initiation, i.e. a three-year long single-handed circumnavigation of

---

chaud?"(*La saga des Béothuks*, 72f.). Similarly, there is a passage discussing the reasons for polygyny in a Beothuk community, which reads in the translation, "That is why there were more [sic!] Beothuk men than women" (*The Beothuk Saga*, 59), whereas Assiniwi wrote: "C'est pourqoi le nombre des homes est moins [sic!] grand que celui des femmes" (*La saga des Béothuks*, 78). Another translation maintains Christian homophobia among Vikings where Assiniwi's original clearly refutes it: "But since the missionaries have come to our land, this pleasant custom has been forbidden. The god Thor, it seemed, did not approve [sic!] of satisfying one's natural needs, such as the mutual satisfaction of physical desires, unless it was between a man and a woman" (*The Beothuk Saga*, 112). Grady mistranslated Assiniwi's original: "Mais avec la venue des missionaries chrétiens dans nos pays, il semble que cette pratique soit à banner. Pourtant, le dieu Thor ne désapprouvait [sic!] pas des besoins aussi naturels que la lutte amoureuse de deux corps, fussent-ils masculins ou féminins" (*La saga des Béothuks*, 177f.). Here, Christian prudishness regarding homosexuality is projected onto the old Nordic gods, simply by omitting the French double negation "ne désappouvait" and 'translating' "did not disapprove" as "did approve".

10   Henceforth indicated as *BS* followed by page number. All quotations are from Assiniwi, Bernard. 2000. *The Beothuk saga*. (Translated by Wayne Grady.) Toronto: McClelland and Stewart.

Newfoundland by *tapatook* (birchbark canoe), which brings the protagonist into contact and combat with "Ashwans, the people who came from the cold" (*BS*, 21) the Inuit, and the "Bouguishamesh" (*BS*, 10), the Vikings, "with hair the colour of dried grass" (*BS*, 11). The omnisciently told narrative follows the perception of Anin, and it is interspersed with words from the extinct Beothuk language, so that a Viking boat is perceived as "a huge Bouguishamesh tapatook with the head of a monster on the bow" (*BS*, 11).

The ferocious Ashwans (or Inuit) are not individualized but appear simply as dangerous and murderous, and Anin perceives them according to an all too well-known (European) racist stereotype: "'They are savages,' he thought. 'They live only to kill'"(*BS*, 23). By contrast, the Vikings are treated more as individuals. Early in the novel Anin observes that, "They laugh like we do" (*BS*, 12), but a moment later he has to defend himself against their attack and kill one of them. Later, he observes a Viking settlement with cattle and sheep, and he encounters a pregnant and wounded Irish woman with hair the colour of dried grass. Together with his first wife, Woasut, he saves her life. Gudruide then becomes his second wife, and their family is later joined by Gudruide's younger sister Gwenid and two Scottish slaves who "can run faster than the wind" (*BS*, 67), Della and Rob. The two Scottish slaves are obviously modelled after Haki and Hekja, the two Scottish thralls mentioned in *Eirik the Red's Saga*.[11] Gradually, the Irish and Scottish captives integrate into Beothuk culture, and together with Anin, Woasut, Gudruide, and their children form the nucleus of a new Addaboutik (Beothuk) tribe, the Bear Clan.

In his depiction of Beothuk and European social interaction Assiniwi explores their differences in physical appearances, beliefs, languages, communal and individual behaviour and survival skills, as well as in matters of sexual practices, but he is careful to show that such "exotic" differences are an enhancement of Addaboutik life, not a detriment. Neither the Natives nor the Europeans are free of prejudices or weaknesses, but together, under the leadership of the initiate Anin, they become a strong community and a model for others to follow. Assiniwi thus goes beyond the self-portrayal of Greenlanders and Icelanders in the Sagas by re-placing the marginalized Irish thralls and Scottish slaves from their marginal

---

11   "When Leif had served King Olaf Tryggvason and was told by him to convert Greenland to Christianity, the king had given him two Scots, a man named Haki and a woman called Hekja. The king told him to call upon them whenever he needed someone with speed, as they were fleeter of foot than any deer. Leif and Erik had sent them to accompany Karlsefni. After sailing the length of the Furdustrandir, they put the two Sots ashore and told them to run southwards to explore the country and return before three day's time had elapsed. They were dressed in a garment known as a kjafal, which had a hood at the top but no arms, and was open at the sides and fastened between the legs with a button and a loop; they wore nothing else. The ship cast anchor and lay during this time. After three days had passed the two returned to the shore, one of them with grapes in hand and the other with self-sown wheat. Karslefni said that they had found good land" (*ERS*, 667).

position into parts of the group at the centre, and by portraying them as members of a common humanity whom the Beothuk learn to respect. Similarly, the novel re-places those individual characters who would be marginalized in their respective communities on account of their gender or their sexual orientation, and gives them the same respect that is due to all Addaboutik. At the same time, the Vikings are seen from a cautious distance. They are undoubtedly human, but they are, in the eyes of Anin and his people, the tough invaders, whom the Vinland Sagas celebrate. Only the Ashwans remain alien and strange and truly marginalized throughout the text. While Assiniwi stresses the differences between ethnic groups, he refrains from essentializing them. While the Ashwans remain hostile and disappear again into the northern cold, the *Beothuk Saga* stresses the common humanity between the Celts and the Beothuk. This may be read as Assiniwi's acknowledgement of the fact that Newfoundland today is ethnically very much an "Irish" part of Canada, but given the fact, that the whole book is a lament for a nation forever destroyed by contact with these very European Newfoundlanders, Assiniwi's revisionist reading of history takes a very generous, and surprisingly conciliatory turn.

Rachael Quitsualik's short story "Skræling" (2004)[12] has a similarly conciliatory ending. Again, we have a culture clash between three ethnic groups, the sedentary archaic Dorset or "Tunit" people, who live along the coast in rectangular houses of rock, the nomadic Inuit protagonist and his dogsled, and the Norse from Greenland, who seem to be bent only on wantonly killing the Tunit. In the beginning, we meet the protagonist Kannujaq standing among a mass of *Inuksuit,* built for the caribou hunt by the Tunit. In this expository opening passage, the omniscient narrative voice steps out of the story and (*Skræling*, 38f.) contextualizes the event in terms of world history around the year 1,000 AD. In this, the text clearly meets a paradigm Linda Hutcheon described as constitutive of historiographic metafiction: "... this kind of metafiction thematizes its own interaction both with the historical past and with the historically conditioned expectations of its readers" (Hutcheon 1988: 65). Quitsualik's text refers to (1) the current strength of the Byzantine empire, (2) the Inuit migration from Alaska, where they had encountered tall, painted and fearsome Indians, (3) the Mayan pyramids in the south, where blood is sacrificed, (4) the philosopher Alhazen in the Osmanic empire, who ponders and explains rainbows, (5) the greed for gold, which ruins Ghana in Africa, (6) the fear of a Mongolian invasion troubling the emperor of China; (7) the Normans, who have invaded France, (8) the Danes, who rule in parts of England, (9) the presence of other Scandinavians in Russia, as well as the fact that competing Norwegians and Danes have settled in Ireland, Iceland

---

12 Henceforth indicated as *Skræling* followed by page number. All quotations are from
    Quitsualik, Rachel A. 2004. "Skræling", in: King, Thomas – Tantoo Cardinal – Tomson
    Highway, 33-66.

and most recently also in Greenland. The passage ends with an omniscient comment that seems ironically to echo the then recent "Y2K" scare (or hype?), by which thousands feared that their computers would break down because the machines were not programmed to accommodate the shift from the year 1999 to the year 2000 (year2kilo). The passage also mocks all Christian millennialist superstitions and at the same time seems to mimic the tone of foreboding fears of the stereotypically 'raping and pillaging' Vikings: "Kannujaq would have been most startled to learn that these were the End Times. A Catholic church was telling all of its flock to expect judgment; for, by their calendar, it was 1000 AD. / And their world was in the grip of the Viking" (*Skræling*, 39).

　　Kannujaq witnesses a Viking raid and massacre of the Tunit village, which otherwise is under the grip of the despotic Angula. There Kannujaq meets two fellow Inuit, beautiful Siaq, and her blue eyed son Siku, who is a "Half Hidden", an *angakoq* or shaman. "He Who Carries Beneath" is the spirit who speaks through Siku, and who says—sounding more like a Christian than a (prelapsarian) pagan—"It is Angula's **sins** [sic!] that have brought the Siaraili among you" (*Skræling*, 52). Siku's mother Siaq is an Inuit captive among the Tunit, and a slave to Angula. Kannujaq learns from her that she once had a relationship with another of Angula's captives, a Viking chief, "The Shining One", who has now returned with his men, apparently to raid the village for the valuable metal weapons Angula once stole from him. While attacking the villagers, the Vikings contemptuously shout "Siaraili", and Kannujaq overhears them talking about "Elulang" or "Hellulan". So, apart from Inuktitut words, we also rediscover Norse words from the Sagas, but heard and misunderstood through the ears of the Inuit protagonist. Eventually, Kannujaq manages to break the power of Angula, whom he kills in self-defence. He then teaches the Tunit how to resist the next Viking raid and how to kill the invaders by baiting and poisoning them like wolves. All through the encounters, The Shining One wears a silver helmet with a mask like visor—much like an early Viking helmet found in Sweden (Magnusson 1965: 20)—and when he finally takes off the helmet while his burning longboat is drifting helplessly out to sea, Kannujaq carefully studies the Viking's facial expression and reads his emotions:

> So they all watched, stared as a current tugged at the vessel, lazily turning it away from the coast. There stood the Shining One, no longer shining, but staring back at Kannujaq. It was a strange thing that there was no hatred in those ice-blue eyes, but only despair, and resignation.
>
> In that moment, Kannujaq recognized the colour of those eyes and knew. The Shining One had never come here for plunder. Siaq had kept a secret from all.
>
> These sea raiders had always had enough weapons and tools to spare. The objects Angula had stolen meant nothing to them. As with Kannujaq, what most mattered was kin. Kannujaq was looking at a fellow stranger in these lands, a newcomer, one who has known that dread of the unknown against him. Perhaps his people were not faring well here.

This was a man with nothing left, whose greatest fear—as with all men—was that
he would fade away, leaving no trace of his passing. And it was such desperation that
had driven his attempts to retrieve his only lasting legacy.
His son.

(Skræling, 64f).

What may be misread as a contrived ending is yet another assertion of a common
humanity across racial and ethno cultural divides, which again, in the face of what
European invaders and settlers brought to the Americas, is a rather generous
reconciliatory gesture on the Inuit author's side. At the same time, the story
undercuts and revises the traditional Indian love story of the Pocahontas-Captain
John Smith type, where the white hero reaps the love of an Indian princess, who
"converts" to his culture; here it is not a princess but an Inuit slave woman who is
wooed by the European, and it is not the Aboriginal female but the European male
who in turn gives up his culture and eventually his life, to be with his Aboriginal
family.

The story closes with Kannujaq's departure from the Tunit village. While
Siku the angakoq decides to come along and join the Inuit, his mother decides to
stay, because "she was no longer comfortable among her own" (65). Kinship, the
story seems to suggest, is not primarily a matter of biology or race, but one of
cultural choice. The omniscient voice then foreshadows the gradual takeover of
the Arctic, from Alaska to Greenland, by the Inuit, who would eventually "speak
of Tunit only in their own legends" (Skræling, 66).

Conclusion

While the Icelandic Sagas tend to celebrate European supremacy, Clark's
postmodern metafictional narratives of historical relations between Skrælings and
Vikings adopt a postcolonial stance and serve to criticize European materialism,
ethno cultural hubris and patriarchal gender norms. Eiriksdottir ends in a fantasy
that may be read as magic realism.

Aboriginal authors Assiniwi and Quitsualik in their narratives tend to meta-
fictionally explore and in the end almost to conciliate the conflicts depicted in the
sagas. Their texts are full of intertextual references to the sagas and world history,
and this far international horizon, and global contextualization, especially in
Quitsualik's narrative, is a fairly new development in Aboriginal literature in
Canada, marking its position on a par with canonized Canadian authors. Both
narratives stress multiculturalism in North America before the Europeans, so they
each depict meetings of at least three ethnic groups: i.e. in Assiniwi's novel the
Beothuk, Inuit and Vikings and in Quitsualik's short fiction between Inuit (Thule,
Copper); Tunit (Dorset) and Viking. Rather than one-sidedly putting the blame for
conflicts and misunderstandings exclusively on the Europeans, these Aboriginal
authors de-essentialize Indigenous ethnicity and argue for a more fluent and

hybrid form of ethnic identities, thus stressing the common humanity of all who met in the Arctic a thousand years ago. They seem to argue for a historical identity tied to place rather than race. Given the colonial legacy of Native—non-Native relations the conciliatory stance of these texts may come as a surprise.

References

Assiniwi, Bernard. 2000. *The Beothuk saga.* (Translated by Wayne Grady.) Toronto: McClelland and Stewart.

Assiniwi, Bernard. 1996. *La saga des Béothuks.* Montréal: Leméac.

Baumgartner, Walter. 1998. "The Grœnlendinga saga interpreted as medieval fiction", in: Peter Easingwood – Konrad Groß – Hartmut Lutz (eds.), 389-400.

Brockhaus Enzyklopädie. 1994. (19th edition.) Vol. 14. F.A. Brockhaus: Leipzig: F.A. Brockhaus.

Brown, Nancy Marie. 2007. *The far traveller: Voyages of a Viking woman.* Orlando: Harcourt Books.

Clark, Joan. 1995 [1994]. *Eiriksdottir: A tale of dreams and luck.* Toronto: Penguin Books Canada.

Clark, Joan. 1995a. *The dream carvers.* Toronto: Penguin Books Canada.

Clark, Joan. 1988. *The victory of Geraldine Gull.* Toronto: Macmillan of Canada.

Easingwood, Peter – Konrad Groß – Hartmut Lutz (eds.). 1998. *Informal empire? Cultural relations between Canada, The United States and Europe.* Kiel: l&f Verlag.

Eirik the Red and other Icelandic sagas. 1976 [1961]. (Translated and edited by Gwyn Jones.), in: Douglas Mead (ed.), 17-21.

"Eirik the Red's Saga", in: *The sagas of Icelanders: A selection,* 653-674.

Encyclopaedia Britannica. 2005. (15th edition.) Vol. 8. Encyclopaedia Britannica Inc.

Engler, Bernd – Kurt Müller (eds.). 1994. *Historiographic metafiction in modern American and Canadian literature.* Paderborn: Ferdinand Schöningh.

Hutcheon, Linda. 1988. "Chapter 4: Historiographic metafiction", in: *The Canadian postmodern: A study of contemporary English-Canadian fiction.* Toronto: Oxford UP, 60-77.

King, Thomas – Tantoo Cardinal – Tomson Highway. 2004. *Our Story: Aboriginal voices on Canada's past.* (Preface by Rudyard Griffith. Foreword by Adrienne Clarkson). Toronto: Random House of Canada.

Klooss, Wolfgang. 1994. "From colonial madness to postcolonial ex-centricity: A story about stories of identity construction in Canadian historiographic (meta-fiction)", in: Bernd Engler – Kurt Müller (eds.), 53-79.

Kulyk Keefer, Janice. 1996. "'Coming across bones': Historiographic ethnofiction", in: Winfried Siemerling (ed.), 84-104.

Magnusson, Magnus. 1965. "Introduction", in: *The Vinland sagas: The Norse discovery of America. Grœnlendiga saga and Eririk's saga*, 7-44.

Mead, Douglas. 1976. *Colonial American literature: From wilderness to independence. An anthology.* New York and Scarborough: New American Library.

Mowat, Farley. 1998. *The farfarers: Before the Norse.* South Royalton, VT: Key Porter Books.

Mowat, Farley. 1990 [1965]. *Westviking: The ancient Norse in Greenland and North America.* Toronto: McClelland and Stewart.

Quitsualik, Rachel A. 2004. "Skræling", in: King, Thomas – Tantoo Cardinal – Tomson Highway, 33-66.

Ross, Colleen. 1996. "The discovery of Joan Clark", *Zeitschrift der Gesellschaft für Kanada-Studien* 16, 2: 101-104.

Siemerling, Winfried (ed.). 1996. *Writing ethnicity: Cross-cultural consciousness in Canadian and Québécois literature.* Toronto: ECW Press.

"The saga of the Greenlanders", in: *The sagas of Icelanders: A selection*, 636-652.

The sagas of Icelanders: A selection. 2000. (Preface by Jane Smiley. Introduction by Robert Kellogg. Translated by Keneva Kunz.) Harmondsworth, Middlesex: Penguin.

Thiersch, Antje. 2002. *The reality b(ey)ond: Triviality and profundity in the novels of Joan Barfoot.* Glienicke: Galda und Wilch.

Salverson, Laura Goodman. 1927. *Lord of the silver dragon.* Toronto: McClelland and Stewart.

The Vinland sagas: The Norse discovery of America. Grœnlendiga saga and Eririk's saga. 1965. (Translated with introduction by Magnus Magnusson and Hermann Pálsson.) Harmondsworth, Middlesex: Penguin.

Whose magic? A comparative reflection on magic realism in Native and white Canadian prose

Ewa Bodal, Nicolaus Copernicus University, Toruń

ABSTRACT

In the last decades magic realism has become not only a major mode of writing in Canadian literature, but also an important concern of Canadian literary criticism. Significantly, magic realism can be detected both in the works by writers belonging to ethnic minorities, and in the books by white authors. Yet, the white writers' usage of magic realism has frequently come under severe criticism, focusing especially on the issue of potential appropriation of the subversive potential of magic realism, for instance by means of utilizing mythology specific for a certain minority.

The present paper attempts to juxtapose the usage of magic realism in the novels written by Native Canadian authors, such as Eden Robinson's *Monkey beach* or Thomas King's *Green grass, running water*, and books by white Canadian writers, taking Margaret Atwood's *Surfacing* and Jane Urquhart's *Away* as examples. The paper analyzes sources of magic realism, paying particular attention to the potential similarities and differences between these in Native and white writing. Furthermore, it attempts to juxtapose the usage of magic realism as based on the beliefs of First Nations in the selected texts, taking Robinson's and Atwood's novels as a case study. Finally, the issue of the appropriation is highlighted in the last part of the paper, as *Surfacing* and *Away* are scrutinized with regard both to the utilization of magic realism stemming from Native Canadian lore in these two books, and to the presence of Aboriginal characters in these texts.[1]

In the last decades magic realism has become a (if not *the*) buzzword on the Canadian literary scene, constituting both a major mode of writing in Canadian literature, and an important concern of Canadian literary criticism. Defined most generally as a medium conveying "alternative approaches to reality to that of Western philosophy, expressed in many postcolonial and non-Western works of fiction" (Bowers 2004: 1), which can be seen to "brea[k] down the distinction between the usually opposing terms of the magical and the realist" (Bowers 2004: 3), magic realism may be detected in texts both by writers belonging to ethnic minorities and by white authors. While the sources of the magical element in such works of fiction differ, they frequently draw on various mythological systems, ranging from Native Canadian beliefs in, for example, Lee Maracle's *Ravensong* (1993) to Japanese legends in Hiromi Goto's *Chorus of mushrooms* (1994) to Scottish folklore in Alistair MacLeod's *No great mischief* (1999), to name but a very select few.

---

1 I would like to thank the participants of the *7th Literature in English Symposium* and, in particular, Prof. Agnieszka Rzepa for the questions and remarks that helped in shaping the final version of this article.

In the present article I focus on prose utilizing elements of Native beliefs as the basis for the magic realism in diegesis, setting out to discuss selected texts by Indigenous and white Canadian authors in order to compare their usage of magic realism with regard to the approach to the source material. Moreover, in the case of the white writers, I analyze the issues related to their turning to the First Nations mythologies as the inspiration for the supernatural in their novels. The works of prose analysed herein are two novels by Native Canadian writers, that is Thomas King's *Green grass, running water* (1993) and Eden Robinson's *Monkey beach* (2000), and two books by white Canadians, namely Margaret Atwood's *Surfacing* (1972) and Jane Urquhart's *Away* (1993). Firstly, I discuss in detail particular instances of magic realism stemming from Native beliefs in the selected texts, arguing that in the Indigenous authors' texts, these can be seen as forming a consistent system, deeply rooted in the communities of the respective protagonists, whereas the herein discussed novels by white writers appear to only utilize selected elements of Indigenous lore. Alternative sources of magic realism in Urquhart's and Atwood's texts that is Irish and Greek mythology, respectively, are also taken into consideration. Subsequently, as I proceed to compare chosen plotlines from *Surfacing* and *Monkey beach*, I point to the extent of correspondences between the magic realist episodes in these two novels. In the final part of the essay I scrutinize the issue of cultural appropriation, arguably detectable in Atwood's and Urquhart's novels, paying critical attention to the notion of magic existing in the land as a possible explanation for the presence of Native magic realism in the texts.

In Thomas King's *Green grass, running water*[2] magic realism appears to be ingrained in the very structure of the narration. Throughout the novel, the unnamed narrating "I" recounts to Coyote[3] four creation stories, centred around mythical figures named First Woman, Changing Woman, Thought Woman and Old Woman, respectively. As Rita Wong comments, "the four transgender Indians … can be interpreted as two-spirited trickster figures who re-present stories to introduce the possibility of change" (Wong 2010: 162). Moreover, it should be noted that in the First Nations' beliefs, Coyote is also a trickster figure; in *Green grass, running water*, he is depicted as a benevolent, yet foolish creature, inadvertently causing mischief wherever he goes. However, rather than faithfully following the Native myths, the creation tales found within the narrative intertwine with key Euro-American cultural texts, such as the Bible, *Robinson Crusoe* or *Moby Dick*, diverging from the subject of creation and into the issue of

---

2   Henceforth indicated as *GG* followed by page number. All quotations are from King, Thomas. 1999 [1993]. *Green grass, running water*. Toronto: Harper Perennial Canada.

3   It ought to be noted that although in Indigenous peoples' beliefs Coyote's gender as a trickster figure may be read as fluid and never fully specified, this analysis follows the convention present in *Green grass, running water* by referring to this character as "he" (*GG*, 145).

the Native people's colonisation. As the stories progress, the four protagonists claim the identities of Euro-American cultural heroes, that is the Lone Ranger, Ishmael, Robinson Crusoe, and Hawkeye. This act may be interpreted as an attempt at a subversion of the Euro-American cultural hegemony which can be seen not only to prioritize white texts of culture over Indigenous ones, but also to usurp fictional Native figures as part of white mythology. Notably, "the four Indians", as the characters are referred to throughout the text (*GG*, 47), are, together with Coyote, both present on the narrative level of the story, and they participate actively in the plot itself, thus contributing to the magic realist dimension of the novel through their mythical identities and abilities.

Interestingly, although the majority of characters in the novel belong to the First Nations, their everyday lives may be seen as fairly ordinary and different from stereotypical perceptions of the Native people. While towards the end of the book the characters gather at a traditional Sun Dance, the event appears to be for them mostly of personal importance, as well as to contribute to the strengthening of familial and communal ties, rather than to possess a mystical meaning. Indeed, it is the actions of the four Indians and Coyote that appear to most significantly contribute to magic realism in King's novel. Following their escape from a psychiatric hospital in the United States, Robinson Crusoe, Lone Ranger, Ishmael and Hawkeye head to Blossom, Canada in order to "fix up the world" (*GG*, 123). On their way, they decide to start by helping Lionel to improve his life (*GG*, 167-168), which they attempt to achieve through singing him "happy birthday" (*GG*, 169-171) and offering him a birthday gift in the form of a jacket of seemingly magical properties (*GG*, 302-303). Although Lionel appears surprised at the relatively small scale of the Indians' actions, they result in an apparent confidence boost for the character, as well as serve to inspire him to make changes in his daily routines. Moreover, the four Indians alter the western movie watched by several characters from the novel, causing the film not only to change from black and white to colour, but also to end in a surprise twist, as John Wayne's protagonist becomes obliterated by the Native forces, again subverting the stereotypes present in the products of white people's culture (*GG*, 321-322). However, it is apparently Coyote who takes responsibility for the most surprising events in the novel, which he affects through his singing and dancing, firstly bringing on the rain (*GG*, 273-274), and later an earthquake (*GG*, 411, 416). What is more, it is due to Coyote's influence that Alberta, one of the book's major human characters, becomes pregnant (*GG*, 412, 416). Amusingly, the four Indians accuse him of being responsible for the conception of Jesus as well, remarking that "[they] haven't straightened out *that* mess yet" (*GG*, 416, italics original, EB).

Finally, the perception of time in *Green grass, running water* can be viewed as a major magic realist feature of the novel. As has already been implied herein, the four old Indians are identifiable with the ancient figures from Native creation myths, who in King's book participate both in the retellings of certain Euro-American cultural texts dating from the 18th, 19th and 20th century, and in the actual plot of the novel. The narrative appears to confirm the possibility that the characters might be incredibly old. Indeed, not only are they repeatedly described as looking over a hundred years old in the present of the story (*GG*, 123), but also it is claimed by Doctor Hovaugh that the four Indians were already old upon their arrival at the hospital in January of 1891 [sic] (*GG*, 96). Following Wong's assertion that "the novel's disruption of time is critical because it signals alternative models of time and of culture" (Wong 2012: 165), the depiction of the passage of time in diegesis can be seen to tie it more closely to the Native systems of beliefs, and thus, alternative means of experiencing the world. Indeed, the very title of the novel draws attention to this issue, as the phrase "[a]s long as the grass is green and the waters run" (*GG*, 267), derived from a treaty between First Nations and white people, refers to time constraints upon Indigenous rights to the land on which they live. Within the narrative, this becomes a subject for a legal dispute between the Native character Eli, who decides to settle in a cabin once owned by his mother (*GG*, 262), and a dam construction company, represented by a white man, Clifford Sifton. The latter's approach to the notion of time is influenced by the language of the Western world's law; as another white character reflects, "no one sign[s] a contract for eternity" (*GG*, 267). Conversely, while for both Eli and other Indigenous characters the eponymous phrase carries a legal meaning, it binds not only the actual signatories of the treaty, but also their descendants, thus essentially becoming literal. As this part of the novel shows, white and Native perceptions of reality differ; in the First Nations' view, the concept of time appears less episodic than for a white person. Indeed, as the figures of the four Indians exemplify, a single person's time-span may seamlessly encompass the creation of the world, early white cultural texts, and the present day events.

In Eden Robinson's 2000 novel *Monkey beach*[4], magic realism may be viewed as being intrinsically connected to the protagonist and narrator of the story, Lisamarie Hill, as well as to her perception of the world around her. Growing up in the Haisla community of Kitamaat, Lisa witnesses or participates in a number of events that can be termed strange, or, perhaps more accurately, described as encroaching firmly upon the territory of magic realism. From her early childhood on, Lisa has recurring dreams or visions of a small, red-haired man, usually preceding some disastrous event in her life, such as the death of her uncle Mike (*MB*, 134-135), or her grandmother's heart attack (*MB*, 234-235). Moreover, Lisa is able to see (*MB*, 267) and, at times, communicate with, ghosts (*MB*, 230-232) or apparitions of people, for example her cousin Tabitha's (*MB*,

---

4   Henceforth indicated as *MB* followed by page number. All quotations are from Robinson, Eden. 2001. *Monkey beach*. Toronto: Vintage Canada.

297-300), as well as to perceive such unusual creatures as "slithering" carnivorous beings in the forest (*MB*, 260-262) or the b'gwugus/the sasquatch (*MB*, 315). The latter, in particular, may be termed a central figure in *Monkey beach*, especially given that the novel's title derives from the place where the sasquatches supposedly tend to dwell. What is more, it is arguably the first sighting of the sasquatch that opens Lisa's perception, preparing her for experiencing other instances of the supernatural around her.

Remarkably, while all these occurrences may be viewed as stemming from the beliefs of the Haisla people, this system appears to be predominantly unfamiliar to Lisa. As Agnieszka Rzepa remarks, "[t]he Haisla community she belongs to no longer has any meaningful connection with traditional beliefs" (Rzepa 2005: 14). Thus, throughout the narrative Lisa slowly uncovers the roots as well as the meaning of her supernatural abilities. Quite early on, she learns a dual lesson from her grandmother, Ma-ma-oo: that not only is the "gift" of seeing the unusual inherited from her mother, but also that it might be dangerous to deal with things one does not understand (*MB*, 153-154). Despite not possessing the gift herself, Ma-ma-oo teaches Lisa about the ancestral traditions, with perhaps most emphasis being put on the issue of "contacting the dead" (*MB*, 139). Thus, *Monkey beach* arguably presents a more internalized case than that found in King's novel, as in *Green grass, running water* the supernatural events happened around the human characters, rather than were caused by them in any way.

In the last part of the novel, Lisa decides to consciously use the skills that she possesses in order to discover what happened to her missing brother. To that end, she offers her blood to the carnivorous beings from the forest (*MB*, 365-366), only to realize their deceptiveness as she is granted a vision of Jimmy's accident, but not of his ultimate fate (*MB*, 368-370). Eventually, as Lisa escapes the creatures, the spirits of her dead relatives, including her grandparents, uncle Mick, and some unnamed ancestors, come to her aid as she struggles not to drown in the lake. In their final messages, the relatives both urge her to keep living, and warn her against the dangers lying in her lack of knowledge regarding her gift (*MB*, 371-373). As the novel reveals, and this encounter may be seen to accentuate, for Lisa "magic realism" seems to be inescapable reality, deeply embedded in the traditions and beliefs of her Native ancestors. Indeed, magic realism in *Monkey beach* can be viewed as a consistent system present throughout the text; while it is unfamiliar to the protagonist and forgotten by the younger members of the community, it is an integral part of the world they live in.

In Jane Urquhart's *Away*,[5] magic realist events may be claimed to stem from a twofold source: firstly, from the Celtic – and more specifically, Irish – mythology, and secondly, from Native Canadian beliefs. Significantly however,

---

5   Henceforth indicated as *Away* followed by page number. All quotations are from Urquhart, Jane. 1997 [1993]. *Away*. Toronto: M&S.

these are arguably utilized to varying degrees in the book. Indeed, not only is magic realism in its Celtic variety present in Urquhart's novel since its very first pages, but also it could be viewed as constituting the very foundation of the plot. As the story begins, Mary, the first protagonist, finds a dying young man on the seashore on Rathlin Island. While the rational explanation is that the man has been a victim of a shipwreck, Mary "recognized ... that he came from an otherworld island, assumed that he had emerged from the water to look for her, and knew that her name had changed ... to Moira," which is the only word uttered by the man (*Away*, 8). This view of the man's origins becomes corroborated by the opinions of the inhabitants of Mary's village, who immediately start perceiving him as her "faery-demon lover" (*Away*, 13). Moreover, they believe that Mary is "away:" that is, that she has been "'touched', and then 'taken'" by the stranger (*Away*, 13), who belongs to "'the Formoire, the ones from the sea, the others'" (*Away*, 12). Remarkably, Mary appears not to be the first person from the village who has been "snatched" (*Away*, 13), although the fact that there were few of them seems to be a matter of pride (*Away*, 13). Afterwards, Mary willingly withdraws herself from the community, preferring solitude to human company, which paradoxically causes her to be more noticeable and attractive to the men of the village. It is the local priest who devises a scheme to save Mary by marrying her to someone from outside the island who does not believe in the possibility of people being taken away (*Away*, 27). Indeed, marriage and bearing children temporarily returns Mary to the world of ordinary people, "[tying] her to the earth" (*Away*, 58). However, upon the family's emigration to Canada, Mary is reminded of her fairy-demon lover when discovering that she lives close to a lake bearing the name "Moira" (*Away*, 152). Having given birth to her daughter, Eileen, Mary leaves the girl in the care of her older brother, and departs from home in order to live by the lake. As she explains, "I am loved by the spirit of this lake ... and he is loved by me" (*Away*, 181).

It is only later that her family discovers that while living in the forest, Mary encountered the Ojibway people, who aided her so that she could survive, as she was unaccustomed to living by herself in the wilderness. In the character of the Ojibway man Exodus Crow, Urquhart may be seen to attempt to construct a bridge between the Irish immigrants to Canada and the Indigenous inhabitants of the land, drawing a link not only between their respective exploitation at the hands of the British (*Away*, 184-185), but also between their mythological systems (*Away*, 180-181). Indeed, in the conversation between Mary and Exodus, the two explicitly express their mutual respect for each other's beliefs. As the narrative has it, "Exodus *did* believe because, he said, it was as if his own mother were telling the stories of the spirits. ... [He] knew that the woman understood him and that he understood the woman" (180-181, italics Urquhart's, EB). What is more, Exodus asserts that Mary "was filled with manitou" (*Away*, 175); thus, through his opinions, Urquhart appears to give legitimacy to the Irish people's usage of

Native myths. As follows from Exodus' pronouncements, it can be argued that within the ideological scope of *Away*, Irish mythology may be interpreted through certain elements of Native beliefs, with Mary's "lover" being possibly akin to a Native spirit guide (Rzepa 2009: 78).

However, certain elements of Native beliefs can be detected in the novel even before the on-page appearance of Exodus Crow. Mary's daughter Eileen since her early years spends time sitting in the branches of a willow tree, talking with a "black bird" (*Away*, 169) – a crow. Not only does the bird bring her "gifts" – such as "belt buckles, a silver ring, coins, watch fobs" (*Away*, 220), but also he reveals to Eileen some glimpses of what her future holds, especially hinting at what kind of visitors Eileen's family might expect (*Away*, 169). The figure of a crow might be seen as being of particular importance here; indeed, as Anna Branach-Kallas puts it, "[t]his magic-realist element of *Away* seems to have been borrowed from Indian mythology in which the crow functions as a messenger of the creator, warning humans against forthcoming threats" (Branach-Kallas 2003: 151). Moreover, crows count also among the Native trickster figures (Schröder 2006: 105). In Urquhart's novel, it is suggested that the crow speaking with Eileen can be identified with Exodus Crow, since both the bird in Eileen's description and Exodus "[wear] a top hat and smok[e] a pipe" (*Away*, 169, 172). Furthermore, when Exodus leaves the farm, Eileen claims that "he turned into a bird" and "flew away" (*Away*, 194), an occurrence that may be linked to the shape-shifting properties of the tricksters in Native people's systems of beliefs.

Arguably, Eileen's relationship with the crow could be perceived as somewhat ambiguous, both in the context of their individual encounters, and that of the entire novel. Already in her first description of a conversation with the crow, she appears uncertain of what happened, telling her brother that "[t]he bird flew to my shoulder and said things... but I don't remember" (*Away*, 169). Importantly, at that point Eileen has had no contact with the First Nations people or their beliefs; therefore, her ability to communicate with the crow might be viewed as puzzling. Furthermore, the problems which Eileen displays when trying to discuss her encounters with the bird seem to indicate that due to her unfamiliarity with Native mythology, she lacks language to describe her experience. Their later relations may be perceived as rather close, as Eileen talks with the crow daily until the family's departure from the farm – an event that itself is facilitated by the information supplanted by the bird (*Away*, 222-225). However, Eileen mysteriously forgets about the crow immediately afterwards, having recollections only of snippets from their conversations (*Away*, 258); moreover, she appears not to remember the meeting with Exodus Crow either (*Away*, 278). She only manages to recall the bird after some time has passed, when during a political meeting her memory is stirred by a moving speech of D'Arcy McGee (*Away*, 338).

Surprisingly, this moment marks also the last occurrence of an element of Native mythology in Urquhart's novel. At around this point, Eileen's brother

Liam marries the half-Ojibway Molly (*Away*, 297), thus potentially opening a space for a fuller exploration of the relationship between the Canadian Indigenous people and the Irish. Yet, the references to elements of Native systems of beliefs appear to cease with seemingly no straightforward resolution following Eileen's remembering of the crow. Instead, the subject of Irish mythology returns as the major source of magic realism, as first Eileen is described as experiencing herself the sense of being "away," while later Eileen's granddaughter Esther becomes romantically involved with another "faery-demon" (*Away*, 353-354).

Although Margaret Atwood's *Surfacing*[6] may be perceived as a predominantly realist novel, the ritualistic experience undergone by the nameless narrator in the third part of the book can be interpreted as the magic realist element in the plot. In this rite of passage, guarded by uncertain, mystical rules, the protagonist appears to distance herself from other people, remaining alone on the island where the novel takes place, and gradually rejecting all links with civilisation available to her. As the ritual progresses, the narrator grows closer with nature around her, to the point where she describes herself as blending into one with a tree or even the island itself (*Surfacing*, 181); moreover, she experiences visions of her dead parents, which arguably enables her to come to terms with her past. Following that, the protagonist declares the ritual to be concluded. Despite the fact that when the novel ends, the narrator seems to hesitate whether she should return to the civilised world, the final message of *Surfacing* may be interpreted as an affirmation of the value of life (*Surfacing*, 191-192).

This part of Atwood's novel has long puzzled critics, who have proposed various potential interpretations of the events therein depicted. On the realistic level, the ritual could be read as an episode of insanity, precipitated by the shock resulting from the discovery of her father's dead body by the narrator. However, critical interpretations more typically tend to focus on the mystical elements of the ritual, as well as on the potential sources thereof, pointing towards either aspects of the gothic in the protagonist's experience, or the possibility of the episode stemming in its description from Native beliefs.

Interestingly, there exists a vein of criticism drawing connections between Atwood's novel and Greek mythology, or, more precisely, the myth of Demeter and Kore/Persephone. These readings of *Surfacing* do not necessarily concentrate explicitly on the ritual, but rather attempt to interpret the events of the book, with the emphasis on the relationship between the protagonist and her mother, through the backdrop of the myth. It has been suggested that the rite could be based on the initiation ceremonies of Eleusis, and thus linked to the cult of Demeter and Persephone. Sherrill Grace enumerates "a creative act of ritual mating, a symbolic

---

6   Henceforth indicated as *Surfacing* followed by page number. All quotations are from Atwood, Margaret. 1994 [1972]. *Surfacing*. Toronto: M&S.

(and literal) act of destruction, and a deeper dive into hallucination and visionary ecstasy" among the "recognized stages in the Eleusian rites" distinguishable in the third part of *Surfacing* (Grace 1988: 41). Even though there are no explicit references to mythology in the novel, this interpretation may appear plausible, given Atwood's preoccupation with Greek mythology in general, visible in her poems (the collection *Interlunar* from 1984) and novels (*Penelopiad,* 2005), and with the myth of Persephone in particular (e.g. the collection of poems *Double Persephone* from 1961, or the poem "Letter from Persephone" in *Interlunar*).

However, it should be noted that both the aforementioned aspects of the ritual and such elements thereof as isolation, purification and personal revelation, might be seen as characteristic not only of the Eleusian ceremonies, but also of the Native American beliefs. According to George Woodcock, this episode may be seen as linked to "the spirit quests which Indians of many tribes ... undertake" (Woodcock 1990: 104). Indeed, specific imagery utilised by Atwood in the description of the ritual, such as its location in the wilderness, or the visions of the ancestral spirits travelling away in a "green canoe" (*Surfacing*, 188), appears directly reminiscent of Indigenous rites of passage (Woodcock 1990: 104). Yet, *Surfacing* contains little if any Native presence; indeed, the only Native characters to feature, albeit very briefly, in Atwood's novel are a nameless family whom the narrator vaguely remembers from her childhood (*Surfacing*, 85-86), who have been "fleetingly glimpsed just outside [her] field of vision on the edge of the woods in Northern Quebec" (Lacombe 2010: 255). Furthermore, although the subject of Native rock paintings which the protagonist's father was searching for before his death recurs throughout the book, only on two occasions are they explicitly referred to as being authored by Indians (*Surfacing*, 102-103, 114) In spite of this virtual absence of First Nations people, the narrator reflects that "[t]he Indians... had once known where [salvation] lived and their signs marked the sacred places... where you could learn the truth" (*Surfacing*, 145), a statement that appears to be closely connected with the ritualistic experience she eventually undergoes. At the same time, she seems to distance her experience from the direct influence of Native beliefs, claiming that it was her father who, having traversed the lakeside in search of the rock paintings, eventually discovered "new places, new oracles" (*Surfacing*, 145), whereas she was only following in his footsteps. Therefore, despite the fact that the protagonist's rite of passage is commonly recognized as drawing on Native spirituality (e.g. Woodcock 1990; Grace 1980: 106), the novel may be arguably viewed to attempt to rebuke such associations by admitting to second-hand knowledge of the matter (via the father's own experiences) only.

The issue of the sources of the mystical ritual in Atwood's work appears especially interesting from a critical standpoint on an occasion when *Surfacing* comes into comparison with Robinson's *Monkey beach*. Although the novels differ in a number of details and plotlines, juxtaposing them reveals striking similarities. Both books feature a female protagonist/narrator who travels into the Canadian wilderness while looking for a missing family member – the father in *Surfacing*, the brother in *Monkey beach*. Moreover, in both cases the protagonists need to submerge themselves into a lake as a part of the ritual they undergo, in what can be perceived as the key scene in the novels: for Lisa, it is the moment of finally making a conscious use of her "gift," while for Atwood's narrator, it is the moment of deciding that she needs to confront her past. As follows from that, another common feature is the fact that both protagonists seek a personal revelation, which the ritual is supposed to facilitate. Arguably, Lisa's participating in the ceremony may be viewed as an intentional act, as she is at least partially aware what steps she must follow in order to attain the help of the carnivorous creatures; conversely, the narrator of *Surfacing* can only intuit the rules governing her rite of passage. Finally, both women come into contact with their dead relatives, who in turn aid them in re-establishing connection with reality and prevent them from remaining in the world of spirits. In both cases the ancestors eventually leave the protagonists on their own; yet, while in *Monkey beach* Mama-oo explicitly urges Lisa "to go back" to life (*MB*, 372), Robinson's character can be seen to "remai[n]… in the fluid borderline zone between the… worlds of humans and spirits" (Rzepa 2009: 90), and it is uncertain whether she survives. On the contrary, as has already been mentioned, *Surfacing* ends with the narrator negotiating her relationship with civilization and praising the value of life (*Surfacing*, 191), having been abandoned by the presences of her parents (*Surfacing*, 188). Additionally, it can be claimed that in *Monkey beach* the ghosts of the protagonist's relatives can be perceived as more tangible than in *Surfacing*, as Lisa is able to communicate directly with her grandparents and uncle, receiving specific messages from them (*MB*, 373). Conversely, Atwood's narrator merely sees the apparitions of her parents: first her mother, surrounded by jays (*Surfacing*, 182), and subsequently, on another day of the ritual, her father (*Surfacing*, 186-187). In the context of this analysis, it ought to be noted that although the protagonist's mother is observed by her in her human form, her father has apparently changed into a figure resembling the prehistoric Native rock paintings he was looking for before his death: part-human and part-animal, with "wolf's eyes" (*Surfacing*, 187), an event arguably further blurring the Native/white distinctions in Atwood's diegesis.

As follows from this, the parallels between Atwood's and Robinson's novels appear to be too extensive so as to be purely coincidental. Certainly, they have not escaped critical attention; for instance, Michèle Lacombe notes that there can be found "gently parodic reminders" of Atwood's novel in *Monkey beach* (Lacombe 2010: 255), although she chooses not to interpret Robinson's book through this particular lens. A different perspective is offered by Coral Ann Howells, who suggests that *Monkey beach* draws on *Surfacing* as on "the paradigmatic Canadian feminist novel about wilderness" (Howells 2004: 202), or, more generally, that

Robinson proposes a retelling of the myth of Canadian wilderness, previously utilized by Atwood (Howells 2003: 187). As she argues,

> Robinson as Native storyteller is recontextualizing that visionary quest [found in *Surfacing*]. Atwood represented the Canadian wilderness of white cultural myth as a mysterious trackless space full of secrets; thirty years later, Robinson leads readers into a different kind of Canadian wilderness where some of those secrets are named, revealing through her Haisla perspective on landscape the answers to questions raised in *Surfacing* where a sense of the sacred pervades the natural landscape
>
> (Howells 2003: 187).

However, while Robinson's novel might indeed consciously refer to the themes explored by Atwood in *Surfacing*, it is equally possible that both books make use of the same source material, namely Native systems of beliefs and, more specifically, Native spirit quests. Yet, on the one hand, not only may Robinson be seen to represent a specific group of Indigenous people,[7] but also her protagonist's world appears firmly rooted in the Haisla traditions, which can be underscored by the fact that the word "Haisla" appears already in the very first paragraph of the book (*MB*, 1). On the other hand, a cursory reading of Atwood's novel might suggest to the reader inexistence of any Native connection; indeed, it could be surmised that the rite of passage in *Surfacing* is but a product of the narrator's damaged psyche. Given the extent of the similarities between the depictions, as well as the personal importance, of the rituals undergone by the protagonists of both books, this divergence seems somewhat puzzling.

As I have attempted to demonstrate in the analytical part of this essay, both Margaret Atwood's *Surfacing* and Jane Urquhart's *Away* showcase elements of Native mysticism in certain magic realist plotlines and episodes connected with white protagonists. Given the presence of Ojibway and part-Ojibway characters in *Away*, these examples of magic realism may be attributed to Ojibway beliefs, whereas *Surfacing* provides no clues as to the potential "source material" of the rite of passage that the protagonist experiences. Yet, while problematic in itself, this lack of attribution in the case of Atwood's novel can be viewed as indicative of a larger problem at hand, namely, the issue of appropriation that, in turn, may pertain to both *Surfacing* and *Away*.

Belonging to the white majority in Canada, both Atwood and Urquhart can be seen to inevitably find themselves in a precarious position when making use of Native lore in their works of fiction. However, the precise characteristics of such references in *Surfacing* and *Away* may yield more specific doubts; while in *Away* the instances of magic realism based on Native beliefs appear to be grounded in the narrative scheme of the book, Eileen's very relationship with the black crow–

---

7   While Lisamarie Hill in *Monkey beach* identifies as Haisla only, the members of Eden Robinson's own family belong to the Haisla and Heiltsuk First Nations.

her apparent spirit guide–seems more than a little happenstance. Indeed, Eileen's conversations with the crow anticipate her meeting any members of the First Nations, as she only has a chance to acquaint herself with Exodus Crow after a period of communicating with her spirit guide. What is more, little to no reflection seems to be offered regarding the reasons for Eileen's ability to speak with the crow, or her loss thereof upon departing from the farm. Thus, it might be claimed that despite the tentative acknowledgement of its source in Ojibway beliefs, the Native magic realism in *Away* predominantly remains a narrative device serving the purpose of providing the white protagonist with pieces of otherwise unobtainable knowledge. While ostensibly Urquhart makes an attempt to open space for a respectful dialogue between the cultures, this may be seen to mostly remain in the sphere of declarations, given the scarceness of the actual presence of Indigenous characters in the novel. Moreover, the sole function of Exodus Crow appears to be that of a guide to the white protagonist; remarkably, the names of Mary's remaining Native helpers are never even disclosed in the text, which may be viewed as relegating them to a marginal position within the story about white women.

A largely similar situation occurs in Atwood's *Surfacing*, a book virtually devoid of the presence of First Nations people, where the protagonist's experiencing a Native-like spiritual quest may be perceived as comparably displaced. Never specifically referenced as connected with the Indigenous systems of beliefs, the ritual's narrative function seems to lie in facilitating resolution of the narrator's personal issues. This may appear especially perplexing in a novel that engages quite thoroughly with the subject of different power relations, be it oppressive male/female encounters, or the (post)colonial relationships between nations and countries. Indeed, in her "Postcolonial guilt in Margaret Atwood's *Surfacing*" Janice Fiamengo points to the fact that even as she claims to be, as a Canadian, a victim of the American colonial practices, the protagonist may be seen to engage into an equally colonial rhetoric towards the Native Canadian people. As Fiamengo argues,

> Native spirituality (as distinct from Native people) becomes the object of the narrator's desire because it holds out the promise of some special knowledge … In taking up Indian subject position [she] re-enacts one of the classic gestures of colonial appropriation in order to escape her own identity, claiming the purity and authenticity of a Native subjectivity
>
> (Fiamengo 1999).

Moreover, the fact that this claim to Native modes of expression appears to be only temporary—after all, the protagonist considers returning to the civilized world at the end of the novel—serves to underline the problematically episodic nature of the usage of an Indigenous ritual in Atwood's book.

Remarkably, both novels also seem to utilize the Native magic realism in order to either establish (in *Away*) or confirm (in *Surfacing*) the existence of a close connection between the respective protagonists and the Canadian land. Drawing on the notion that magic originates in the land itself, rather than in the people inhabiting it, the books arguably attempt to demonstrate that by possessing the ability to access this magic, the protagonists may contend to boast clear ties to the place it derives from. Indeed, this interpretative possibility can be corroborated by textual evidence, as demonstrated by the aforementioned fact that Elaine goes through her experiences without any prior knowledge of the tenets of Native spirituality. Similarly, Atwood's narrator ostensibly finds the incentive for her spiritual quest, which includes escape from civilization and humanity, during her time spent in the wilderness of Northern Ontario, and thus draws it from the land rather than its inhabitants. Moreover, as she is a representative of the first generation of Irish settlers born in Canada, Elaine's ability to communicate with a Native trickster figure/spirit guide characteristic for the place she lives in may be seen to serve as a legitimization of her Canadianness. Conversely, it is only through re-discovering the depth of her connection with nature and the land that the protagonist of *Surfacing* becomes able to reconcile herself with her past as well as establish her identity as being rooted in the "pristine space" (Fiamengo 1999) of the world before a colonial intrusion.

It could be argued that the Canadianness of the protagonists may be viewed as a sufficient reason for them to have access to the magic imbued in the Canadian land. However, an argument to the contrary may be that regardless of the existence of a genuine connection between the protagonists and Canada, it is still through the usage of specific imagery associated with Native beliefs, namely trickster animals as spirit guides, or spiritual quests, that Elaine and Atwood's narrator experience this magic. Thus, by turning to Native means of expression in that matter, the novels may be seen to perform an act of appropriation with regard to the Indigenous people's beliefs. Moreover, it should be noted that even though Urquhart in *Away* provides a tentative justification for its utilization of Native spirituality by suggesting that there exists a parallelism between Irish and Native beliefs, these declarations can still be viewed as coming from the privileged and dominant, white perspective. Indeed, while it may be the Ojibway secondary character who refers to the correspondences between Irish myths and Indigenous spirituality, it is nonetheless the white protagonist, Eileen, who experiences first hand a Native variety of magic realism.

In the present article I have attempted to trace and analyse some of the instances in which magic realism based on the beliefs of the Canadian First Nations people is utilised in the prose written by both Native and white Canadian writers. As I have demonstrated, Thomas King and Eden Robinson use the elements of their own people's mythologies in order to imbue their novels with magic realism; moreover, they present those beliefs in a clear, systematic fashion throughout their books. Conversely, Jane Urquhart's utilisation of magic realism based on Native beliefs may be viewed as somewhat haphazard, while her attempts to reconcile Irish and Native Canadian mythologies could be perceived as predominantly declarative. Finally, despite depicting a rite of passage most probably based on the First Nations spirituality, Margaret Atwood's *Surfacing* appears to largely shy away from featuring any Native Canadian characters, as well as from acknowledging the roots of the protagonist's experience in Native Canadian beliefs. Indeed, in Urquhart's and Atwood's books it is frequently only certain select elements of Indigenous beliefs which seem to be utilized. Moreover, in these texts such a variety of magic realism appears to predominantly serve the interests of the white protagonists, who themselves can boast little to no awareness either of Native mythologies or customs or of the Native people themselves. This issue may be perceived as especially puzzling upon juxtaposing Robinson's *Monkey beach* with Atwood's *Surfacing*, two texts sharing a very similar magic realist episode of a ritual undergone by the respective protagonists, one of which explicitly refers to First Nations (Haisla) system of beliefs, while the other disavows such connections. Following this, the final issue I have discussed is the problem of appropriation of Native Canadian mythology, and thus, a particular mode of expression, by the writers belonging to white majority.

As critics analysing the subject of magic realism tend to point out, this mode frequently appears to serve a subversive function, becoming "a means to write against dominant ... culture" (Bowers 2004: 46), as well as allowing the heretofore marginalized voices to tell their own stories by utilizing their own particular means of expression. As I have argued, this feature is especially visible in Thomas King's *Green grass, running water* and its usage of the four Indian characters who disrupt conventional notions of time and influence reality with their supernatural powers. However, this aspect of magic realism comes under question when it is the white writers who make use of the mythology specific for a certain minority, such as, in the works herein discussed, the Indigenous peoples of Canada. Atwood's or Urquhart's usage of Native spirituality may be defended on the basis of the conviction that the magic their protagonists experience may be seen as inherent in the Canadian land the characters were born on. Nevertheless, it ought to be noted that the instances of magic realism in the novels are recognizably influenced as having been mediated by the authors' knowledge of specific elements of Indigenous beliefs. Moreover, it may be argued that in the case of these particular writers utilizing Native beliefs, links may be drawn between the patriarchal oppression of their female protagonists and the colonial oppression of the First Nations people. However, as the former turn to the means of expression characteristic for the latter on the basis of common marginalisation, the issue remains that by belonging to white majority, the authors as well as their characters may be seen as dominant with regards to the Native people.

References

Atwood, Margaret. 1994 [1972]. *Surfacing*. Toronto: M&S.

Bowers, Maggie Ann. 2004. *Magic(al) realism*. Abingdon, Oxon-New York: Routledge.

Branach-Kallas, Anna. 2003. *In the whirlpool of the past: Memory, intertextuality and history in the fiction of Jane Urquhart*. Toruń: Wydawnictwo Uniwersytetu Mikołaja Kopernika.

Fiamengo, Janice. 1999. "Postcolonial guilt in Margaret Atwood's *Surfacing*". *American Review of Canadian Studies*. (http://findarticles.com/p/articles/ mi_hb009/is_1_ 29/ai_n28724699/) (date of access: August 16, 2011).

Grace, Sherrill E. 1988. "In search of Demeter: The lost, silent mother in *Surfacing*", in: Kathryn VanSpanckeren – Jan Garden Castro (eds.), 35-47.

Grace, Sherill E. 1980. *Violent duality: A study of Margaret Atwood*. Montreal: Véhicule Press.

Howells, Coral Ann. 2004. "Writing by Women", in: Eva-Marie Kröller (ed.), 194-215.

Howells, Coral Ann. 2003. *Contemporary Canadian women's fiction: Refiguring identities*. Houndmills, Basingstoke, Hampshire: Palgrave Macmillan

King, Thomas. 1999 [1993]. *Green grass, running water*. Toronto: Harper Perennial Canada.

Kröller, Eva-Marie (ed.). 2004. *The Cambridge companion to Canadian literature*. Cambridge: Cambridge University Press.

Lacombe, Michèle. 2010. "On critical frameworks for analyzing Indigenous literature: The case of *Monkey beach*", *International Journal of Canadian Studies/Revue internationale d'études canadiennes*, 41: 253-276.

Robinson, Eden. 2001. *Monkey beach*. Toronto: Vintage Canada.

Rzepa, Agnieszka. 2009. *Feats and defeats of memory: Exploring spaces of Canadian magic realism*. Poznań: Wydawnictwo Naukowe UAM.

Rzepa, Agnieszka. 2005. "Beyond Hodgins and Kroetsch: Other spaces of English-Canadian magic realism", *Central European Journal of Canadian Studies/ Revue d'Etudes Canadiennes en Europe Centrale*, 5: 7-17.

Schröder, Nicole. 2006. *Spaces and places in motion: Spatial concepts in contemporary American literature*. Tübingen: Narr.

Sojka, Eugenia – Tomasz Sikora (eds.). 2010. *Embracing otherness: Canadian minority discourses in transcultural perspectives*. Toruń: Wydawnictwo Adam Marszałek.

Urquhart, Jane. 1997 [1993]. *Away*. Toronto: M&S.

VanSpanckeren, Kathryn – Jan Garden Castro (eds.). 1988. *Margaret Atwood: Vision and forms*. Carbondale and Edwardsville: Southern Illinois University Press.

Wong, Rita. 2010. "The laughter of law-unbiding bodies in Thomas King's *Green grass, running water* and Ashok Mathur's *Once upon an elephant*", in: Eugenia Sojka – Tomasz Sikora (eds.), 158-173.

Woodcock, George. 1990. *Introducing Margaret Atwood's* Surfacing: *A reader's guide*. Toronto: General Paperbacks.

Let the crow speak: Magic realism and Indigenous knowledge as beak(on)s of light in Robert Kroetsch's ecological gothic text *What the crow said*

Alanna F. Bondar, Algoma University, Sault Ste. Marie, Ontario

ABSTRACT

Canada's cultural and literary critics continue to debate definitions of Canada and what it is to be Canadian. "Instead of answers," Robert Kroetsch argues, "we have questions. Instead of resolution, we have doubt" (1989: 25), and thus Canadian authors and readers find themselves in a space wherein, "being skilful shape-changers" (1989: 28) becomes a necessity. Through literary critical theories and practices such as postmodern politics and aesthetics, postcolonialism, magic realism, the gothic mode, and ecological philosophies, Canadian authors have begun to create new rhetoric, interpretations, and shifts in cultural values that speak less about the politics of representation and more about the need for accountability, respect for otherness, and sustainability. This paper explores the ways in which theoretical perspectives have opened avenues for the inclusion of Indigenous Knowledge Systems, and how they may be recognized in Kroetsch's novel, *What the crow said* (1978) as positive revisioning and revaluing of Canadian cultural identity, and responsible citizenship within (biotic) communities. By parodying earlier definitions (Frye, Atwood, et al.) of Canadian literature as thematically based in "survival" – wherein its explorers and settlers are seen to battle against a wilderness (and often Indigenous) other – Kroetsch dismantles European and Western-identified views of "Canada" as they have been placed within a strict and confining colonial history. In so-doing, he exposes dangerous cultural mythologies contained within the logic of binary oppositions, and their capacity to silence voice and cultural perspectives in a privileged, unified, and "assumed [colonial] story".

Literary critic, Northrop Frye influentially observed that the question of Canadian identity is not "who are we?" but rather "where is here?". W. H. New in *Articulating West* notes Frye's influence and suggests that authors, in response, have shown a "land [that] becomes a stronger presence than the human figures in Canadian fiction, a character … an actor as well as an activating power in the psychological and metaphysical dreams being unveiled" (New 1972: xii). Albeit a half century later, Frye's musings have remained in the cultural consciousness of Canadians, and with them, speculations about the ambiguity of Canada's cultural identity. Thus derived through its literary imagination, Canada saw a mapping of itself psychologically to its physical "wild uncultivated land, which in Canada includes vast tracts of forest and innumerable lakes and also the Arctic North," wherein a wilderness-territory containing "multiple functions," does "not exist … exclusively as a thing-in-itself" (Howells 1996: 21). Canada unfolded as, "a state of mind … the space you inhabit not just with your body but with your head . . . the kind of space in which we find ourselves lost" (Atwood 1972: 18). Because of the "survival" of such literary "obsessions" (which made nature suspect and the wilderness something to be simultaneously loved and feared) an emerging ecological theoretical perspective necessarily returns to "thematic" literature and criticism of the 1970s and 1980s as a place to begin dismantling the logic of binaries that helped construct and perpetuate these wilderness myths. In addition, critical theories and practices, and the interstice amongst them – including but not limited to postmodernism, postcolonialism, the gothic mode and magical realism – offer the possibility for new rhetoric and shifts in cultural values that may prove to be more about accountability, respect for otherness, and sustainability, and less about the politics of representation. These shifts in consciousness redefine Canada as a nation-state whose emerging ethics concerning biotic community are anathematic to earlier colonial-identified ideas of conquest, resource-extraction, wilderness-extinction, and the annihilation of the other. Thus, Canada's "love-hate" relationship with nature, which "missed the (ecological) mark" on issues of territory, ownership, belonging, and community, may find its way through its literature, its application and interpretations of theoretical modes, and its ability to teach a better awareness of ecological consciousness and practice so that it might, in the process, learn something about what it now means to be Canadian.

Canada's cultural and literary critics continue to debate definitions of Canada and what it is to be Canadian—particularly given historical, economic, and social tendencies to be subsumed by the stronger cultural forces of Britain and the USA. A conference at the University of Manitoba in 2000 asked the question "Is Canada Postcolonial?" and gathered critics still examining definitions of Canadian cultural identity; they responded by suggesting it is complicated. This conference echoes Canadian writer and critic, Robert Kroetsch's critique of thematic criticism in 1989 when he asked, "Is Canada postmodern?" (1989: 21-33). Conference critic Neil Besner offers:

> Canada is not simply postcolonial because the formulation suggests that the story of Canada is only and simply a narrative about its evolution out of a colonial status, (…). Canada is not postcolonial because the very idea of Canada implied in the question is too univocal, monolithic, monocentric, monocultural. Canada is not unilaterally postcolonial; the various kinds of *difference* increasingly manifest in the culture – differences that were always integral to, even when not recognized by, the critical institution – are too vital to be subsumed, hitched together at any post. … Canada is not postcolonial because it is various, its histories are ambiguous and intertwined, and its regions disparate and not themselves to be understood simply as colonies in another, or in an "other," Empire. Canada is not postcolonial because vital elements of Canada – like, for example, First Nations, or, in another sense, different waves of immigrant in several centuries – were never simply "Canada" and certainly never pre-colonial
> (Besner 2003: 48).

Likewise, according to poet and critic George Eliott Clarke, "this fusion and fission of various minority cultures *was* and *is* what confirms the *uniqueness* of the majority Anglophone and Francophone populations – and, thus, of Canadian culture as a whole" (Clarke 2003: 34, Clarke's emphasis, AB). As a nation divided into regions, multicultural recognitions, and two official languages, English and French (though regionally, nine aboriginal languages make the list in the Northwest Territories, New Brunswick is the only bilingual province, and Quebec remains officially unilingual) Canadian multiculturalism is reflected in a literature that resists colonial definitions of stability, centrality, unity, and history. The second half of the twentieth century shows an attention to postmodern and postcolonial literatures that illustrate, instead, the celebration of a many cultured citizenship while simultaneously showing the dangers of silencing multifarious voices within a unified and "assumed story" (Kroetsch 1989: 21). However, Canadian literature continues to deal with the tension inherent in critic Neil Bissoondath's charge of a "multicultural fallacy" which highlights cultural and racial differences and then defines individuals by them. Bissoondath suggests that "to accept the role of ethnic is also to accept a gentle marginalization [. . . and] that one will never be just a part of the landscape but always a little apart from it, not quite belonging" (Bissoondath 1998) Ultimately, it creates "mental ghettos for the various communities" (Bissoondath 1998). Yet, as Clarke further advises, there is "value" in "[Canada's] *great* contradictions – as a site of both *attempted* imperial re-inscription and a much more successful resistance to (and rejection of) "Britain First-ism", and as represented by the effort to construct an English-Canadian culture and literature open to "America", Francophones, ethno-cultural and racial minorities, and First Nations peoples" (Clarke 2003: 31, Clarke's emphasis, AB).

Introducing the debate in "Disunity as unity: A Canadian strategy", Robert Kroetsch (1989: 25) maintains that it is "this willingness to refuse privilege to a ... restrictive cluster of meta-narratives [that] becomes a Canadian strategy for survival". Herein, he suggests:

> The centre does not hold. The margin, the periphery, the edge, now, is the exciting and dangerous boundary where silence and sound meet. It is where the action is. In our darker moments we feel we must resist the blind and consuming power of the new places with their new or old ideas that now want to become centres. In our happier moments we delight in the energy of the local, in the abundance that is diversity and difference, in the variety and life that exist on any coastline of the human experience
> (Kroetsch 1989: 22).

"Instead of answers", Kroetsch continues, "we have questions. Instead of resolution, we have doubt" (Kroetsch 1989: 25), and thus Canadian authors and readers find themselves in a space wherein, "being skillful shape-changers" (Kroetsch 1989: 28) becomes a necessity. Recognizing that the Canadian literary tradition in fiction is only a half-century-old and emerged largely within the post-structural and postmodern climate of the 1960s and early 1970s, much of its texts strive to decentre identity (yet simultaneously questing for it) while parodying literary tropes and cultural mythologies as a means of finding solace in an ever-shifting cultural environment. These texts, which manage to tie any number of theoretical investigations into the narrative as strategies for reflecting "all the reality of the story", do so because they recognize what it is to be "Canadian" and articulate it as the place where "speech against ... silence is on the circumference. The margin. [Since] we live a life of shifting edges, around an unspoken or unspeakable question" (Kroetsch 1989: 30).

In *Gothic Canada* (2005), Justin Edwards likewise explores how Canada defines itself in liminal terms—"caught in-between colonization and post-colonization" where a number of political, cultural, and historical concerns "cannot but generate paradoxes within Canadian identity and textuality" (Edwards 2005: xiv-v). As such, Edwards (2005: xix) finds that "nations like Canada rely upon delusions that call attention to the fictions that exist at the heart of their national metanarratives". He concludes that Canadian gothic literature is well-situated for mapping the "articulation of, and anxiety about, a range of borders that define identity and oppositional relationships [that] fracture specific national conceptions of self," and which exist "at the heart of 'Canadianness'" (Edwards 2005: xiv). His findings are consistent with a much earlier critical Atwood who identifies how imprisoning fortresses (home, hearth, garrison) are ironically pitted against a feminine-identified wilderness as an "icy and savage *femme fatale* who will drive you crazy and claim you for her own" (Atwood 1972: 89).

Emerging Canadian gothic and magic realism—as genres and as tropes within a literary context—may be used to better articulate complex layers of the psychological and physical "realities" of living and being in a Canada no longer defined by its psych-social colonial boundaries. This miscegenation of literary modes explore "unfamiliar logic" where "we find isotropes based on the non-disjunction of contradictory elements (myth/history, *naturalia/mirabilia*) – not either/or, but both/and" which "censure ... the principle dictating the reality of the social order" (Linguanti 1999: 2). Linguanti (1999: 3) further argues that magic realism, with its "metaphors built on analogical links with quantum theory, the theory of chaos, and fluid dynamics" has a "tendency to connect rather than separate, to recover and salvage rather than scatter or deconstruct". In Stephen Slemon's "Magic realism as postcolonial discourse", Slemon suggests that the interstice between postcolonial and magic discourse, particularly outside Latin America and the Caribbean, has expanded as a literary mode that "seems most visibly operative in cultures situated at the fringes of mainstream literary traditions" (Slemon 1995: 408). Its "strange seductiveness" as a literary mode particularly adept at articulating "living on the margins" and a "resistance toward the imperial center and to its totalizing systems of generic classification" contains, for him, a "startling development" in terms of its extension to English Canada since, unlike other regions such as India and Nigeria, Canada is "not part of the Third World" – "a condition long thought necessary to the currency of the term in regard to literature, though not to art" (Slemon 1995: 407-8).

The appearance and development of magic realism in a Canadian literary context allows authors to reflect common Canadian experiences—whether physical, psychological, cultural, historical, etc.—of a constantly changing natural environment. Thus, coming to terms with indefinable spaces in a Canadian literary context may be assisted by magic realism and means that, in some cases, we require a retraining of Canadian audiences, while in other circumstances, we need to secure what is already a Canadian understanding of "reality". As Kroetsch remarked in a 1980 interview with Enright and Cooley, Canadians are not used to seeing themselves in their literature, and "right now, we have a literature about ourselves and it's the audience that's having the crisis. Ten years ago the writers were. Now it's the audience's turn. It's unreal" (Enright – Cooley 1980: 32). In *What the crow said* (1978), Kroetsch establishes a division between humanity and nature that is consistent with mid-century themes of "survival"; nonetheless, he does so in ways that challenge Western epistemological ways of seeing "reality". This division stands systemic throughout the text as readers bear witness to a community's "war with the sky". Nonetheless, Kroetsch's text avoids perpetuating Atwood's thematic prescription and categorization of Canadian literature as a series of survival stories (see Atwood's *Survival*, 1972).

What the crow said[1] reads as a postmodern parody – with elements of the gothic and magic realism literary modes – of Canadian literature based in thematic representations of survivorship when it playfully maims and tortures its male characters with wilderness-threats, oftentimes killing them in the most extravagant and unexpected ways. Critic Christine Jackman articulates the complexities of Kroetsch's parody when she deems it a "topos of excess", and suggests that:

> Kroetsch undermines binaries, collapsing them in parodic extremeness. He also undermines his undermining. So the question is not whether Kroetsch destroys or perpetuates binaries. He does both; he does neither. ... [this text takes] a position where binaries are forces of "becoming" rather than rigid structures which unambiguously shape our lives"
>
> (Jackman 1991: 1).

These characters sometimes suffer maladies associated with foolish and "useless" tasks but oftentimes succumb to the treachery of the mythology of Canadian wilderness-space and weather. Rose marries a war-veteran, hired as a farm-hand, who is missing his "private parts" and one leg but who still manages to impregnate her; Isador Heck breaks his big toe "by dropping a post maul on it" but "heal[s] himself by disallowing the theory of gravity" (*WCS*, 67). Vera's three husbands die in fairly rapid succession, seemingly trying to escape her: the first, Ebbie Else dies charging a bull ("in some unnamable agony, or fear, or

---

1   Henceforth indicated as *WCS* followed by page numbers. All quotations are from Kroetsch, Robert. 1978. *What the crow said*. Edmonton: The University of Alberta Press.

desperation"; *WCS*, 152); the younger Adams' body is found by "an Indian woman, pulling frozen fish out of a net with her bare hands" where it had been "swimming away from the hole he'd fallen into (*WCS*, 154); finally, Vera's third husband is found sacrificed on the windmill, his "hair the color of dust .... trailing behind his fixed head, one sock loose on a locked foot, his arms outspread" (*WCS*, 159). This binary contained within death/wilderness (countered by a survival/ homestead linked to the feminine) is associated solely with men who die by choice, foolishness, and/or bad luck.

A synergy developing in Canadian literature is, perhaps, why critic Steven Slemon named the emergence of magic realism in Canadian postcolonial literature a "startling development" (Slemon 1995: 407). Canadian authors have, from the onset, struggled with tensions between colonial models and the New World experience—articulating self and other in Native, non-Native, colonial, immigrant, settler, explorer, post-colonial, racial, religious, gender relationships and paradigms. Likewise, finding "unity in disunity," as Kroetsch speculated, has been embraced by authors and scholars seeking positive interpretations of a country plagued by cultural destabilization that can never (or ought not to ever) resolve issues of unity. An evolving literary tradition in Canada shows how its contemporary writing seeks non-traditional modes of narrative, representation, and form, to articulate its self-declared paradox of identities which desires the simultaneous collapse *and* the determination of (shifting) territories "between the extremities of the self and the Other, the sublime and the abject, the real and the virtual, American and Europe" (Edwards 2005: xv).

Exploring Native literatures from non-Native perspectives is fraught with political and social challenges. Teaching Canadian readers how to see "equality in difference" (a third wave feminist mantra) and how to understand, recognize, and respect both self (one's own cultural and personal ideologies) and the position of cultural otherness is key to resolving what Kroetsch described as an audience in crisis in the 1980s. Educating readers of strategies for identification and interpretation of texts that construct "realities"—including historical perspective, philosophies, spiritual practices, and Western models of interpreting the world— has transformed the author's ability to integrate aspects of post-colonialism and Indigenous Knowledges (IK), without appropriating voice, and creating further denigration of racial/religious otherness. Indigenous Knowledges (IK) or Indigenous Knowledge Systems (IKS) currently defines an area of theoretical and practical investigations into Indigenous philosophies, wisdoms, methods of education, ways of knowing, etc.—*by* Indigenous writers, philosophers, elders, and critics – that distinguishes itself from colonial interpretations, and Eurocentric theories and practices. Canadian critic, Helen Hoy in *How should I read these?* (2001) explains that, while "race and gender (among other identity classification) may well be inventions, constructed categories that signal the deviation of marked races and gender(s) from the norm," nonetheless, "their effects are tangible, producing distinctive racialized and gendered subject positions" (Hoy 2001: 7). Her criticism explores the complexities of non-Native readers/instructors who read/teach Native literature in a Canadian context, and identifies strategies of inclusion of Indigenous literatures and oral traditions in the study of Canadian literature, history, and culture. She explains:

> The appropriation-of-voice debate in Canada—which flourished in the late 1980s and early 1990s, with Native people challenging non-Native creative writers particularly to stop "stealing our stories"—invoked this question of difference. Although it pivoted also on questions of Native copyright, racist structures of publication and reception, and arrogation of profits, the challenge insisted on perspectives and knowledges located in the particularities of Native histories, culture and political experiences, and story-telling traditions
>
> (Hoy 2001: 7-8).

Furthermore, when non-Native authors usurp subject positions (particularly in first-person narratives) from the cultural "other" they are ultimately "seen as both displacing the Native author and subject and presuming—and, in the process, producing—knowledge of realities at some remove from his or her own" (Hoy 2001: 8). Though this debate has quieted somewhat, members of Indigenous communities in Canada are "still pressing to be recognized as socially differentiated subjects whose understandings are distinctive, not simply interchangeable with those of other groups or instantly accessible to outsiders" (Hoy 2001: 8).

Cultural climates that allow for the coming together of colonial, postcolonial and Native literatures offer us the opportunity to discuss the recognition of and respect for difference in cultural and/or racial otherness. Hoy asks us to reject the "metaphor of Canada as a conversation ... [as] part of a wrongheaded quest for a national mythos [that] missed the mark" (Hoy 2001: 14), but maintains an openness to resisting the "retreat response" common to non-Indigenous writers and readers. Hoy concludes that issues of race, voice, identity, etc. will remain contentious until equalities are achieved but in the meantime, offers a text that is "tracing a process, rehearsing areas of contention, proffering analysis that is then often itself challenged, modified, or displaced, and ending with partial and provisional answers that invite further challenge" (Hoy 2001: 25). Bridging cultural, philosophical and pedagogical gaps between Native and non-Native Canadians is becoming possible in the early twenty-first century; it is *becoming*, that is, if the politics of representation are sincerely shifting to a politics of accountability. Recently, Canada has witnessed the formations of The Indian Residential Schools Truth and Reconciliation Commission (2008, with a budget of $60 million), Aboriginal Healing Foundation (1998), and a public apology on 11 June, 2008, from Canada's Prime Minister, Stephen Harper to all residential school students. However, Canadians still have a long way to go to right the wrongs and bridge gaps between communities.

By reading Indigenous Knowledge Systems (IKS), and by following traditional teachings, or teaching bundles, readers find strategies for entering into Indigenous literature that insist on self-identification through symbolic and mythological imageries, and as such, they may engage in a transnational healing process. In this way, the learner enters into the literature to explore how 'reality' is not simply understood through a fixed and strictly empirically obtained objectivity but through the recognition of an "ever-shifting fabric" of *intersubjective* phenomenology—articulated at the turn of last century by philosopher Edmund Husserl (Abram 1996: 38)—but likewise supported by centuries-old native philosophies and educational systems. American critic and writer, Paula Gunn Allen explains:

> One of the problems with the Western world, in all of its aspects today, right now in white folk's time, is that we don't understand the spirits. We don't understand the supernaturals. We don't understand that right here standing with us are multiple worlds coexisting, cohabiting, and occupying the same space with us. What the tribal people all recognize is that those communities are absolutely real and have everything to do with us
>
> (Allen 2008: 140).

Essential to Indigenous education and understanding reading strategies in Native literature is the goal to be "fully knowledgeable about one's innate spirituality"—to learn the "pathway of vision" within a "process that unfolds through a variety of dimensions" (Cajete 1994: 69). It is within this context that magic realism has emerged in late twentieth-century Canadian literature as a site of discovery; as a place for potential and powerful shifts in consciousness; and as a reflection of the integrated and authentic Canadian experience—one which is not easily placed within simple confines of strict epistemological evidence.

In its Canadian literary context, magic realism allows for incompatible worlds to "come into being," and "remain ... suspended [and] locked in a continuous dialectic with the 'other;'" it thus becomes a situation which creates disjunction within each of the separate discursive systems, rending them with gaps, absences, and silences" (Slemon 1995: 410). Herein, magic realism works as a textual strategy that does not always "suggest a seamless interweaving of, or synthesis between, the magic and the real" (Slemon 1995: 424)—nor does it need to fulfill this criteria since the Canadian seamless and definitive sense of identity has already been actualized as a meta-narrative, impossible and undesirable to create. Placed within a unique Canadian (post)colonial context, the incorporation of magic realism with aboriginal philosophies and Indigenous "ways of knowing" provides opportunity for genuine understandings of the complex and oftentimes contentious Native and non-Native political and social dynamic. Nonetheless, it is important to note that Native writers and critics resist conflating and connecting postcolonialism with Indigenous thought and knowledge systems; yet non-Native critics continue to both respect "Indigenous desires to separate their project at this crucial stage in the decolonization process" (Brydon 2003: 58) and see positive and empowering overlaps between and within these theoretical modes and conditions.

Combining traditions provides "startlingly" new possibilities for answering Frye's question, "where is here?" as it eludes any definition of cultural identity and celebrates, instead, how Canada's literary imagination is discovering the ways in which "here", continues to be "resistan[t] to monologic political and cultural structures" (Zamora – Faris 1995: 6). By destabilizing binary oppositions that are key to Canadian discussions of culture in literature and criticism, magic realism creates and defines "home" as a place eager to have the walls built between nature/humankind, aboriginal/settler, and wilderness/garrisons, which persist as anathematic to social and political well-being. Herein, the boundaries between "mind and body, spirit and matter, life and death, real and imaginary, self and other, male and female" are "to be erased, transgressed, blurred, brought together, or otherwise fundamentally refashioned in magic realist texts" (Zamora – Faris 1995: 6). As Zamora and Faris (1995: 6) remind us, "the propensity of magical realist texts to admit a plurality of worlds means that they often situate themselves on liminal territory between or among those worlds—in phenomenal and spiritual regions where transformation, metamorphosis, dissolution are common, here magic is a branch of naturalism, or pragmatism.

Integral to this discussion of text and politics are the ways in which Kroetsch creates an organic space filled with infinite possibilities and unanswered questions in *What the crow said*; this novel investigates how magic realism may be respectfully explored as a means of incorporating elements of Indigenous culture and knowledge systems, to better articulate an inclusive Canadian cultural consciousness, within regenerative aspects of the postmodern novel. As Slemon maintains, "binary opposition between control in one dimension and incompetence or bewilderment in the other" in *What the crow said* "reflects the dialectic operative in post-colonial cultures between inherited, sure, and constraining codes of imperial order and the imagined, precarious, and liberating codes of postcolonial 'original relations'" (Slemon 1995: 415). Kroetsch too attempts "an imaginative projection into the future, where the fractures of colonialism heal in the 'revisioning' process that produces a 'positive imaginative reconstruction of reality'" (Slemon 1995: 417). Thus, binaries in Kroetsch's text may be read as "legacies of the colonial encounter" which "undergo a process of dialectical interplay between opposing terms which undermine ... the fixity of borders between them" and where "each term invades the other, eroding its absolute nature and addressing the gaps or absences, the distanced elements of 'otherness', that fixed systems inevitably create" (Slemon 1995: 418). Likewise, Kroetsch's critical perspective on "prairie fiction" describes an engendered dynamic of space and creative paralysis wherein the male figure, who "works by trespass" "is violently rivaled by a fear of woman as the figure who contains the space, who speaks the silence" (Kroetsch 1989a: 76). Resolution of this dynamic, when the figures are already "in exile from paradise" (Kroetsch 1989a: 77), is, however, temporary, and appears to exist only in the liminal spaces created when binaries are destabilized, and social modes of behaviour and expectation are collapsed into androgynous thinking and being.

Thus, echoing Northrop Frye's inquiries concerning space and identity, Kroetsch asks "how do you make love in a new country?" Stories, Kroetsch suggests, contain the answers to the queries concerning "any sort of *close* relationship in a landscape ... whose primary characteristic is *distance*" (Kroetsch 1989a: 73). It is what happens on the closed insides of a book that paradoxically, he explains, "might be made to ... contain space" (Kroetsch 1989a: 73, Kroetsch's italics, AB). Critic John Clement Ball suggests that identifying the house/horse binary and the Coyote/God binary are key to reading Kroetsch's fiction. These tropes associated with gender difference and social practice herein represent "the failure of male-female unity: the failure of sex and the failure of the dance" (Ball 1989: 5). Thus, what creates possibility in *What the crow said* is the promise of change and shifts in consciousness made possible (if only to the reader) by entering into a liminal and magical space; infused with metaphors and miracles capable of converting, as Kroetsch does, skeptical characters like Isador Heck who "claim[s] to believe in nothing" (*WCS*, 67), bear witness to a carnivalesque mode of circus travelling and change his/her "conviction [to a belief] that anything that can be imagined exists" (*WCS*, 162). Heck, who fails to integrate horizontal and vertical spaces into an androgynous psyche, is ultimately misguided when he tries to reach heaven through man-made devices; nonetheless, he becomes symbolic of the pilgrimage of change and the futility of maintaining masculine-identified notions of motion-as-power.

Given the choice between creative styles of authorship—God (Western, Christian, binaries, controls the narrative of the "other") and Coyote (Aboriginal, IK, holistic, tells his own stories)—Kroetsch offers us possibilities for positive change that act against stasis, boredom, and social hegemonies associated with maintaining binary oppositions in everyday practices and mythologies. As such, the author who chooses to be Coyote, "lets in the irrational along with the rational, the pre-moral along with the moral" and becomes "a shapeshifter," "a charlatan-healer" and "the low-down Buddha-bellied fiddler midwife" (Kroetsch – Bessai 1978: 209). Choosing "energy over stasis" (1978: 215) becomes the preferred choice for change since Coyote "lets everything into his art" and as such, shows art to be more than an "artifact" by enabling "not meaning but the possibility of meanings" (Kroetsch – Bessai 1978: 208). Critic John Clement Ball explains (in his exploration of the text *Word*) that Kroetsch ultimately "breaks down the dualities in a number of ways ... bring[ing] horse and house, male and female together and in ways that do not diminish the man's heroic stature or threaten the integrity of his role as cowboy, orphan, and outlaw" (Ball 1989: 6). Ball (1989: 6) insists that, "by unifying elements that he has said are not unified in Prairie fiction, Kroetsch is writing against the prairie mythology that he himself has identified".

In *What the crow said*, the community of Bigknife, the dissolving of political and historical borders remains seemingly unimportant since its citizens co-exist within cultural diversity (including men, women, Indigenous, Europeans, Hutterites, etc.) without too much notice of cultural difference, at least by its inhabitants. For example, the "Indian List," a "racist term for the list of those proscribed from being served alcohol" (Slemon 1995: 419), registers, "every white male over the age of twenty in the Municipality of Bigknife" (*WCS*, 114), but does not include names of any Aboriginal characters. While Kroetsch seems, on one hand, to be collapsing the Native/Non-Native boundary, on the other hand, he simultaneously gives a critical recognition of colonial violence consistent with the historic erasure of aboriginal peoples, names, heritage, etc. from Canadian cultural recognition. Indigenous characters certainly set the standard for loyalty, leadership, and for being among the successful visionaries in the text. Native-Canadian, Joe Lightning is the only person to whom Tiddy Lang confesses that her only son, JG, "sang in her womb" (*WCS*, 139), as if suggesting that *he* would not contest her lack of epistemological evidence. Also, Joe Lightning is the only character who revalues JG's "stepping from the top of the tree" as a reasonable attempt to "enter ... the sky" (*WCS*, 139) and uses it as inspiration for his own "plan for learning the sky's own secret;" after all, "Joe Lightning was opposed to the war against the sky; he believed in the union of the elements" (*WCS*, 139). Furthermore, JG could communicate with the crow, and walked in a figure eight—symbols of eternity and endless possibilities—read as "strange" or "abnormal" to the Western reader but interpreted as powerful and "visionary" to those schooled in IK.

In a novel that repeatedly uses trinities, Joe's vision quest, instead, begins, "on the morning of the fourth day" when Joe attempts to "learn about the sky" (and not necessarily conquer, destroy, enter into it, etc. as other characters profess) as he grabs hold of the legs of an eagle in flight. Symbolically, the number four is associated in IK with the four corners of the earth, the four directions, and the four sacred plants, four realms of human experience, etc.—all reflected in the tetradic structure of the medicine wheel. Unlike other characters who respond to simple binary reflections of space as either horizontal or vertical, Joe is afforded the privilege of reflection and perspective, particularly when "he let go of the eagle or the eagle let go of him" on the third day (traditional vision quests last for four days) and understands how, "his fall was as new to him as his rise; the vertical world was all a mystery" (*WCS*, 140). Significantly, the eagle, in IKS, is the closest to the Creator and serves as the principle messenger. Like Vera's scream that pierced the ears and consciousness of everyone in Big Knife,

Joe too releases a "laughter" or "cry of terror" or "simple laugh of pleasure" that serves as "a version of prayer, a kind of holy laugh" (*WCS*, 142). Like JG, whose death might have been prevented, so too might Joe Lightning's death have been prevented; however, "the fall was messy and everyone had their church clothes on" (*WCS*, 143). Significantly, JG falls from the tree, arms stretched out (like a Christ-figure) and is impaled by homemade crosses in Rose's animal and china cup graveyard. Likewise, Joe Lightning dies, landing "on the ladies' outhouse behind the Church of the Final Virgin. Or, rather, he landed where the outhouse should have been. Pranksters, the previous Halloween, had set it behind the toilet pit" (*WCS*, 142); in sacrificial death, Joe remains entangled in the metaphor of Christian protocols and leftover pagan ritual.

Kroetsch's use of "space", as it is associated with the Canadian consciousness and obsession with "place" marries magic realism with elements of gothic as a means of shifting an inherited (European) consciousness—which has shown a tendency to maintain locks on categories associated with race, nature (pastoral vs. culture/urban) and class—to a more inclusive hybrid space (Wilson 1995: 222). Through a theory of "spatial folding" in magic realism, Wilson argues that Kroetsch uses the magic realist mode to show "two worlds, distinct and following dissimilar laws that interpenetrate and interwind, all unpredictably but in a natural fashion" (Wilson 1995: 222). In this way, Kroetsch finds the necessary flexibility to continue postcolonial and postmodern agendas of destabilization, but also offers deeper and continuous overlappings of physical/psychological and imaginative/spiritual pairings as a means of re-addressing staid categories of literary landscape/biotic community. Critic Luca Biagiotti comments on "geographical miscegenation" in *What the crow said*, suggesting that:

> The ambiguity of the geographical collocation is significant, insofar as the town becomes not so much a *trait-d'union* or a 'link' (a synthesis) between the two colonial cultures as a morphological point of contact and fusion between two different cultural 'tectonic plates.' It is a moment of spatial and cultural 'folding' where different languages decide to listen to, rather than silence, each other
>
> (Biagiotti 1999: 106).

Clearly, Big Indian and its surrounding municipality of Bigknife folds two distinct cultures—European-colonial and Aboriginal—into a land that "has no precise borders" (Biagiotti 1999: 106). Kroetsch's narrator explains: "No one, due to a surveyor's error, had ever been able to locate conclusively where the boundaries were supposed to be. The south end of the municipality, beyond the poplar bluffs and the fields of grain, faded into bald prairie and a Hutterite colony; the north end vanished into the bush country and an Indian reserve" (*WCS*, 36). Taken into this spatial folding, readers readily accept Kroetsch's employment of the liminal as a place of thresholds between opposing subjectivities and perspectives and enter, without hesitation, a space where the unfamiliar, hauntings, mutilations, beauty, strange and unnatural occurrences, and the grotesque cohabit, as though timelessly familiar with the movement—in and out, vertically and horizontally—of each other's boundaries. As Wilson asserts, this novel "incorporate[s] the extratextual world even while constructing a textual space that makes unlikelihoods possible" (Wilson 1995: 220).

Kroetsch has often been quoted as a writer who is aware of the ways in which Canadian authors enter into a dance with nature, wilderness, land, and landscapes. In an interview with Enright and Cooley, Kroetsch, when asked about his writing and its exploration of place, responded by saying: "The idea of landscape is incredibly complicated emotionally. It's no accident that a lot of poets work out of that notion of a place as a reality, as a metaphor, as a story, as a myth" (Enright – Cooley 1980: 31). This sentiment is consistent with what Indigenous philosopher and educator, Gregory Cajete has deemed "the geopsyche." The *geopsyche*, Cajete explains, is the recognition of one's own psycho-spiritual relationship with rocks, trees, and nature as a means of re-engaging with self, and the "pathways of vision … [that may] unfold through a variety of dimensions" (Cajete 1994: 69). Ecofeminist critic, Patrick D. Murphy revisions the *geopsyche* as a theoretical and psycho-spiritual space in which shifts away from cultural perceptions that divide self from other (and thus ghettoize difference as "strange" and/or "dangerous") become possible (Murphy 1998: 41). *What the crow said* may not be categorized as strictly as ecological literature; but, as protoecological literature, it does tend to incorporate and foreshadow the emergence of more clearly defined ecological concerns of place and an ethics of behaviour in recent Canadian ecological literature and ecocriticism. This literary landscape is not tropological in the text, but serves as a character or characters, acting in its own sense of self-preservation and oftentimes, indifference to 'the other'. For example, after the snowstorm that takes Martin Lang's life, bodies of dead animals are seen as becoming part of the landscape and not divided from it (*WCS*, 30); instead, they are incorporated into a folded "reality" that is simultaneously aesthetic, physical, metaphoric (particularly in terms of historical resonance with war), environmental, and psychological. Herein, men hired to retrieve Martin Lang's dead body become stand-ins for fence-posts, their heads, "above the drifting snow" and "knock[ing] the staples out of a row of willow posts" (*WCS*, 27). Significantly, men's bodies too are incorporated into the natural environment as they replace missing visual lines in the open prairie fields, and return the architectural or skeletal backbone of the fence to the prairie "wilderness"—a common metaphor in prairie fiction for boundaries and thresholds.

Kroetsch describes a Prairie "landscape" that is *in actuality* a kind of magical and liminal encounter that exists, for his characters, on an on-going and a regular basis, as if nature and humankind live in a symbiosis, not always interpreted as cooperative. Given the unpredictability of sudden, violent weather in Canada and correspondingly, in *What the crow said* (namely, snow, lightning and wind storms) Kroetsch uses its known presence as the site of focusing, blurring, illuminating and erasing, and de-mythologizing the contextualization and reality of place. When Liebhaber first entered the snowstorm that would later leave Martin Lang dead, how "the hardware store ... wasn't quite where it should have been, its dark windows full of rakes and hoes and garden seeds, unsold because spring had never come" (*WCS*, 17). The "landscape" draws Liebhaber and two others attempting to journey home from the bar, deeper into a gothic and magically real territory. The narrator further explains:

> They passed the last caragana hedge surrounding the last house, the last and final street lamp, the myriad snowflakes eating its light. ... The grain elevators weren't there. The string of elevators, slope-shouldered, red; they weren't visible along the railway tracks that weren't visible either. Liebhaber sawed at the horse's reins. He might have turned back, had he known how. Perhaps he thought he had turned back when he felt the wind. He faced into the wind. Liebhaber couldn't see. The snow rattled on his stiffening cheeks. The hard, broken snowflakes pecked at his eyes. He was already turning back, he believed he was turning back, when the muffled squeak of hoofs on the snow-buried gravel road became, abruptly, a hollow drumming. They were onto the bridge. They were not so much onto the bridge as out into the air itself, into the blizzard
>
> (*WCS* 17-18).

Though the "othering" of nature is generally inconsistent within literary traditions of magic realism, herein Kroetsch plays with a Canadian critical tradition which sets wilderness against the colonizer and uses Canadian motifs to create a uniquely Canadian sense of the magically real and the Prairie gothic—as if to say they are inseparable in the Canadian (Western) literary imagination.

Notably, "landscape" is never gendered as feminine but exists as an entity outside the purview of the townspeople who find the vertical world baffling and mysterious. However, Kroetsch continues to engage in the collapsing of binaries—particularly those constructions of opposition which purport to be consistent with a Canadian literary imagination. Thus, Kroetsch does not resist imaginatively venturing into a psychological landscape wherein nature and humankind coexist in an ebb and flow of conquest and surrender. For example, the swarm of bees that problematically colonize and eroticize Vera in the opening chapter continue to be blamed throughout the text and associated with "the war with the sky"; failed weather and crops; and a consciousness that remains a mystery throughout the text. Kroetsch's layers of complexity within rings of meaning (colonial, postcolonial, IK, magic realism, gothic, feminist, etc.) is profound. First, Vera's erotic encounter exists in the meadow—a liminal space between town and wilderness, farmed and unfarmed, domesticated and wild, house and frontier, which serves as a literary metaphor for infinite possibility and transmogrification, including the miscegenation between wildlife and humans. Second, Vera's encounter is juxtaposed in the text with the anaphoric and parceled out narrative of the journey her five sisters take, within mock epic proportions, all at the "urgent request" of their mother who sensed something had gone awry (*WCS*, 2-3). These sisters venture into the attic, cellar, grandmother's trunk, barn and garden—all places consistent in a female gothic tradition with metaphors of escape, madness, incest, ancestral secrets, etc. (see Gilbert and Gubar's *Mad woman in the attic*). Third, the only other character entering this space is Vera's father, who, despite having "a wife and six daughters and a mother-in-law in the house, he liked on a Sunday afternoon to take a pail and go by himself into the valley of the Bigknife River" (*WCS*, 10). Martin Lang's physical body disappears and reappears in landscape-erasing snowstorms; he remains a snow-ploughing spectre throughout the text, caught in the in-betweens of the home-front, between the garden and the house, "at the clothesline" and whose story, whether it contains an incest or not, nonetheless, remains silent, hidden, and secret. Finally and symbolically, Vera's encounter happens in the springtime when new beginnings for transformations, hope, rebirth, fertility, etc., abound in literary symbolism.

Significantly, by juxtaposing seemingly psychological and 'natural' opposites within the same liminal spaces, Kroetsch builds a ring of "speaking mirrors" into the text, through which the reader can begin to process "the 'shreds and fragments' of colonial violence and otherness into new 'codes of recognition'" (Slemon 1995: 422). In this way, as Slemon (1995: 422) addresses, "the dispossessed, the silenced, and the marginalized of our own dominating systems can again find voice and enter into the dialogic continuity of community and place". Consistently, it is within long "realistic" and descriptive passages of the land that Kroetsch sets life-altering, consciousness-shifting, and human physical and spiritual metamorphosis. The natural environment is key when Vera is inseminated by the bees; when the town's men are resurrecting and burying bodies; and when Joe Lightning takes flight in eagle-talons for a three-day vision quest. The only significant exception to this textual pattern is the final chapter when Liebhaber, with the use of Isador Heck's human-canon, takes Vera's new batch of bees, and "pump[s] them into the sky itself, ramm[ing] them into the sky's night, into the sky's blue breaking" (*WCS*, 194), to end "the war with the sky" (or the war between horizontal and vertical planes) and to finally enter into a sexual, legal, spiritual, and psychological "marriage"—"one androgynous moment of heaven and earth" (*WCS*, 193)—with mother and keeper of the home-hearth, Tiddy Lang. By engaging in a marriage of equals, Tiddy and Liebhaber effectively create their own "naked circle" (*WCS*, 194) within one "androgynous moment" (*WCS*, 193) or, as defined within IK, a "sacred hoop of being" (Allen 1992: 11). As Peter Thomas (1980: 5) suggests, *What the crow said* "is a parody of metaphysics in its cosmic religious and existential dramas, ... a Kroetschian pun on bee-ing and bee-coming.

Gestures which collapse male/female social boundaries within this final scene serve as agents of dissolution between genders, between humankind and nature, between the past and the present, and between standardized meaning and mysteries, that finally bring a resolution, of sorts, to the reader and to the novel's main characters. Since "resolution" suggests finality, closure, and potentially stagnation, this final scene decentres its resolution as much as it promotes it; what is required by readers in Kroetsch's conclusion, is not so much "resolution" (though it is there) but "awareness" in new perceptions that allow stability in organic and ever-shifting territories of the psyche, the spirit, the body, and the biosphere. In this psycho-spiritual space, Liebhaber's quest for meaning in language and lettered symbolism dissolves: "Liebhaber hears the crow. The crow is outside the bedroom window. It is talking, not listening, croaking endlessly on. Liebhaber cannot quite understand what the crow is saying" (*WCS*, 195), and Cathy, Joe Lightning's widow, walks through the pasture, "barefoot", where "the crows are cawing" (*WCS*, 195). Instead of engaging with a "wilderness" that exists exclusively in the exterior, this final scene takes place within the farmhouse's interior; bees and rain continue to fall, outside, from the "opened" sky but inside another kind of collapsing and joining occurs. Here, assuming a shift in consciousness, "sometimes [Cathy] does not wonder at all, squinting against the slant of fine rain, trying to spot the motionless cows. Sometimes she talks to herself. Sometimes she looks up at the sky, at the slant of rain, hoping that Joe Lightning will fall into her arms" (*WCS*, 195).

As if to bookend the novel, Vera's desires are awakened by the bees falling *outside* the house; this time, however, Vera rejoins the bees "at home" thereby collapsing the cultural strictures that exist throughout the text (and in the reader's ideology) between house/wilderness, internal/external and male/female as a way of unburdening the reader from hegemonies that result when self and other are divided. The narrator explains:

> [Vera] spied a bee, on the dry side of a rock. She plucked the bee like a berry; she opened her large leather shoulder bag and dropped the bee inside. ... They fell from the sky; they appeared, now and then, a bee on a Saskatoon bush, on a strand of barbed wire, on the dry side of a willow fencepost. She gathered the fallen bees into her careful hands, into her bag. They were too wet to fly, the bees. Vera's desire was more than she could contain. Her eyes were bright, hot, intense when she met her sisters. She hardly knew them. She refused to go with them, back to the house. She touched her son. She actually touched her son's wet hair
>
> (*WCS*, 171).

Thus, Vera returns to the beginning of the novel, to complete a full sexual cycle (including the trinity of three husbands in the text) when Kroetsch returns the text to that earlier anaphoric listing of timed events associated with Vera's encounter with the bees. While Tiddy and Liebhaber consummate an androgynous relationship inside the house, Vera creates an external space of resolution, simultaneously, outside the text—here too, Vera becomes the nurturing mother and thoughtful lover. Finally, the reader is invited to join the holistic sexual circle of meaning and mystery when judgments concerning the initial encounter (was it mutual, incest, rape, unnatural, grotesque, horrific, glorious?) are laid into a similar acceptance of being and bee-ing that requires no definitive meaning or resolution.

Ultimately, the binaries that Kroetsch collapses at the novel's close, present themselves within a cyclical dynamic, or "naked circle" (*WCS*, 194) which Christine Jackman describes as "mandala-like in both image and effect" (Jackman 1991: 10). Through the miscegenation of gothic and magic realist literary modes, Kroetsch enables critically explored aspects of a Canadian cultural consciousness to be exposed as both valid and fraudulent. That is, whether or not Canadians experience real or imagined tensions between home and wilderness, this definition of a Canadian cultural consciousness cannot ultimately hold meaning. Interpreting Frye *et. al.* as "seeds of intensions" (as Cajete might call them), Canadian ecological criticism requires a committed cultivation of the ideas in order to engage in other (and othered) ideas within the discussion of a Canadian cultural consciousnesses. By naming this organic journey as one that requires broader perspectives and *ways of knowing* Kroetsch asks his readers to re-examine gothic as a place of horror; magic realism as a place of mystery; and the wilderness as a place of fear. In so-doing, Kroetsch collapses these boundaries within postmodern and post-colonial arenas, thus enabling him to expose a more respectful complexity of a necessarily ever-shifting Canadian consciousness. His question is one that probes beyond "where is here?" and "what is community?" From an ecological perspective, Kroetsch moves away from literature that explores "how are we living *with* the wilderness", to writing that asks its readers, "how are we living *in* the wilderness", respectfully and within a broader perspective of a biotic community.

References

Abram, David. 1996. *The spell of the sensuous: Perception and language in a more-than-human world.* New York: Pantheon Books.

Allen, Paula Gunn. 2008. "She is us: Thought woman and the sustainability of worship", in: Melissa K. Nelson, 138-144.

Allen, Paula Gunn. 1992. *The sacred hoop: Recovering the feminine in American Indian traditions.* Boston: Beacon Press.

Atwood, Margaret. 1995. *Strange things: The malevolent North in Canadian literature.* Oxford: Clarendon Press.

Atwood, Margaret. 1972. *Survival*. Toronto: Anansi.

Ball, John Clement. 1989. "The carnival of Babel: The construction of voice in Robert Kroetsch's 'Out west' triptych", *Essays on Canadian Writing*, 39: 5-16.

Besner, Neil. 2003. "What resides in the question, "Is Canada postcolonial?"", in: Laura Moss (ed.), 40-48.

Bessai, Diane – David Jackel (eds.). 1978. *Figures in a ground: Canadian essays on modern literature collected in honour of Sheila Watson*. Saskatoon: Western Producer Prairie.

Biagiotti, Luca. 1999. "Bees, bodies, and magical miscegenations. Robert Kroetsch's *What the crow said*", in: Elsa Linguanti – Francesco Casotti – Carmen Concilio (eds.), 103-114.

Bissoondath, Neil. 1998. "No place like home", *New Internationalist Magazine* 305. (http://www.newint.org/features/1998/09/05/multiculturalism/) (date of access: April 2, 2012).

Bissoondath, Neil. 1994. *Selling illusions: The cult of multiculturalism in Canada*. Markham, ON: Penguin Books.

Brydon, Diana. 2003. "Canada and postcolonialism: Questions, inventories, and futures", in: Laura Moss (ed.), 49-77.

Cajete, Gregory. 1994. *Look to the mountain: An ecology of indigenous education*. Durango, Colorado: Kivaki Press.

Clarke, George Elliott. 2003. "What was Canada?", in: Laura Moss (ed.), 27-39.

Edwards, Justin D. 2005. "Introduction", in: *Gothic Canada: Reading the spectre of a national literature*. Edmonton: University of Alberta Press, xi-xxxiv.

Enright, Robert – Dennis Cooley. 1980. "Uncovering our dream world: An interview with Robert Kroetsch", *Essays on Canadian Writing*, 18/19: 21-32.

Frye, Northrop. 1971. "Conclusion to a *Literary history of Canada* (1965)", in: *The Bush Garden*. Toronto: Anansi Press, 213-251.

Gilbert, Sandra M. – Susan Gubar. 1984. *The madwoman in the attic*. London: Yale University Press.

Howells, Coral Ann. 1996. *Margaret Atwood*. London: MacMillan Press Ltd.

Hoy, Helen. 2001. "Introduction", in: *How should I read these? Native women writers in Canada*. Toronto: University of Toronto Press, 3-31.

Jackman, Christine. 1991. "What the crow said: A topos of excess", *Studies in Canadian Literature/Etudes en Litterature Canadienne* 16, 2: 79-92.

Kamboureli, Smaro. 2000. *Scandalous bodies: Diasporic literature in English Canada*. Don Mills, ON: Oxford University Press.

Kerridge, Richard – Neil Sammells (eds.). 1998. *Writing the environment: Ecocriticism and literature*. London: Zed Books.

Kroetsch, Robert. 1989. "Disunity as unity: A Canadian strategy", in: *The lovely treachery of words: Essays selected and new*. Toronto: Oxford UP, 21-31.

Kroetsch, Robert. 1989a. "The fear of women in prairie fiction: An erotics of space", in: *The lovely treachery of words: Essays selected and new*. Toronto: Oxford University Press, 73-83.

Kroetsch, Robert. 1978. *What the crow said*. Edmonton: The University of Alberta Press.

Kroetsch, Robert – Diane Bessai. 1978. "Death is a happy ending: A dialogue in thirteen parts", in: Diane Bessai – David Jackel (eds.), 206-15.

Leggatt, Judith. 2003. "Native writing, academic theory: Post-colonialism across the cultural divide", in: Laura Moss (ed.), 111-126.

Linguanti, Elsa. 1999. "Introduction", in: Elsa Linguanti – Francesco Casotti – Carmen Concilio (eds.), 1-7.

Linguanti, Elsa – Francesco Casotti – Carmen Concilio (eds.). 1999. *Coterminous worlds: Magical realism and contemporary post-colonial literature in English*. Amsterdam: Rodopi.

Moss, Laura (ed.). 2003. *Is Canada Postcolonial? Unsettling Canadian literature*. Waterloos. ON: Wilfrid Laurier University Press.

Murphy, Patrick D. 1998. "Anotherness and inhabitation in recent multicultural American literature", in: Richard Kerridge – Neil Sammells (eds.), 40-52.

Nelson, Melissa K. (ed.) 2008. *Original instructions: Indigenous teachings for a sustainable future*. Vermont: Bear and Company.

New, W. H. 1972. *Articulating west: essays on purpose and form in modern Canadian literature*. Toronto: New Press.

Slemon, Stephen. 2003. "Afterword", in: Laura Moss (ed.), 318-324.

Slemon, Stephen. 1995. "Magic realism as postcolonial discourse", in: Lois Parkinson Zamora – Wendy B. Faris (eds.), 407-426.

Thomas, Peter. 1980. "Robert Kroetsch and silence", *Essays on Canadian Writing* 18/19, 33: 2-17.

Wilson, Rawdon. 1995. "The metamorphoses of fictional space: Magical realism", in: Lois Parkinson Zamora – Wendy B. Faris (eds.), 209-233.

Zamora, Lois Parkinson – Wendy B. Faris. 1995. "Introduction: Daiquiri Birds and Flaubertian Parrot(ie)s", in: Lois Parkinson Zamora – Wendy B. Faris (eds.), 1-11.

Zamora, Lois Parkinson – Wendy B. Faris (eds.). 1995a. *Magical Realism: Theory, History, Community*. Durham NC: Duke University Press.

Magic realist and utopian discourses in Margaret Sweatman's *When Alice lay down with Peter*: negotiating paradigms of belonging

Agnieszka Rzepa, Adam Mickiewicz University, Poznań

ABSTRACT

The present article probes into the confluence of magic realist and utopian discourses in Margaret Sweatman's novel *When Alice lay down with Peter* (2001) that allows the author to examine the intricacies of the notion of "belonging" in Canada. In Sweatman's novel the cyclical drama of the exile from Eden is written ironically and in the spirit of self-questioning into the story of the creation and maintenance of the Canadian national project emblematised by the notion of Canada as a Peaceful Kingdom. Sweatman's approach to constitutive components of "white civility", as defined by Daniel Coleman, her questioning of progress and peaceful public order as Canadian ideals and realities, the interrogation of class, colonialism, capitalism she works into the novel promote a "cross-hatched, multiply vectored dialogue", which, according to Coleman can "generate ... a wry or critical civility" (Coleman 2007: 27). The utopian discourse that propels the plot is supported by a number of magic realist devices, which help visualise the processes that destabilise the intertwined notions of nationhood and belonging in the contemporary Canadian, and to a certain extent also global, context. The text undermines the normalisation of the Canadian nation-making project, at the same time placing it within a global network of historical developments and influences.

Margaret Sweatman's epic family saga *When Alice lay down with Peter* (2001)[1] develops under the sign of the utopia of the peaceable kingdom. Prefaced by the well-known quote from Isaiah (11:6-7, 9; "The wolf also shall dwell with the lamb, and the leopard shall lie down with the kid ..."), the text follows four generations of a family of Scottish extraction, whose venture into the New World starts with the vision of "a land without landlords ..., a green and verdant place where man could be free from tyranny, free from history itself ... a country where nobody can own you" (*AP*, 2001: 8). Some vestiges of the utopia are still there when the Scottish protagonists arrive in the land soon to become Manitoba, but it all quickly unravels before their eyes. The biblical quote resonates throughout the novel not only as an ironic reminder of an ideal unreachable and lost, but as a teleology that guides the family in their espousal of utopian idealism through a series of lost political causes into the final, though temporary and spatially circumscribed, reinstatement of the utopian solidarity and freedom in nature through the agency of fire and the cleansing waters of the Red River.

The ideal of Canada as a peaceable kingdom, the quest for which Northrop Frye associated with what he called "the pastoral ideal" (Frye 1965: 848) central,

---

1   Henceforth indicated as *AP* followed by page number. All quotations are from Sweatman, Margaret. 2001. *When Alice lay down with Peter*. Toronto: Alfred A. Knopf Canada.

he claimed, to the imaginative development of Canada and Canadian literature, goes hand in hand with the construction of the colonisation of Canada as a process of peaceful "settlement". Both have contributed to what Daniel Coleman sees as the trance of "white civility" in Canada, which—he argues—has actively acted against the possibility of creating a nation founded on inclusivity, whether racial, ethnic, gender or sexual. Sweatman's novel addresses various aspects of the problem by making the settler family constantly negotiate its "belonging" in the Canadian national project and its belonging to the land in the context of the ever returning utopian hope and crisis. The complexities of the settler project of belonging are presented partly through the use of magic realist devices, which in effect both support and question the utopian discourse of the novel. *When Alice lay down with Peter* may then be placed among the magic realist texts that "inhabit ... an 'ambivalent temporality,' that is, an alternative sense of time appearing, to use Foucault's terms, simultaneously 'outside of history, as well as in it.' ... Through the overlapping of different temporalities, these texts put forward a 'projective past' that speaks about the disjunctive present" (Benito – Manzanas – Simal 2009: 121). In consequence, the text undermines the normalisation of the Canadian nation-making project, at the same time placing it within a global network of historical developments and influences. All of the historical events are positioned not only within the linear, historical time, but also within the utopian regime of eternal return.

The McCormack family both become part of the place they settle and remain forever conscious of their imposition and their "squatter" status on the Métis land. The final utopian un-settling of the settler (and the settler narrative)—unmoored and dislodged by the flood, willingly reverting to the squatter status, but still tethered to the land by the feeling of belonging—suggests Coleman's notion of "wry civility." Coleman sees "wry civility" as a way to remedy the "white civility" project. While he defines it as "a critical positioning" occupying a space of ambivalence "between the gains and the losses of nationalism" (Coleman 2006: 44), Sweatman's novel suggests its literary uses. The McCormack saga she creates addresses and problematises all the constitutive elements of the construct of "white civility" as Coleman sees it. The multifaceted "civility" rests on the alliance between the concepts of "civilization as progress" (Coleman 2007: 29), based on the linear notion of time, and that of a "peaceful public order ... fundamental to the politics of the modern nation-state" (Coleman 2007: 29). These, Coleman says, have been assumed to be best supported and evinced by "civil", polite behaviour into which citizens should be educated. The model was that of a British gentleman, hence Britishness, whiteness and masculinity function as defining elements of the concept. "The idea of civility as a (White) cultural practice," Coleman maintains, "made it not only a mode of internal management and self definition, because it distinguished the civil from the uncivil, but also a mode of external management, because it gave civil subjects a mandate for managing the circumstances of those perceived as uncivil" (Coleman 2007: 31).

As succeeding generations of MacCormacks make their way through Canadian history—from 1869 till 1979—they witness, contribute to and attempt to disrupt the rise of "white civility" as a mode of being and as a parameter of belonging. Though they become in many ways paradigmatic Scottish settlers, Peter and Alice McCormack start their New World adventure because they do not want to be settled; they want freedom. As the novel develops, the couple participate in and show as bankrupt the vision of the utopia of the Prairies; or, to be more specific, the three visions of the Prairies as the Promised Land deployed at the turn of the nineteenth and twentieth centuries in order to draw European immigrants. The three visions are those of the Prairie West as the "Arcadian Paradise" of simplicity and happiness in nature, embodying the pastoral ideal; as the land of opportunity and individual freedom; and as the laboratory of the perfect society of the future (Francis – Kitzan 2007: 10-12). The intertwined utopian visions were both a corollary of the earlier persistent myth of America as the Promised Land, and clearly constituted part of the creation of the myth of Canada as a Peaceful Kingdom:

> It was to be a gentler, milder west. Here the ideals of "peace, order, and good government" would be placed above that of the "inalienable rights of the individual", and British culture and British law and order above American frontier culture and vigilante rule. (...) The Canadian Prairie West as Promised Land would uphold values of harmony, co-operation, and the good of society as a whole. It was a different – and superior, Canadians believed – utopian vision of the Promised Land than that of the American West
>
> (Francis – Kitzan 2007: 14-15).

The MacCormacks arrive in Rupert's Land when it has just been sold by the Hudson's Bay Company to the Canadian Confederation, and is about to be settled. They are still in time, however, to become enamoured with the life of the Métis even as it is slipping into oblivion. Alice, following Peter from Scotland, disguised as a man, in search for freedom even though she thinks she is just looking for her "underfed crofter" (*AP*, 10), joins him in the party of Métis buffalo hunters, and then the party of Métis hunters reduced to driving cattle. The freedom of the prairie, the freedom of being a man (for Alice), and the hard work spur them. For a while, they live in a thoroughly utopian space that allows for a reinvention of one's relation to nature and to others, for a reinvention of oneself, seemingly even in gender terms. While this paradise is not absolute—there are, after all, overseers, and racial as well as gender distinctions do apply—from their point of view it is as close to a utopia as possible.

The much bemoaned crisis of their utopia starts with the surveyors and the commodification of the land they herald, which Peter sees as a process of selling the Garden of Eden (*AP*, 14), a hunt which results in the land being ensnared in the grid of surveyors' maps (*AP*, 18), which the protagonists perceive as a murder

(*AP*, 14). This, however, is also the moment when Alice and Peter become aiders and abettors in the murder, a vanguard of the empire. While witnessing the crisis of the "natural" utopia they imagined and lived, the one preceding the concerted settlement effort in the Prairies, they start to participate in the government-sanctioned process of the building of the West as a land of financial success on the community and individual level. Pregnant Alice needs "home," which Peter provides by buying 160 acres of land on the Red from a Cree couple. This is when it becomes their "property," always referred to in the novel in quotation marks. The ostensible land title that Peter receives from the Cree turns out to be a drawing of a buffalo: "a neat metonym for the historical transaction (and transition) between Native peoples' nomadic lifestyle and European settlement," as Herb Wyile (2006: 741) comments. Alice literally "projects" the national future resulting from the exchange as she vomits "things she'd never eaten, food not available in the Red River valley in 1869. Oranges and mango, artichokes and lichee nuts. The future cuisine of the Dominion" (*AP*, 21) right before she voices her desire for "home."

It is important to mention, in relation to this aspect of the novel that Frye emblematises the pastoral tradition in Canadian literature, based on the motive of „a quest for the peaceable kingdom" (Frye 1965: 848), through a reference to one of well-known versions of "The Peaceable Kingdom with Seated Lion" by the American primitivist painter Edward Hicks, painted in the 1830s. The picture shows a peaceable group of animals and children seated in the foreground amid American nature, while the background depicts the moment of signing the peace treaty between Quaker settlers led by William Penn and a group of Delawares. According to Frye, the painting visualises the ideal of "the reconciliation of man with man and of man with nature" (Frye 1965: 848), which he himself attempts to identify as the leading, idealistic impulse of Canadian social and literary tradition. Hicks, however, not only combines a prophetic biblical vision with a historical event, but also—as Kokotailo (1998: 4-5) points out—mythologizes history, as such a ceremonial act of signing the agreement most probably never took place. At the same time, the scene of the signing itself—copied from another well-known painting by the loyalist Benjamin West—"conflates colonial commerce with brotherly love" (Rigal 2000: 557): an element, whose significance Frye omits in his interpretation. The motive of "the reconciliation of man with man" is then revealed as ambivalent: it is based on a commercial transaction rooted in the commodification of the land, it is "conquest … presented as an act of magnanimity" (Fowkes Tobin 1999: 56). It is the idealisation of the illegitimate transaction that through Frye's influential intervention becomes in consequence consecrated as one of the foundations of Canadian literary tradition. What is more, while Frye stresses that the propelling force of the tradition is a quest for the peaceable kingdom as an ideal, by the 1970s Canada itself begins to be theorized as a realisation of the ideal, a true peaceable kingdom (Kokotailo 1998: 7): a process noted also dryly in Sweatman's novel ("After the war, Canada became a tragedy-free zone" [*AP*, 391]).

The illegitimacy of the above mentioned transaction becomes the pivotal element in Sweatman's text. Alice and Peter, instead of becoming legitimate owners of the land become squatters, and their right to the land is constantly questioned and undermined not only by the lingering Native claims on it, but also by the state and the forces of big capital allied with it. The latter demand constantly that they prove their ownership by "improving" the land, changing it into a commodity and an object of monetary exchange.

Peter's transition to the settled life is neither easy nor desired. He himself, and later his descendants, enact and in different ways embody the settler dilemma as Alan Lawson and other postcolonial critics see it: they are "liminal sites at the point of negotiation between the contending authorities of Empire and Native" (Lawson 2004: 155). They are sites with a difference, however. They come into the Imperial and national project without cleansing the land of "prior signification" (Lawson 2004: 155). Peter and Alice are painfully aware of the pre-colonial social and political signification written into the land, which further complicates their negotiations of belonging. Peter, in particular, "the Orkney buffalo hunter who had spent his youth travelling the surface of life" is trapped in "the torment of ambivalence" (*AP*, 68) when he is about to turn into a farmer. Declaring that he "hate[s] belonging to *anything*" (*AP*, 67, Sweatman's emphasis, AR), conscious that he could never truly belong with the Métis, loathing the "murder" of the land he witnesses and the government that sanctions it, he feels nevertheless compelled to build fences and buildings, which the government requires to prove his claim to the land. Claiming the land, he nevertheless remains conscious of the falsity of the claim. His belonging is always in flux and tenuous; he accepts his future as a farmer, but only when he conceptualises it as a dark necessity. At the same time he clings to his idealism flooded now with "the dreary light of compromise" (*AP*, 69) and adopts the cause of impossibilism.

Alice seals her belonging to the land when she and Peter join Louis Riel's Red River rebellion; and she does it in a way that is more complete and visceral. Her ties, and the ties of her daughter Blondie, to the land and the river are—literally—the ties of blood; of blood, violence, death and a new life. The crucial moments in the development of this sense of belonging are both related to the period of Alice's participation, in male disguise, in the Riel rebellion. As pregnant Alice, lying in snow, witnesses the brutal murder of the "simple Parisien" by the Orangeman Thomas Scott and feels blood seeping between her legs, she thinks, in the words of her daughter, about "our mutual blood, how it would melt with spring and confirm for the river its English name" (*AP*, 36). She perceives Scott as an agent of anti-utopian forces, a danger to life, a blemish on "an otherwise blameless world" (*AP*, 39). Propelled by hatred, she takes her revenge by willingly joining the firing squad that kills him, and then descends into the depths of guilt. Her participation in Scott's execution, the execution which turned to be a pivotal event in the fate of Riel's rebellion and the history of the West, exiles Alice finally from her Paradise. As the scene in which Alice and Peter meet Riel indicates, he functions as a God, or at least an inspired Prophet (a role which he imagined he was indeed fulfilling), in the utopian community of rebels that promises that the paradisal West is not yet lost. He arrives on his horse when Peter and Alice are taking a bath on their "property" and does not notice their nakedness, which for the couple also seems quite natural. They follow the man who seems to penetrate with his eyes to the core of their being. For Alice, it is not sexuality that precipitates her fall from innocence into experience, but rather her participation in Scott's execution, which compels her to look with compassion "on the catastrophe of human nature" (*AP*, 42). At the same time, the advent of guilt and understanding seals her claim to the land. When Alice and Peter return to their "property," she enters into "a heathen's communion with the Red" (*AP*, 44), learns from it the lesson of death and regeneration. In the fashion characteristic of Second World magic realism, there exists a clear link between the character, and later her descendants, and place/landscape which seem alive and active (Delbaere-Garant 1995: 252-253). Alice is *of* the river and *of* the land even as she is haunted by, and accommodates, the specter of the Empire, in the form of the ghost of Thomas Scott soon to appear; and the specter of the Native in the form of the ghost of Metisse Marie, the former inhabitant of the McCormack "property". While the ghost of Scott functions "as … a reminder of a history she is unable to forget" (Braz 2010: 49), the spectral presence of Marie, while functioning in a similar way, additionally constantly undermines attempts at full, uncomplicated settlement.

The presence of the river, the constant floods that change the shape of the land question the permanence of the settlement effort, its rationale, the very notion of property. Land itself is not a "thing" in the novel, but almost a living being, changing, merging with the river. The river, with its floods that destroy, but also fertilize and cleanse, suggests the circular notion of time, a cyclical repetition, the beginning that is also the end. This cyclicity, repetition, with its suggestion of permanence to be found in constant flux, constant unsettling of belonging, is in fact the sign under which the narrative unfolds. As the narrator declares at the beginning: "I'm dipping my pen into the Red River, always at the same spot, and like they say, all the time into a different river. I have hauled this story out of the fish-smelling muck of the Red" (*AP*, 1). Repetition of the natural events, coupled with the magical repetition of the fates of the McCormack women, creates, as in many other magic realist texts, "a narrative hall of mirrors" (Faris 2004: 127). The linear notion of time, one of the foundations of "white civility", is thus disrupted. The disruption is confirmed by the presence of ghosts, which accompany the MacCormacks in their Canadian odyssey.

The ghosts are not only those of Scott, Marie, later of Helen (Alice's granddaughter). Crucially, the narrator is also a ghostly presence. The story is told by Alice's daughter, Blondie, "dead as a stick" (*AP*, 2) at 109, lying in her vegetable garden and displaying for all the world to see her birthmark, devil's kiss, the sign left on her by Thomas Scott. All those ghostly presences question the view of history as linear development, as progress. As Wyile comments, "a crucial effect of the spectral point of view is the way in which, structurally, it stages a dialogue between myth and history. While Blondie's tale progresses forward in time and is divided into chronologically ordered, dated sections, her narrative has a cyclical structure and a mythological resonance" (Wyile 2006: 739). Wyile's comment suggests also a specific cultural and textual "metissage" enacted in and by the novel: a coexistence of two, seemingly opposing perspectives that are never fully reconciled, but inhabit, nonetheless, a common geographical, historical, mental and textual space. The story, as the opening statement of the narrator proclaims, is fashioned out of the "muck of the Red". The solid-fluid medium that both devours and shapes local geography already written by forces of history and myth is turned into the text. Additionally, figuratively speaking, the narrator, whose blood had mixed with the waters of the Red even before she was born, makes the body of the text out of her own body. She is always already "written" into the story of the land and the river, makes it and is made by it, as much as all those others who had lived and died there, which is stressed by the tenacity of the ghostly presences, who continue to influence and meddle into the lives of the protagonists.

The ghostly presences of Marie and Scott underline also the violent foundations of the state, which are further exposed by various wars and conflicts the MacCormacks, especially the McCormack women, participate in. Thus the novel exposes also another assumption underlying the construct of "white civility": social organisation, while it changes, does not necessarily develop into higher forms guaranteeing the "peaceful public order". Rather the myth of such order is achieved by the suppression and marginalisation of "disruptive" elements, and nationally sanctioned forgetting of events that might contradict the ideal. The ghosts visualise these violent and paradoxical foundations of "white civility," the "repressive violence that haunts the borders and stratifies the layers of civility" (Coleman 2007: 36). While Coleman in his conceptualisation of "white civility" focuses on race and ethnicity as most clearly showing the hierarchies and "striations" of civility, Sweatman's text enters into a dialogue with the concept by focusing additionally on the question of class and social privilege. "While Sweatman adopts a somewhat satiric attitude towards the excessive idealism of the Canadian left," comments Wyile, "the novel's critical energies are directed principally at the forces of colonialism and capitalism, both of which thrive by manipulating and / or erasing the past. Ghosts play a pivotal role *within* Blondie's narrative in resisting such a strategic cultivation of amnesia" (Wyile 2006: 741, Wyile's italics, AR).

In order to survive the impositions of the state and capital the MacCormacks cling to visions of future social utopias, and in a variety of ways engage in social protest. Peter espouses the anti-reformist, revolutionary doctrine of impossibilism. Alice actively promotes utopian social visions by her engagement in educational undertakings which provide quasi-utopian spaces for participants, at the same time exposing the omissions and lies of the story of Canada in the process of congealing into history. She establishes a school for children of recent immigrants, "a boot camp for anarchists" (*AP*, 181) in which, among others, she educates the children in the history of Canadian uprisings and social protests. Later she establishes a theatre, which gives to the audiences stories that counter the government propaganda. Alice and Peter's granddaughter, Helen, participates in the On-to-Ottawa Trek in 1935 and the Regina riot; and then defends the Republican cause with the Mackenzie-Papineau Battalion. She dies by a firing squad in Spain: a tragic, inverted repetition of Alice's misguided shooting of Scott. Dianna, Helen's daughter, joins the anti-imperialist protests of the 1960s. Throughout the text, the McCormack women take male disguise to experience freedom, which allows them to participate actively in traditionally defined "history" of large-scale, violent events. The only exception is Dianne, who can enter the public space of political participation as a woman because she takes benefit of the relative freedom granted women since the 1960s. These wars and conflicts are formative experiences that allow the women to get a better understanding of human capacities, a better understanding of men and therefore also of themselves, and to test their own limits. For example, Alice's realisation of her own capability for hatred and violence, which she exhibits volunteering to the firing squad that kills Scott, allows her later to scorn the visions of a social utopia which accompany the introduction of female franchise in Manitoba in 1916. At the same time, though, Alice's case is an exception, as the other women, while they participate in the violent events, actively avoid committing violent acts. All ventures and causes the MacCormacks participate in or espouse, in one way or another, finish in defeat; yet this does not destroy the yearning for a utopia, nourished periodically by the ever repeating "utopia of the flood" (*AP*, 2001: 406). The MacCormacks want civility based on solidarity and comradeship, a utopia of social relations, the peaceful kingdom.

On the individual level, the promise and betrayal of utopia appear also under the guise of the yearning for the ideal coupledom, the marriage that would constitute a perfect union, a totality in which two become one. Alice and Peter, Blondie and Eli, Helen and Bill, Dianna and Jack all achieve, temporarily but with lasting effects, the perfect fusion. The first intercourse of each couple, always in the storm, is blessed by the magically recurring event: a strike of lightning symbolically fuses each couple forever, each fusion resulting in conception. Additionally, the lightning "engraves" each couple "upon the land" (*AP*, 167) making it a three-way union. At the same time, coupledom is described in the novel in terms of the impossible utopia of the lion lying with the lamb. This is true not only in the emblematic case of Helen's misguided marriage to Richard, which expectedly proves an unmitigated disaster. Even in the case of the perfectly matched couples, their magical fusion guarantees the desired totality only for a moment.

The second marriage ceremony of Blondie and Eli constitutes a perfect visualisation of the "terms" of coupledom. Performed by the ghost of Marie, Eli's stepmother, at her behest, it indicates the tragic entanglement of the individual in the social and the historical, which is never cancelled by individual happiness. What functions as the wedding vow, are the words of Chief Mawedopenais spoken at the conclusion of Treaty #3, which helped open Manitoba to settlement; and the first of the numbered treaties in which also Métis rights were taken into account (Dickason 1992: 279). The words, as the narrator indicates, are "a beautiful misunderstanding" (*AP*, 175-176); the promises in her interpretation have both a utopian and clearly satiric ring: "we gave each other everything, and in exchange we were promised security and peace everlasting" (*AP*, 176). In this way, Blondie and Eli enter into an even more intimate, and no less vague transaction than Peter did with the Native who "sold" him the land. Their union is a constant reminder of the fraudulent terms under which it starts. Both for Blondie—a daughter of settlers born symbolically with the new province of Manitoba—and Eli—the adoptive son of Metisse Marie, harbouring within him the memory of the subdued and vanquished way of life—the landscape they enter is the impossible landscape of Hick's painting. Crucially, by making Eli both an inheritor of a Métis tradition, and by putting in question his origins, the author sidesteps the danger of "indigenising" the McCormack family and thus legitimising their claim to the land.

The MacCormacks remain wedded to the impossible future, and contest the Canada that slowly congeals into the shape of "white civility". The force of "white civility" as well as its constructed nature are embodied by the figure of Richard Anderson, Helen's husband. Richard is the child of social privilege, the son of a wealthy and educated British-American merchant and lawyer, white and civil. As the narrator comments, "his wealth and prestige acted as the perfect insulation" (*AP*, 197), protecting him not only from the effects of Blondie's "electric" handshake, but also from the compassionate engagement with the world and from the consciousness and results of his own crude errors and inequities. When Richard attempts to shoot a friend of the family during the Winnipeg General Strike (1919), and instead shoots Eli, he comes to apologize. His apology combines self-righteousness and politeness; he admits his error even as he claims the justifiable nature of his motive and places the guilt on the victim. The scene exemplifies metonymically the "history-denying tendency", which allows Canadians, in Coleman's view, "to claim unblemished civility and a moral high ground" (Coleman 2007: 40) and is propped up by the structures of privilege. The striking workers, Eli and the MacCormacks, the poor immigrants are erased or marginalized: they do not belong into the national project, or—to be specific—the injustices they suffer put their belonging into question. They "vanish" as the national project develops. Richard's "blue looking, that displaced you, did not take you in, but knocked you out of way, that he may take your place" (*AP*, 245) best describes the process.

Helen's marriage to Richard is presented in the novel as another utopian experiment, the lamb dwelling with the wolf. For Helen it is a logical conclusion to her discovery that "it is safe only behind danger, inside its ribs, to go to the adults with the mad hearts and soft hands" (*AP*, 184). Like any utopia, it concludes with a revolution, the "revolution taking place within Helen" (*AP*, 310). She flees her flawed Eden, but Richard remains part of the family's life. When he shoots Eli, Richard finally becomes for the family "our very own Orangeman" (*AP*, 296), as Blondie comments with disgust. Richard cannot be sidestepped or avoided. He is a social and historical necessity. While existing at a different level of the narrative, the character plays a role comparable to that of the spectral presences of Marie and Scott, reminding the McCormack family about the fallibility of human nature and about the fact that through their family history they are implicated not only in utopian fights for a variety of peaceable kingdoms, but also in the machinations of the darker historical forces. Richard, unlike the ghosts, has agency and a hold on the land and the family because they owe him money, and he finally threatens to put the land up for sale if Dianna does not evict her lover. Like "white civility" itself he is both attractive and repulsive, benevolent, banal and monstrous.

When Dianna helps the elements and sets fire to their "property" during a lightning storm, the family revert to their squatter status in its unadulterated form: the only mode of belonging possible for them in Canada. The world is fresh again, there is a new beginning, in accordance with the biblical motto: "in the world of peace, as the weird old prophet Isaiah would tell us, *the waters will cover the sea*" (*AP*, 303, Sweatman's italics, AR); "water being the wisdom of the earth" (*AP*, 303) it becomes the agent of the utopia. The fire and the flood have cleansed the world; they have almost wiped out the signs of their houses, "the land has changed shape. The river comes close. ... It is Dianna's ideal environment, at the cusp between the dead and the living. Saplings, moist green against black ash. Paradise" (*AP*, 454). They build again, start an orchard, a vegetable garden; Dianna's daughter is born; all the family ghosts witness the event; Blondie dies. The McCormack "property" on the Red becomes again, though temporarily, simply part of the land, though it can never cease to be a site of constant negotiations of belonging.

In Sweatman's novel the cyclical drama of the exile from Eden is written ironically and in the spirit of self-questioning into the story of the creation and maintenance of the Canadian national project. Sweatman's approach to constitutive components of "white civility," her questioning of progress and peaceful public order as Canadian ideals and realities, the interrogation of class, colonialism, capitalism she works into the novel promote a "cross-hatched, multiply vectored dialogue," which, according to Coleman can "generate ... a wry or critical civility" (Coleman 2007: 27). The utopian discourse that propels the plot is supported by a number of magic realist devises, which help visualise the processes that destabilise the intertwined notions of nationhood and belonging in the contemporary Canadian, and to a certain extent also global, context.

References

Benito, Jesús – Ana M. Manzanas – Begoña Simal. 2009. *Uncertain mirrors: Magical realisms in US ethnic literatures.* Amsterdam, New York, NY: Rodopi.

Braz, Albert. 2010. "The Orange devil: Thomas Scott and the Canadian historical novel", in: Andrea Cabajsky – Brett Joseph Grubisic (eds.), 39-52.

Cabajsky, Andrea – Brett Joseph Grubisic (eds.). 2010. *National plots: Historical fiction and changing ideas of Canada.* Waterloo, ON: Wilfrid Laurier University Press.

Coleman, Daniel. 2007. "From Canadian trance to TransCanada: White civility to wry civility in the CanLit Project", in: Smaro Kamboureli – Roy Miki (eds), 25-43.

Coleman, Daniel. 2006. *White civility: The literary project of English Canada.* Toronto, Buffalo, London: University of Toronto Press.

Delbaere-Garant, Jeanne. 1995. "Psychic realism, mythic realism, grotesque realism: Variations on magic realism in contemporary literature in English", in: Lois Parkinson Zamora – Wendy B. Faris (eds.), 249-263.

Dickason, Patricia Olive. 1992. *Canada's First Nations: A history of founding peoples from earliest times.* Norman: University of Oklahoma Press.

Faris, Wendy B. 2004. *Ordinary enchantments: Magical realism and the remystification of narrative.* Nashville: Vanderbilt University Press.

Fowkes Tobin, Beth. 1999. *Picturing imperial power: Colonial subjects in eighteenth-century British painting.* Durham, NC: Duke University Press.

Francis, R. Douglas – Chris Kitzan (eds.). 2007. *The prairie west as promised land.* Calgary, AB, CAN: University of Calgary Press.

Frye, Northrop. 1965. "Conclusion," in: Carl F. Klinck (ed.), 821-849.

Howard, Victor (ed.). 1998. *Creating the peaceable kingdom and other essays on Canada.* East Lansing, MI: Michigan State University Press.

Kamboureli, Smaro – Roy Miki (eds.). 2007. *Trans.Can.Lit: Resituating the study of Canadian literature.* Waterloo, Ontario: Wilfrid Laurier University Press.

Klinck, Carl F. (ed.). 1965. *The literary history of Canada: Canadian literature in English.* Toronto: University of Toronto Press, 1965.

Kokotailo, Philip 1998. "Creating the peaceable kingdom: Edward Hicks, Northrop Frye, and Joe Clark," in: Victor Howard (ed.), 3-11.

Lawson, Alan. 2004. "Postcolonial theory and the 'settler' subject", in Cynthia Sugars (ed.), 151-164.

Rigal, Laura. 2000. "Framing the fabric: A Luddite reading of Penn's *Treaty with the Indians*", *American Literary History* Vol. 12, 3: 557-584.

Sugars, Cynthia (ed.). 2004. *Unhomely states: Theorizing English-Canadian post-colonialism*. Peterborough, Ontario: broadview press.

Sweatman, Margaret. 2001. *When Alice lay down with Peter*. Toronto: Alfred A. Knopf Canada.

Wyile, Herb. 2006. "'It takes more than mortality to make somebody dead': Spectres of history in Margaret Sweatman's *When Alice lay down with Peter*", *University of Toronto Quarterly* 7, 2: 735-751.

Zamora, Lois Parkinson – Wendy B. Faris (eds.). 1995. *Magical realism: Theory, history, community*. Durham & London: Duke University Press.

City, identity and wartime narrative in *De Niro's game* by Rawi Hage

Monika Włudzik, Nicolaus Copernicus University, Toruń

ABSTRACT

The article is an attempt to reflect on the idea of wartime narrative as a metatextual means of identity creation on the basis of *De Niro's game* (2006) by Rawi Hage, an Anglo-Lebanese Canadian author. The novel recounts the story of two friends, George and Bassam, who live through the Lebanese Civil War. By referring to numerous cinematic and literary accounts of war, Hage seeks to dismantle the conflation of narratives aimed at rationalising and domesticating the discourse of war, thus unmasking the invisibility of everyday suffering in times of war. To Bassam, the narrator, it seems that the city infects its inhabitants with violence, as they become oblivious to cross-generational war and self-perpetuating destruction. The banality of violence and boredom associated with atrocities are counterbalanced by Hage's use of the marvellous in an effort to render war less abstract by introducing wondrous imagery and events. It could be said that, through destabilising the relation between memory and nationhood, the writer strives to find a language that would convey the vulnerability and desperation felt by those who fear daily for their personal safety and choose "forced immigration" (Christoff 2007). *De Niro's game* is viewed as a celebration of the metatextual and intersubjective self which is assumed to provide a valid commentary on the experience of war trauma in the global and political sense.

The present article is an attempt to reflect on wartime narrative as a metatextual means of creating space and identity on the basis of *De Niro's game* by Rawi Hage, an Anglo-Lebanese Canadian author. The generative power of the narrative and the agency provided by semi-autobiographical narrativity are explored in the story of George and Bassam, two friends who grow up during the Lebanese Civil War of 1975-1990. Hage recreates the emotional reality of the civil war by drawing on a variety of popular representations of war, thus bringing war-torn Beirut closer to Anglophone readers. The book is written in a distinctive variety of English, heavily indebted to the metaphoricity of Arabic and French, his first two languages. The position Hage holds in-between languages and discourses can be regarded as a marker of postcolonial hybridity related to the primary undertaking of the novel: conveying collective trauma through memory-mediated and culture-bound resources of images (Mostafa 2011: 2; Rahman 2009: 806). Although so far Hage has published two novels, *De Niro's game* (2006) and its continuation *Cockroach,* the present article focuses exclusively on the former, as it pays attention to the issue of wartime narrative.

As a writer of the Arab diaspora, Hage seeks to oppose the dehumanised and depersonalised accounts of the civil war by dismantling the conflation of narratives aimed at rationalising and domesticating the discourse of war. In the novel, the atrocities of war are conveyed by establishing similarities between the game of Russian roulette as depicted in Michael Cimino's 1978 film *The deer hunter* and the actual warfare, since both are understood as death-defying games of chance with survivors but without winners. Hage conjures up a bleak vision of a community in crisis, torn between loyalties to Christian or Islamic militias and foreign military powers, and riven by ethnic clashes. The universal character of the novel and its self-conscious historicity point to the fact that civil wars can be said to precondition human relations in the postmodern world (Nancy 2003: 23-24), symbolising a state of extremity and hollowness that cannot be supplanted with any stable doctrine or dogma and resulting in the self-annihilation of entire populations. Simultaneously, the wartime loss of traditional values and human civility is also represented as a demystification that suggests a new beginning for the protagonist. This duality of civil war is examined in the novel from a first-person perspective which combines the elements of magic realism and dark humour for political reasons.

The first part of the article is devoted to the experience of civil war and its influence on the community, in an attempt to analyze the imaginary aspects of social unity and disunity explored in *De Niro's game*. Subsequently, the elements of magic realism that can be found in the novel are discussed in relation to the portrayal of urban space and in the context of Cimino's film and Albert Camus's 1942 novel *L'Étranger*. It is argued that the derealisation of urban space and the universalisation of the Lebanese Civil War experience have presumably contributed to the popularity of Hage's much acclaimed novel.[1] The aim of the article is to present the narrative as a model of subjectivity and to discuss possible modes of self-creation with reference to urbanity and cinema. Furthermore, the novel is viewed as a celebration of a metatextual and intersubjective self which is assumed to provide a valid commentary on the experience of war trauma in the global and political sense.

Not unlike other Canadian writers who use the convention of magic realism (Bowers 2004: 52; Rzepa 2009: 24), Rawi Hage touches upon the issues of collective memory and nationhood. In order to express the instability and imaginary quality of these concepts, the writer prefers to concentrate on the immediate and the intimate in the experience of war mediated or even mediatised through representations. Strangely enough, while the events take place outside the protagonist's control, they seem to exist independently inside his psyche, a phenomenon which exacerbates Bassam's feelings of estrangement and isolation. In addition, it could be said that his feelings of desolation and despair are expressed in the mode of narration, wherein Bassam describes his actions in a methodical and disengaged manner, thereby achieving a doubly-fictionalised

---

1   *De Niro's game* was a finalist for numerous prestigious national and international awards, and won the IMPAC Dublin Literary Award. Hage's second novel *Cockroach* (2008) received the Quebec Writers' Federation Award and was shortlisted for numerous prestigious awards including the Scotia Bank Giller Prize, the Governor General's Award, The Writers' Trust Award, and the Prix des libraires du Québec (www.anansi.ca DOA 01/04/11).

status. He interweaves two types of accounts, shifting phantasmagorical and poetic descriptions of a life during the civil war, as well as dry report-like conversations and quotes from everyday events in the city under siege. This multiperspectival stance allows for a presentation of the civil war as a half-magical fissure in the centuries-long structure of Beirut. Bassam can be said to translate his trauma into fabricated memories of distant and marginalised past, unrelated to the official discourse of history. Granted the stance of an individual outside the community, Bassam rebels against the existing state of affairs and severs family and community ties, slowly spiralling into psychotic paranoia and desperation. It has to be said, however, that his rebellion is not so much a heroic act of a peace-loving human spirit, but rather a matter of a gradual derealisation of events and paralysing helplessness. In fact, Bassam experiences the collapse of everyday certainties and is forced to live with a constant realisation of an impending death and the futility of life-saving efforts. In other words, the civil war is depicted as a multilayered discourse of violence conducted at the heart of the community, not only destroying its urban structure, but also damaging the self in the quest for order in dehumanizing narratives of difference and cleansing.

According to Dalia Said Mostafa, it is possible to recover the structured progression of a character through the discourse of violence in the fiction of contemporary Lebanese authors (Mostafa 2011: 21). She explores the relations between violence, masculinity and sexuality, specifically referring to the marginalised position of those who resort to violence as a means of expression and liberation (Mostafa 2011: 21). The main characters of Hage's *De Niro's game* are members of the Christian minority in Beirut; they inhabit an enclosed part of the city and, in consequence, their identity is as if prescribed to the territory of the Achrafieh district. Their marginality or position as outsiders is also highlighted by the absence of father figures (Mostafa 2011: 26); George's father left his mother before his birth, and Bassam's died early during the conflict in an air raid. The two friends are described as "aimless beggars and thieves, horny Arabs with curly hair and open shirts and Marlboro packs rolled in [their] sleeves, dropouts, ruthless nihilists with guns, bad breath and long American jeans" (*De Niro's game*[2]: 16). George and Bassam rely on each other and try to make the most from their alienation from the community to which they cannot fully belong, as due to the fact of having been brought up by single mothers, they possess inferior social and financial standing. George works in a casino, where he tastes the life of shady business, easy money and violence, while Bassam finds odd jobs at the harbour, unloading smuggled goods. George seems to have an inclination towards ruthless and violent behaviour; after the death of his mother, he joins the Christian militia and tries to pressurize his best friend into following his steps. Bassam's refusal

---

2   Henceforth indicated as *DG* followed by page number. All quotations are from Hage, Rawi. 2008 [2006]. *De Niro's game*. London: Old Street Publishing.

ultimately separates the childhood friends and is followed by a series of betrayals on George's part, including making false accusations in order to have Bassam arrested and tortured. All these events disrupt Bassam's sense of reality, making him "closer to birds and away from humans" (*DG*, 91) and preparing him for his eventual journey from Beirut to Paris.

Influenced by American war and gangster films, Bassam and George grow up with a longing for heroic masculinity and a tendency to glamorize violence (Mostafa 2011: 37). The boys speed on George's motorbike down the bombed streets and find their place of comfort in the forest where they try their hand at hunting for birds. Their attempts at impersonating cinematic war heroes constitute a significant source of dark humour in the novel. For example, George tries to imitate the harsh tone and authority of Brando's Godfather (*DG*, 39), while Bassam assaults and robs the family owners of a corner shop only to take a pack of sanitary towels for a young girl befriended by his mother (*DG*, 79-80). Influenced by the films they have seen, the boys absorb ready-made scripts of violent male behaviour in an attempt to deal with the violence that surrounds them, yet all their efforts are revealed to be horrendously unsuited to their situation (Mostafa 2011: 35). On the whole, it is argued that the tragicomic inadequacy of cinematic role-models is presented as an emptifying narrative of masculine mastery, although initially it appears to be "the perfect mediation" (Fanon 2004: 44), at least to the teenage outsiders.

Hage draws on Cimino's compelling cinematic portrayal of friends who are sent from a small industrial Pennsylvanian town to fight in Vietnam in *The deer hunter*. The film centres on the relationship between two of them, Nick (Christopher Walken) and Michael (Robert De Niro); the former is the informal leader of the group, while the latter is his quiet, less socially-able companion. They work, live and spend most of their time together and every so often hunt deer in the nearby woods, living a life of companionship and adventure. According to their code of conduct, killing a deer is a privilege and as such should be performed with one bullet only, in order not to disrespect the animal and to demonstrate the mastery of sufficient skill and precision. They consider death by one bullet to be honourable, almost visually pleasing; it is quick, virtually painless and leaves the game untouched, as if it were still alive. Uprooted from their life in a close-knit community, they take with them their code of friendship and the one-bullet rule to Saigon, where, as soldiers, they become both hunters and prey. In the jungle, fighting against an unpredictable and largely invisible enemy, they duly take the lives of other people. When imprisoned in a prisoner-of-war camp and forced to play Russian roulette against each other for the amusement of their guards, they have to embrace the idea of leaving one's life to chance and the possibility of imminent death. Although eventually they manage to kill their captors, Nick is saved by a rescue helicopter, whereas Michael is left behind floating down a river with a seriously wounded comrade. Under the impression that he has betrayed his friends, Nick begins playing Russian roulette for money and slowly descends into insanity. Once Michael returns home, he learns that his friend is still alive and decides to fetch him home. When they meet again in a gambling den in Vietnam, Nick does not recognize Michael who in an act of desperation challenges him to play Russian roulette in this way instigating his friend's suicide.

In the novel, Rawi Hage inverts the motif of a wartime male friendship: his Nick is the rather unassuming Bassam, who refrains from any engagement in the militia and by his isolation manages to escape death in Beirut. George, on the other hand, plays De Niro's role and grants himself the right to kill and mete out justice in accordance with his internal code of rugged masculinity, thereby following the laws of nature. Not fully realising in what he decides to participate, George imitates American action movie characters both in their ability to distinguish between right and wrong and their tendency to glamorise violence. The extreme mental and physical stress of combat as well as the sense of detachment from their previous civilian life make Bassam and George develop a tendency to fictionalise their own lives. Similarly to Michael, Bassam is tragically complicit in the death of his childhood friend. It is implied that George was under such mental distress after taking part in mass civilian executions that he confessed his deeds to Bassam and challenged him to play Russian roulette, as a result of which he committed an honourable suicide in line with the vision of war presented by Cimino. Nevertheless, it is equally possible that Bassam, a clearly unreliable narrator, had to protect his own life and narrates only a structurally satisfying version of events. His wartime story-telling gains an epic dimension when he finds George's sister in France and describes life in the city torn apart by civil war to her. To her delight, Bassam portrays his friend as a brave man of action, conveniently omitting all the shameful details. At the end of the novel, however, he appears to be ready to tell the whole story and eventually discloses the suspicious circumstances of George's death. In brief, it could be said that both the film and the novel try to illustrate the paranoia and internal destruction brought on by the war in which the protagonists reluctantly participate.

Bassam and George's inner havoc and turmoil are reflected in the crumbling cityscape of Beirut. The city is steeped in an immensely complex and perplexing history; its rulers changed, empires rose and fell, while the city found a *modus operandi* in times of scarcity and crisis. The fictional world of the novel can be said to be organized around a colonial consciousness, understood as an incentive to seek liberation both in and through violence. As Franz Fanon wrote "[a]t the individual level, violence is a cleansing force. It rids the colonized of their inferiority complex, of their passive and despairing attitude. It emboldens them, and restores their self-confidence" (Fanon 2004: 51). To the boys growing up in times of war, cinematic narratives of violence may become an empowering and simplifying force that would help them to overcome the differences of tribalism or sectarianism in a national struggle for a common purpose (Fanon 2004: 51). Adopting foreign role models, Bassam and George attempt to look for narratives that would explain their status as a minority, a side in the conflict and meaningful agents in a process of liberation; it transpires that their violent behaviour helps them to silence despair and act in self-defense. In this conflict there is no space for recreating the identity of Lebanon, as the region is internally divided and wilfully destroyed by Israeli, Syrian and Palestinian forces for their own ends. Furthermore, securing a peaceful co-existence among the various religious and political groups would require finding one common denominator outside the enclosed cycle of violence. As, in Hage's eyes, "Lebanon had become a theatre, a convenient venue to resolve issues that had nothing to do with the country" (Hage in Salvador 2011), his fictional Beirut is consequently presented as a space of de-territorialised conflict, abstracted from the interest of its citizens, playing into the hands of international political and corporate powers. By superimposing images of a centuries-long occupation of Lebanon on contemporary atrocities, the writer seemingly attempts to challenge the idealistic view of violence held by Fanon. Judging by Hage's fictional Beirut, it could be said that the boundary between the colonized and the colonizers is permeable, the enemy impossible to identify and the ravaging effects of armed conflicts in the region are far from an imagined unity and equity under local rule.

Furthermore, Hage's novel bears witness to a stultifying loss of stability and a dilution of identity. Although violence seems to free the protagonists of their timidity and low self-esteem, it leaves them emotionally exhausted and psychologically wounded. In a war against the colonisers, as Fanon (2004: 51) wrote, the benefits of violent behaviour may outnumber its drawbacks, yet in the novel the question of who plays the game and who is the game is not satisfactorily resolved. This artificial distinction between the colonised and the colonisers is epitomised in the character of Monsieur Laurent, a discontented old man, once a young businessman who emigrated from a small Lebanese village and became a successful international entrepreneur. Now a stranger in his own country, presumably trading in African diamonds, he feels as if he has betrayed Lebanon and his former self. In consequence, it can be observed that Monsieur Laurent has spent his life walking a thin line between enemies and allies to become a self-made man. His commercial success is dependent on the complex ties between the centres and the peripheries of the contemporary world, influenced by the precariousness of the global economic and political situation. Still, unlike other wealthy people of Beirut, he decided to stay in the city, presumably, with business in mind. Similarly, the border line between friends and foes seems to be at its thinnest on the front, where soldiers stay in the trenches and engage in humorous exchanges of insults, keeping each other company rather than fighting (*DG*, 59). Although they have all the paraphernalia of war, they do not use their guns to kill other soldiers, only manifest the possibility of doing so in a ritual of male bonding; thus it may be said that the image of violence in the novel amounts to a discourse that precedes and determines human relations, only partially concealing its cinematic, or rather simulatory, qualities. When it comes to Bassam and George, they are most certainly fearless because they have grown up putting their lives at risk. As a matter of fact, neither of them commits the error of regarding an armed conflict as a purifying act; they appear to regard violence as a means in itself, a career choice or a way of settling scores.

George joins the militia and engages in a series of appalling acts, reminiscent of the massacres of Palestinian refugees in the camps of Sabra and Shatila in 1982.[3] His lack of scruples and cruelty allow him to rise through the ranks and achieve a respected status in Mossad, Israel's intelligence agency, which is also responsible for covert paramilitary operations abroad. In contrast, Bassam does not engage directly in combat, but keeps to himself, until he finds himself arrested and tortured. Routinely beaten and humiliated, he channels his anger and despair into vengeance. He slaughters his torturer, nicknamed Rambo, and would kill anyone who would try to prevent him from making enough money to go abroad. In his desperation, he is not afraid to commit crimes and settle scores with former oppressors. Interestingly, George and Bassam could be seen as mirror characters; they represent two types of coping mechanism during the conflict as they both refuse to be victimised by engaging actively in the war or by trying to refrain from any involvement. George has chosen to become a war hero and risk his life in the combat, while Bassam has decided to survive the hell of the civil conflict. Even though the choices made by the characters result in their separation, they share memories of their childhood and notions about masculinity.

The structural logic of the narrative makes them meet again for the last time and resolve the tensions between fraternal love and bitter hatred. In an emulation of the eponymous game, George challenges Bassam to play Russian roulette; it is quite clear that they shall not part before one of them dies. In an act of appropriation, Bassam and George reverse the cinematic narrative: "De Niro" kills himself, while his friend survives and leaves his place of birth. This fictionalised transposition of the game onto the reality of the Lebanese Civil War may be said to provide an account of violence as a ritualised and globalised mode of self-definition. Hage seems to share the opinion that violence is not a matter of theory, but rather of practice, since there is no violence without context (Mostafa 2011: 31; Fanon 2004: 51). Moreover, the ideological plane in *De Niro's game* is scarcely stressed, as the soldiers do not devote their lives to a greater cause but want to achieve power and financial gain. Hence, it could be stated that the sectarian context of the conflict is largely omitted or written out of the action in

---

3   For more information on the history of Lebanon please refer to historical sources on the subject, e.g. Laffin, John. 1985. *War of desperation (Lebanon 1982-1985)*. London: Osprey Publishing.

the novel. George, in his approach to guns and fighting, appears to be adamant not to die for the cause but to kill for it whereas Bassam, in spite of being outside any military structures, kills to achieve his goals. To quote Elaine Scarry, a fighter needs to go through a process of extreme desensitisation in order to

> ... wrench around his most fundamental sanctions about how within civilization ... another embodied person can be touched; he divests himself of civilization, decivilizes himself, reverses not just an "idea" or "belief" but a learned and deeply embodied set of physical impulses and gestures regarding his relation to any other person's body
>   (Scarry 1987: 122).

Apart from capturing the essence of combat that involves reversing the relation to another's body, Scarry's statement also reflects how the fictional world of the book is stratified according to gender: men go out to fight, women stay at home, cook and look after the children. If there is anything left of a community, it is not in the trenches but in the shelters where women, the elderly and children keep to themselves. However, the underground place of refuge can also be a scene of a crime, as in Bassam's ambiguous account of rape. His victim, a little girl, changes after the incident; at first, she seeks his company then leaves him for older boys (*DG*, 156). Unable to stay in the shelter, Bassam chooses to go outside and, like George, "he consents to 'unmake' himself, deconstruct himself, empty himself of civil content" (Scarry 1987: 122). His decision to leave the maternal space of the shelter and remain outside, oblivious to the raids of the militia and high-altitude bombing, could be regarded as a rite of passage for a boy who grows up in war-torn Beirut watching American soldiers in Vietnam on the silver screen.

In Hage's novel, the reversal of values and civility, as well as the breakdown of community, is also implied through a lack of distinction between animals and humans. It could be said that this reversal reaches its full force when the inhabitants of Beirut go underground and leave their city to dogs. Packs of pedigree dogs, abandoned by their wealthy owners who fled the war, and mongrels roam the streets, gorge on garbage and attack humans. Many, among them George's aunt, cannot tell the difference between what is human and what is animal: "Nabila hung up the phone, lit a cigarette, and noticed she was alone in an empty house, all alone in a war, and surrounded by dogs, human dogs, dogs in men's masks, dogs with guns, dogs in banker's suits, dogs that pee on one's couch and pant their filthy breath on one's breast" (*DG*, 65). Bassam also perceives his fellow-humans to be like animals: "the faithful trotted past, like horses" (*DG*, 109); and animals like humans: "Christian cats walked ... nonchalantly, never crossing themselves or kneeling for black-dressed priests" (*DG*, 16). He associates the violence done to animals with that done to humans; for instance, large-scale dog killing is alluded to as "the night of the big moon and the final howl" (*DG*, 66). The protagonist's reflections on the bestiality of humans and the humanity of beasts are a painful realisation of one's loneliness and vulnerability during urban warfare. It is an enduring part of Bassam's self-image who, confronted with the Christian concept of sin, deems himself to be without exception corrupted and bestial: "George and I had knelt in white robes with mumbling lips, and chewed the son of man's body, and cheerfully sipped His blood, and knew that He always loved us, cannibals, petty bandits, hormonal misfits, candle thieves, and masturbators that we were" (*DG*, 219). Bassam's pessimistic view of himself as intrinsically capable of cruelty and crime is, by its existentialist implications, extended to the reader.

The Lebanese Civil War is represented as a state of being that encapsulates all contradictions; allies and enemies, victims and oppressors, home and battlefield escape proper definitions and create overflows of meaning that cannot be accommodated:

> That world ... produces an illimitation of its own worldness, in such a way as to appear able only either to implode or to explode: because at the centre of the illimitation a deepening rift is appearing which is nothing other than an unequalness of the world to itself, an impossibility of endowing itself with meaning, value and truth, a precipitation into general equivalence that is progressively becoming civilisation as a work of death
>
> (Nancy 2003: 24).

In the writings of Nancy, civil war is a particularly deceptive type of conflict: an urban war of civility that destroys the meaning of the world as it is understood by the community involved in the conflict. Furthermore, civil war is an internally-conflicted concept that incorporates military strategy, economic and social regulations, gross injustice as well as resistance and revolt. The lethal potentiality of civil war is perhaps best rendered in the term "urbicide", pertaining "to an assault on buildings in order to destroy urbanity ... defined as an existential condition of plurality or heterogeneity. Urbicide is thus an attack on buildings as the condition of possibility of a plurality or heterogeneity" (Coward 2009: 12). In a place where military uniforms and occupied territories are turned into identities, any conditions for independent self-fashioning are indeed limited.

It could be said that Hage writes about the exhaustion of his native city by war. In his magico-apocalyptic Beirut, violence tears apart meaning structures and reveals hallucinatory mythic signifiers of human suffering. The city is populated by neither winners nor losers, only injured and traumatised individuals who have to cope with religious anxieties, moral dilemmas as well as material implications of war, poverty and desperation. Nancy's reflections on civil war are consistent with Hage's fictional representation of it; they both stress the importance of truth and meaning in the face of military aggression and describe civil war as a case of extreme relativism. To Nancy, a community affected by war is in a state of permanent crisis; on the personal and the social level what was distinct and autonomous in the past, now lacks essence and is almost impossible to distinguish in a spectacle of mutual destruction. Likewise, Hage's characters have to live through the cognitive confusion of a collective trauma, while their breakdowns are symptomatic of a more universal collapse of civility.

The city in *De Niro's game* is not a human settlement nor a miniature of community, but rather a rhizomatic space of living in conditions of uncertainty with regard to personal safety and global politics. It is a chaotic multicultural site of meaning creation as well as a heterogeneous and plural area of interaction. A space of and inside language, the city can be said to be both mythological and textual in Hage's fiction. Moreover, the troubled voice of his protagonist signals "the need for an interpretative approach that would disclose the intersubjective meanings and symbolism of the urban landscape" (Hubbard 2006: 59). To the protagonist, the city is a paradoxical destination, a place of imprisonment and liberation; he dreams of leaving Beirut and finding refuge in his imaginary Rome, the city of marble squares, pigeons and fountains. In his eyes, war-torn Beirut is nothing short of normal; bombardment is a fact of life to which one should grow accustomed, while hunger and blackouts are only another part of daily household drudgery. The disproportions between the ravages of war and Bassam's criticism of his mother's taste in music seem to illustrate the tensions accumulating within his perception of the world; in his mind, war is nothing when compared with the songs of Fairuz, a singer to whom his mother continually listens on the radio (*DG*, 15). Bassam's complaints and down-to-earth problems of adolescence give his wartime testimony a rather comic, but also in a sense universal, characteristic of a young adult rebelling against his mother.

At some points in the novel, the civil war is depicted as a backdrop to Bassam's coming of age. The two friends are presented as no different than any other youngsters growing up in a gang culture; they smoke, experiment with drugs, fall in love, despise their parents, speed, steal, mug and carry guns. The boys share a frame of mind that could be termed a "frontier mentality" – they trust only each other and believe in making laws for themselves. Yet their outward nihilism is a marker of the underlying condition of civil war, characterised by a heavy death toll and no identifiable differences between the fighting fractions. Deprived of any frame of reference, Bassam and George are equipped to live in a senseless world envisioned by Nancy:

> The present state of the world is not a war of civilizations. It is a civil war: it is the internal war of an enclosed city, of a civility, of an 'urbanity', which are in the process of fanning out to the very limits of the world, and … spreading right to the extremity of their own concepts. At its limit, a concept breaks, a distended figure shatters, a yawning gap appears
>
> (Nancy 2003: 23).

In addition, life in a war zone shatters the distinctions between well-known concepts, such as home, usually perceived as a place of comfort and cordiality, and is re-inscribed as a part of the battlefield (Nancy 2003: 23). Despite this intrusion of war into the personal sphere, Bassam suffers from a strange dislike of shelters; he feels nausea at the very thought of such crowded, pitch-black spaces and would rather stay at his bombed-out flat than go with his mother down to the shelter. One fateful day, his mother comes up to implore him to go underground during a particularly intensive air raid. While she is upstairs in the flat, a bomb falls and kills her instantaneously, symbolizing the ultimate disintegration of Bassam's family in their most intimate space. As has been indicated, the story of the protagonist's life is consistently subsumed into the grand narrative of war.

The condition of alienation associated with the transition to adulthood is further developed in the novel as the narrator changes from a blasé youth to a mature flâneur (Hubbard 2006: 101). It is understandable that living in the circumstances of civil war, Bassam wishes to achieve the ideal of disengaged observation and an impersonalised recording of events in order to maintain his sanity. In an attempt at self-preservation, the protagonist slowly sheds all his ties with the outside world and resorts to a state of profound loneliness and exile within. Bassam forsakes the clarity of his narrative in order to represent the experiential realism of his situation in its particularity and uniqueness. He selectively employs various historical discourses to redefine and personalise the lived experience of the civil war, blurring the boundaries between allies and enemies, war and peace, sanity and madness. The city in a state of war stands for "the nadir of human civility" which signifies "anonymity, alienation, immorality, disorder" and mass executions (Hubbard 2006: 60). It is presumed that George and Bassam are traumatized by a rapid transformation of their former well-known homes into sites of conflict and their friends into potential enemies. Those who die become heroes or martyrs, irrespective of their courage or merits, whereas those who stay alive become survivors, constantly reliving their trauma. In the face of such cognitive anxiety, what was previously held to be true and what was known as false is no longer relevant to the main character who creates archaeological images of Beirut, delving further into its history with every phrase:

> I climbed onto George's motorbike and sat behind him, and we drove down the main streets where bombs fell, where Saudi diplomats had once picked up French prostitutes, where ancient Greeks had danced, Romans had invaded, Persians had sharpened their swords, Mamluks had stolen the villager's food, crusaders had eaten human flesh, and Turks had enslaved my grandmother
>
> (*DG*, 16).

In the eyes of Bassam, Beirut is inseparably connected with bloodshed and war. He renders the self-perpetuating history of violence less abstract by referring to the story of his family and by compulsively compiling lists that are often startling descriptions of well-known phenomena. In this way, Rawi Hage consistently utilises the conventions of magic realism to unmask the invisibility of everyday suffering in times of war.

Although there are no straightforwardly magical or supernatural elements in the novel, its plot may be deemed magical, as it not only "presents reality from an unusual perspective without transcending the limits of the natural, but [also] induces in the reader or viewer a sense of unreality" (Franz Roh in Klonowska 2006: 12). Bassam's heightened theatricality and sense of history are reconciled in strikingly contradictory versions of events and their perception, which, in turn, constantly question the stability of received truths in a manner reminiscent of other magic realism texts. Hage's protagonist is a lager than life character "[f]or ... whom the real world becomes real images, mere images are transformed into real beings, tangible figments which are the efficient motor of trancelike behavior" (Debord 1994: 8). Even though Bassam is incredibly loquacious, the spectacle he presents in his wartime memoirs "is the opposite of dialogue" (*DG*, 8), his chooses exile and divests himself of all social interaction. Quite understandably, the protagonist seeks refuge in his imagination as a way of voicing dissent from the actuality of the civil war, of which survival seems to be a merely accidental by-product. Hage's magic realism is in the eye of the beholder and as such it could be said "to have clear affinities with modernism in that it is concerned with looking for mythical resonances and structure of the world under the incidence and fragmentation of the present" (Rzepa 2009: 15). One of such recurrent mythical structures in the novel is fratricide, usually associated either with the foundation of Rome by Romulus, who famously murdered his brother in a struggle over its location, or with Cain, who killed Abel out of envy for God's favour. The first account of fratricide irreversibly links urban space to the killing of one's brothers and heralds the imperial greatness of Rome, whereas the second one connects fratricide with the punishment of rootlessness and a restless wander of the earth. Speaking from the position of survival, Bassam looks back on the narcissistic fictions of nationhood and attempts to reconstruct his identity outside the rigid distinction between friends and foes. This mythical structure provides coherence to Bassam's story and allows for a radical reconfiguration of the soldier figure from a freedom fighter to an archetype of a fratricidal murderer.

Notwithstanding its apparent lack of clarity, the imagery evoked by Bassam points to the impossibility of describing any painful experience, for it is "an unmaking of the world" (Scarry 1987: 19). A similar observation is made by Slavoj Žižek who, while discussing concentration camps, points out that "realistic prose fails, where the poetic evocation of the unbearable atmosphere of a camp succeeds" (Žižek 2008: 5). Three representative features of Roh's magic realism can also be found in *De Niro's game*: denaturalisation of realism, intertextuality and metafictional foregrounding (Klonowska 2006: 111). With regard to the first one, it could be said that Bassam appears to be deliberately distorting the realistic mode of description in order to raise suspicion against any factual account of the events depicted in the novel. In fact, his line of narration suggests that a civil war is, in its essence, indescribable. Hage has chosen mottoes from Ezekiel, Heraclitus and Jean Paul Satre to set an apocalyptic tone for his novel and create a network of intertexual relations between the Lebanese Civil War and other narrations of catastrophe and calamity.[4] Moreover, the estrangement felt by the main character is conveyed by means of metafictional foregrounding: Bassam often imagines himself to be a character in a gangster movie or in a book. Significantly, he relives the life of Mersault from Camus's *L'Étranger* in war-torn Beirut; they both adopt a position of an outsider and simply let life happen with their minimal participation and, if possible, none at all. It would seem that they are passers-by and spectators rather than agents in the narrative, curiously detached from their own existence, indifferent to the deaths of their mothers and ruthlessly violent, if need be (Taylor 2011). In Camus's novel, Mersault is a Frenchman living in Algiers, who killed an Arab at his friend's request; in Hage's novel, Bassam is an Arab, guilty of wartime crimes and at least one murder. As a civil war survivor, Bassam comes across Camus's novel and reads it during his first days as an illegal immigrant in Paris. Rawi Hage can be said to critically invert Camus's character and revise his mode of writing in times of civil war while the conventions of magic realism along with dark humour in *De Niro's game* comprise a vital part of the narrative and character presentation.

Hage uses the image of a war-torn city to create a contradictory space of belonging and perpetual political violence. Whether it is Beirut or Paris, Bassam looks through the permeable boundary of a cityscape and sees war and destruction at its very core. Accordingly, it can be said that the civil war is portrayed as the driving force of a self-perpetuating urbanity. Leaving aside the storyline, *De Niro's game* could be said to excavate urban meanings without referencing the topography of Beirut, which implies that the fictional city could be everywhere and nowhere at the same time. Being the principal targets of modern warfare, modern cities become universal images of destruction that make the news:

> A bomb has torn open the side of a house. To be sure, a cityscape is not made of flesh. Still, sheared-off buildings are almost as eloquent as body parts (Kabul; Sarajevo; East Mostar; Grozny; sixteen acres of Lower Manhattan after September 11, 2001; the refugee camp in Jenin) ... This is what war does. War tears, rends. War rips open, eviscerates. War scorches. War dismembers. War *ruins*
>
> (Sontag 2002, Sontag's italics, MW).

The images of bombed-out cities themselves represent casualties in their annihilation of inhabited space; the painful realism of press photographs calls attention to the materiality of buildings which, in turn, is suspended to emphasise their metaphorical significance as the markers of shattered communities and lost lives. For Hage, Beirut's cityscape is a pliable material, not only a figure for local, national and global tensions,

---

4   See Najat Rahman's *Apocalyptic narrative recalls and the human: Rawi Hage's* De Niro's game for an extensive discussion of apocalyptic imagery and its meaning.

but also a fertile source of narratives that often incorporate "virtual, filmic, and televisual representations of city killing and actual urban war" (Graham 2004: 45). Under Bassam's regard, any cityscape has an underlying structure of war; when in Paris, he walks the streets with Napoleon's soldiers following their every step, sees Rommel's army heading south or leads the French revolutionaries preparing to hang the aristocracy (*DG*, 257-258). For this reason, it could be inferred that Bassam cannot fully disengage himself from the discourse of war; he becomes obsessed with it and is unable to function outside zones of conflict, real or imaginary.

Bassam's flight from Beirut marks a turning point in the novel. Even outside the war torn city, Bassam retains his ability to perceive and visualize past wars long after they are over. The meaning of his archaeological images is twofold. Firstly, the urban landscape becomes a character in its own right with patterns of conflict and guerilla fights that are similar around the globe. Secondly, war is shown to be the driving force of all civilisations. The narrator seems to reach the conclusion that relative peace and calm in the privileged parts of the world is balanced by military actions conducted in other regions. To Bassam, however, no-one is exempted from the state of war. This can be illustrated by Rhea, George's half-sister, who is depicted as an inconspicuous Parisian society girl, yet as it turns out later, she is also entangled in a web of close associations with military agents, passed on by her father. The circle of self-perpetuating violence is extended to Europe, and even though it is not visible on the outside, it is still lurking behind the marble façades of modern-day Paris. Although the French capital is not in a state of war, a military presence pervades its cityscape. For instance, its centre, shaped by centuries of human activity, was demolished by Baron Georges-Eugène Haussmann in the nineteenth century in order to build wide boulevards, garnished with theatres and cafés to control the unruly populace and avert the threat of rioting (Graham 2004: 36). Despite the visual appeal of Haussmann's design, its main purpose was the creation of a space that could be easily monitored by armed forces (Graham 2004: 36); thus, it can be inferred that Paris, like Beirut, is revealed to be a hybrid space of dialogue and war that cannot be fully investigated or ordered. Only Bassam's imaginary Rome, a place of refuge and secular heaven, is a city free of conflict and violence, symbolically populated by pigeons, despite its violent past and mythical fratricidal foundations. In its peace and quiet, Paris strangely resembles the war-torn Beirut where all human activity has gone underground. Bassam longs for an urban space without violence and history to break with the surrealist images of war and destruction that haunt his imagination. Therefore, it seems understandable that, at the end of *De Niro's game*, with his usual dramatic flair, Bassam decides to flee Paris and buys a ticket to Rome, subconsciously reviving the history of his native Beirut that was once a French colony and an important Roman city.

The correlation between city and identity at the time of war is a central point of reference in *De Niro's game*. In Bassam's tormented mind, Beirut is a surrealist space populated by dogs, thugs and bombs. His departure from realism appears to be a political choice, a decision to speak about the unimaginable impact of mass violence, using cinematic and apocalyptic metaphors. Perceptive as he may be, the protagonist creates an ambiguous and subjective version of events, knowing that a lyrical discourse, rather than a realistic one, could better describe the appalling atrocities of the civil war. Looking down on the city from the rooftops, he tells the tragic histories of its people with almost archaeological precision, going back generation after generation to recover the personal and the human amidst collective violence. Beirut, in his view, is an accumulation of narratives that are "normally socially, politically incremental and [are] often perceived and experienced by perpetrators, collaborators, bystanders—and even, eventually, by victims themselves—as ordinary, routine, even justified" (Scheper-Hughes 2003: 192). Such banality of violence and boredom associated with atrocities is counterbalanced by Hage's use of the marvellous and thriller-like technique of writing (Salvador 2011), which highlights his preoccupation with the issues of identity and nationhood often addressed in other Canadian works of fiction. Hage develops Bassam as a character with an inherent hybridity, never quite at home in his native land and in the foreign lands his visits. The protagonist is haunted by his failure to construct a stable identity related to any religious denomination or politico-geographical construct and, by extension, his experiences could be interpreted as a covert commentary on Canadian multiculturalism policies.

Writing from across the ocean, Hage recreates Beirut as a vague and surreal place. The topographical elements of the actual city – its streets and geography – are hardly mentioned in the minimalistic descriptions that could refer to any contemporary war zone, it can be said that every evocation of Beirut's history in the novel is an attempt at universalising the experience of the civil war. By the same token, the city in its extremity appears to infect its inhabitants with violence as, after centuries-long occupation and local conflicts, there is no life outside the self-perpetuating circle of conflict. For Hage, hostilities are not isolated acts but rather mimetic and readily-available legitimate means of expression and identity-formation. In order to find to a way out of the conflict, Bassam tends to describe his actions rather than his feelings. The obsessive use of the first person perspective could be interpreted as a symptom of posttraumatic stress disorder, presumably related to his feelings of depersonalisation and isolation. Drawing on his past, Hage strives to find a language that conveys the vulnerability and desperation felt by those who fear daily for their personal safety and choose "forced immigration" (Christoff 2007).

It could be said, moreover, that Hage describes Beirut as a city witnessing its own destruction, undergoing the process of killing memory of collective coexistence (Coward 2009: 6). Despite his miraculous escape, Bassam still has to answer the key question asked by Jalal Toufic, how "not to remember – without forgetting" (Toufic 2007: 9); that is, how to survive the trauma of the civil war and come to terms with the memory of those who died during the conflict. Contemporary Beirut is said to be a place with no memory, legislating amnesty for war-lords and criminals without any official recognition for those who died during the war (Christoff 2007, Toufic 2007: 9-10). Memory, especially in the case of Bassam, is regarded as a source of fractured national and cultural identities, open to manipulation and speculation. When he recounts the story of George's life to Rhea, he states that "I changed names, I planted trees, ... I made people dance and laugh, even under falling bombs" (*DG*, 212). Like Scheherazade, the narrator of *One thousand and one nights*, Hage's protagonist needs to tell stories to be granted the privilege of life. A nihilist and a cynic, he does not hesitate to betray the story in exchange for survival, making his readers complicit by listening. This inclusive side of Hage's novel points to the role of global bystanders in international conflicts, since in his account of mass violence there are no neutral positions. *De Niro's game*, in its extension of the discourse of civil war from Beirut to Paris, reminds its readers that "war is the norm and peace is the exception" (Sontag 2002).

References

"Author's profile: Rawi Hage". (http://www.anansi.ca/authors.cfm?author_id=441&return_id=593) (date of access: April, 1 2011).

Bowers, Maggie Ann. 2004. *Magic(al) realism.* New Critical Idiom. London and New York: Routledge.

Christoff, Stefan. 2007. "Lebanon: Shadows of war." *The dominion. News from the grassroots.* (http://www.dominionpaper.ca/articles/1114) (date of access: August 25, 2011).

Coward, Martin. 2009. *Urbicide: The politics of urban destruction.* London and New York: Routledge.

Debord, Guy. 1994. *The society of the spectacle.* (Translated by Donald Nicholson-Smith.) New York: Zone Books.

Fanon, Franz. 2004. *The wretched of the earth.* (Translated by Richard Philcox.) New York: Grove Press.

Graham, Stephen. 2004. "Cities as strategic sites: Place annihilation and urban geopolitics", in: Stephen Graham (ed.), 31-53.

Graham, Stephen. 2004a. (ed.). *Cities, war and terrorism: Towards an urban geopolitcs.* Oxford: Blackwell.

Graham, Stephen. 2004b. "Introduction: Cities, warfare, and states of emergency", in: Stephen Graham (ed.), 1-25.

Hage, Rawi. 2008 [2006]. *De Niro's game.* London: Old Street Publishing.

Hubbard, Phil. 2006. *City. Key ideas in geography.* Routledge: London and New York.

Klonowska, Barbara. 2006. *Contaminations: Magic realism in contemporary British fiction.* Lublin: Maria Curie-Skłodowska University Press.

Laffin, John. 1987. *War of desperation (Lebanon 1982-1985).* London: Osprey Publishing Ltd.

Mostafa, Dalia Said. 2011. "Journeying through a discourse of violence: Elias Khoury's *Yalo* and Rawi Hage's *De Niro's game*", *Middle East Critique* 20, 1: 21-45.

Nancy, Jean Luc. 2003. "The confronted community", *Postcolonial Studies* 6, 1: 23-36.

Rahman, Najat. 2009. "Apocalyptic narrative recalls and the human: Rawi Hage's *De Niro's game*", *University of Toronto Quarterly* 78, 2: 800-814.

Rzepa, Agnieszka. 2009. *Feats and defeats of memory: Exploring spaces of Canadian magic realism.* Poznań: Wydawnictwo Uniwersytetu Adama Mickiewicza.

Salvador, Faustus. 2006. "War and movies. Rawi Hage's acclaimed debut re-imagines Beirut". Interview with Rawi Hage. *The Montreal Review of Books.* (http://www.aelaq.org/mrb/feature.php?issue=19&article=545&cat=1) (date of access: August 22, 2011).

Scarry, Elaine. 1987. *The body in pain: The making and unmaking of the world.* Oxford and New York: Oxford University Press.

Schreper-Huges, Nancy. 2003. "Genealogy of genocide", *Modern Psychoanalysis* 28, 2: 167-197.

Sontag, Susan. 2002. "Looking at war: Photography's view of devastation and death". *The New Yorker.* (http://www.newyorker.com/archive/2002/12/09 /021209crat_atlarge?currentPage=all) (date of access: August 25, 2011).

Taylor, Craig. 2006. "Review: *De Niro's game* by Rawi Hage", *Quill and Quire.* (www.quillandquire.com/reviews/review.cfm?review_id=5105) (date of access: August 25, 2011).

Toufic, Jalal. 2007. *Undeserving Lebanon.* Forthcoming books. (http://www.jalaltoufic.com/publications.htm) (date of access. August 30, 2011)

Žižek, Slavoj. 2008. *Violence: Six sideways reflections.* New York: Picador.

'There, time juggles fire…' – A Jewish *shtetl* revisited in Lilian Nattel's *The river midnight*

Dagmara Drewniak, Adam Mickiewicz University, Poznań

ABSTRACT

Lilian Nattel's first novel *The River Midnight* is an attempt to show a fictional Polish-Jewish *shtetl* of Blaszka near Plotsk from a perspective of Jewish women who play substantive roles of a mother, a midwife, and a healer in the community and yet they remain insignificant and in the shadow of male-dominated society. Lilian Nattel, a Jewish-Canadian writer, though culturally distant from the most of magic realist fiction can be located within this spectrum owing to her unique style of portrayal of Jewishness as consisting of both spiritual (thus pertaining to religion, death) and physical (illness, sex) elements.

The present article endeavours to read Nattel's novel as a magic realist work where the harsh reality of the 19th century poor village is juxtaposed with a series of magical factors and events like traditional healing practices, mysticism of religious observances, frequent intrusions of Yiddish and a collective experience of womanhood, to name only a few.

Franz Roh, whose name is frequently associated with the first definition of the term "magic realism," saw magic realist painting as a post-impressionistic return to realism. His views on this kind of art function nowadays as an important background for the changes the term has undergone since Roh's famous text of 1925. Although Roh's argument referred mainly to painting,[1] Irene Guenther claims that "Roh never gave a concise definition of Magic Realism" (Guenther 1995: 34). Zamora and Faris at the very beginning of their preface to a seminal anthology of articles devoted to the phenomenon explain that "Roh praises … the text's *departure* from realism rather than its reengagement of it" (1995: 15, italics original, DD). The term itself had already been mentioned earlier, first by Novalis in the 18th century in connection with the field of philosophy, and then by Gustav Hartlaub, who two years before the publication of Roh's text had discussed the so-called *Neue Sachlichkeit*, a trend in art which declared a return to realistic art. However, it is still Franz Roh's text which is seen by scholars (Zamora and Faris 1995; Guenther 1995) as a foundation of the definition of magic realism and its later departure from painting into literature. The present paper endeavours to read Lilian Nattel's, a Jewish-Canadian writer's, first novel *The River Midnight* (1999) as a magic realist work in which the harsh reality of a poor, 19th-century village is interwoven with a series of magical factors and events such as traditional healing

---

1   The full title of Franz Roh's text is *Nach-Expressionismus, Magischer Realismus: Probleme der neuesten Europäischen Malerei*, which sets his definition of magic realism exclusively within the field of painting, which, however, gave a beginning to further discussions on the concept.

practices, mysterious religious observances, frequent intrusions of Yiddish and a collective experience of womanhood, to name only a few.

Irene Guenther, in her essay on magic realism in the visual arts, lists a series of features called for by Roh and explains connections between verism and uncanniness with their reference to the marvellous (Guenther 1995: 36). She emphasizes Roh's differentiation between the 'magic' and 'mystic' and attributes the former to magic realist practices in the arts and thus eradicates the latter: "The term 'magic' as opposed to 'mystic' is meant [by Roh] to imply that the 'secret' should not enter into the realistically depicted world, but should hold itself back behind this world" (Guenther 1995: 35).[2] This particular feature has also been ascribed to literature and a vast body of diverse texts,[3] although Roh's "influence on the contemporary literary genre ... is debatable" and "clear parallels between the visual arts and the literary arts" (Guenther 1995: 61-62) are difficult to be found. Nevertheless, the importance of the early 20th-century connotations of the term are worth mentioning.

With the post-World War II establishment of *lo real maravilloso americano* (the American marvellous real) and the works of Borges, Marquez, and Carpentier, to name only a few, literary magic realism started to develop and expand into other continents and, according to Wendy B. Faris, it has become "an important component of postmodernism" (Faris 1995: 163). As such, magic realist texts are becoming more common, and through their popularity appeal to a wide variety of readers. They join a certain 'lightness' of reading[4] with a penetration of the themes and places that are rediscovered through, for instance, the postmodern revisions of fairy tales or postcolonial subjects in Angela Carter's and Salman Rushdie's works respectively. The interplay of the central and the marginal so typical of postmodernism is also traceable in magic realist fiction, and apart from such emblematic locations as India and Latin America, Faris adds Eastern Europe as a forceful periphery appealing to the centre and thus creating the magic realist convention (Faris 1995: 165).

The study of magic realism in literature has been a relatively new enterprise, although according to Barbara Klonowska, already quite established (Klonowska 2006: 10), especially within the scholarly discussions on Roh, Carpentier and Borges, to list only a few famous names. As a result of the multiplicity of similar

---

2   In a translation of Roh's 1925 essay the final statement reads: "... but rather hides and palpitates behind it" (Wendy B. Faris's translation from Spanish 16). This clearly presents 'magic' as being an inherent part of the otherwise realistic world.

3   The diversity of texts ranges from Kafka to Chesterton (Klonowska 2006: 16) and includes the works of such artists as Jünger and Döblin among others (Guenther 1996: 56-60).

4   Faris (1995: 161) juxtaposes the "accessibility" of these texts with the "hermeticism of many modernist texts" by authors such as Joyce, Proust, or Faulkner. She also argues that the fact that these texts are more "youthful and popular" (Faris 1995: 161) locates them among works read for entertainment.

definitions, Klonowska (2006: 11) arrives at the conclusion that since the term "seems ... [to] be used to describe practically every novel which is only slightly different from classical realism, ... it ceases to be useful at all". She manages to escape this paradoxical cul-de-sac by asserting that probably every field of study needs specific categorization, at least for the sake of discussion, and quotes Frederic Jameson's declaration that the term possesses "a strange seductiveness" (Klonowska 2006: 11).

Both Faris and D'haen in their essays link magic realist texts with postmodernism and present a series of features that are typical of magic realism and can be distinguished in such texts. Looking at Faris's list of traits, one may find such aspects as the element of unexplainable magic inherent in the text, a literary convention where the details flee from simple mimetic descriptions like the appearance of eternal mythic truths, a constant feeling of the "closeness or near-merging of the two realms" (Faris 1995: 172), metafictional references, repetition, local folk traditions, communal affinity and elements of the carnivalesque, among others (Faris 1995: 163-170). As an illustration of these features Faris lists quite conventionally the most 'typical' magic realist texts such as Gabriel Garcia Marquez's *One hundred years of solitude,* Salman Rushdie's *Midnight's children,* or *Ironweed* by William Kennedy to name just a few, but she quite forcefully explains the core features of the convention claiming that such "fiction exists at the intersection of two worlds, at an imaginary point inside a double-sided mirror that reflects in both directions. Fluid boundaries between the worlds of the living and the dead are traced only to be crossed" (Faris 1995: 172). These elements together with a certain reversal of the logic of time or space and especially a constant intertwining of life and death appear in current definitions and discussions on the magic realist convention in literature. Klonowska, in her study, refers to some aspects of anthropology and ethnology, turning to the work by Michał Buchowski on magic as a cultural phenomenon.[5] It turns out that, according to cultural anthropologists, "magic realism is only an oxymoron if we treat magic as implying the existence of the supernatural, and reality as something material ... To primitive cultures, then, magic was not merely a part of reality: it was the reality as such and the dichotomy between these realms did not exist" (Klonowska 2006: 13).

It should also be noted that magic realism is not the only term that has been coined by critics to name the same phenomenon in the arts. Apart from the disjunction of magic and magical realism, there are a few more designations, such as psychic realism, grotesque realism and mythic realism (Delbaere-Garant 1995: 256; Rzepa 2009: 13-14). The phenomenon can also be linked to the fairy tale, the carnivalesque and even fantasy (Klonowska 2006: 61). Despite certain, but

---

5   Michał Buchowski analyzes magic as a primitive and original element of human nature. His views echo Mircea Eliade's anthropologist perspective.

usually minute, differences among these terms, they can all be applied to the majority of magic realist texts. Variations appear more on a national level. As Rzepa argues, while "early magic realist novels in Canada were written by white, Euro-Canadian writers, the majority of current magic realist output comes from non-white authors, many of them women, who write from and into widely differing historical and cultural contexts and literary traditions" (Rzepa 2009: 62). This particular new trend in Canadian magic realist literature has much to do with the rediscovery of the space of memory (Rzepa 2009: 63). In this context, Lilian Nattel, though not being a member of any sexual or cultural minority, can still be seen as a writer who reconsiders her ethnic origins and thus reinvents the memory of the pre-war Jewish communities from Eastern and Central Europe. The personal story of this Toronto-based author can be traced back to Poland, where her family emigrated from with "their history lost in prewar memory", as we read on the cover of the novel. They settled in Montreal, where Nattel was born and raised. In this way her writing pertains to the Jewish pre-war Poland, and strives to reclaim the lost past in the form of story-telling.[6]

This is why Lilian Nattel's debut novel *The River Midnight*,[7] which presents the life of a fictional *shtetl* called Blaszka, near Plotsk, may serve as an example of a magic realist text in which the Western perception of the realistic world is modified by the 19th-century Eastern European traditions and vivid Judaism present in the story.[8] The idea of the periphery is further suggested by the fact that Blaszka is a small village which, though geographically not very distant from Plotsk and Warsaw, is spiritually remote from large cities. Even the presentation of the village is based on this contrast and equipped with some magical elements. For example: "Time is a trickster in Poland. In Warsaw they have electric lights. On the farms, peasants make their own candles. And in Blaszka? There time juggles fire, throwing off sparks that reach far into the past and spin toward the future" (*RM*, 19). Similarly, D'haen (1995: 194) refers to such a phenomenon as writing "from the margin, from a place 'other' than 'the' or 'a' centre," and calls it "ex-centric" writing. It has to be noted that the novel written by a female writer and about women fits the tendency of latest Canadian magic realism as seen by Rzepa (2009: 62-63). By putting women at the pivot of the story, Nattel subverts the traditionally male-dominated society of the 19th century and shows how

---

6   Lilian Nattel is also the author of *Singing fire* published in 2004, in which she depicts the 19th century London and the Jewish communities. She has also written *Web of angels*, which was published in February 2012.

7   Henceforth indicated as *RM* followed by page number. All quotations are from Nattel, Lilian. 1999. *The River Midnight*. New York: Scribner.

8   Although there is scarcely any reference to Nattel in scholarly publications, her novels have been frequently categorized as magic realist by publishers and bookstores. In an anthology of *The year's best fantasy and horror* from 1999, Terri Windling, describes *The River Midnight* as "Yiddish magic realism" (2000).

women, deprived of power, are still able to influence the world through their innate powers of giving life, creating closed circles of healers, sisters, and *zogerins* – leaders of prayers in synagogues.

The story concentrates on four women, Hanna-Leah, Faygela, Zisa-Sara and Misha, who become close friends in childhood and are called by the locals *vilda hayas*, which means "wild creatures" in Yiddish. Their nickname creates a collective experience and "collective relatedness" (Faris 1995: 183).[9] This communal dimension remains visible throughout the entire novel. The girls grow up and follow various paths, but remain closely connected to each other, both physically and spiritually. The novel is the story of their lives, fears, tragedies and small joys in the harsh conditions of the village of Blaszka. Misha, the midwife, connects them all and represents feminine power. She is the most independent one of the group – she is divorced, a village healer knowing the mysterious ways of curing, a midwife helping the *shtetl* women give birth to their children as well as get rid of unwanted pregnancies, and has a secret lover and a son and daughter of her own. She also fits a magic realist convention herself, not only through her occupation, but also because she is the biggest woman in the village, a descendant of large women who have always talked to demons and had contact with the spirits. She is presented as "dangerous as a mother bear. And because Misha is a man's name among the Russians, she would also be as fierce as a Cossack ... When a woman is in childbirth, even the Angel of Death is afraid of Misha" (*RM*, 16).[10] Hanna-Leah's life is marked by her inability to have children, which is expected of women in a 19th-century Jewish community. Faygela, on the other hand, has many children and thus has very little time left for her childhood friendships. Zisa-Sara's life is depicted only in the background, since she marries an intellectual and leaves Poland for the USA to seek better opportunities, and

---

9   In her usage of the term, Faris refers here to other important studies devoted to the discussion on the appearance of magic saying: "As Seymour Menton has pointed out, a Jungian rather than a Freudian perspective is common in magical realist texts; that is, the magic may be attributed to a mysterious sense of collective relatedness rather than to individual memories or dreams or visions" (Faris 1995: 183). Despite her inspirations in the usage of the term, it is Faris's interpretations of the collective relatedness which seems valid for the present study as it concerns to the fact that the magic in such novels is "unrecuperable" and presents "a communal magic of storytelling" (Faris 1995: 183), both of which can be easily traced in Nattel's *The River Midnight*.

10 There yet another example of Misha's communication with the Angel of Death at the end of the novel, when she is called to Emma's side, who is dying of a fever. Misha negotiates Emma's recovery with the Angel of Death and offers to give herself instead. Her offer is rejected since she is pregnant and the demon is sent to take just one girl, but Misha is still able to rescue Emma. This long conversation (*RM*, 383-386) exhibits many magic realist traits, as Misha says that pregnant women see more, and readers are able to view the strength of the woman, healer, and midwife in one, a description of the devil, and the proximity of the two realms.

eventually dies there. Her children, Emma and Izzie, return to Poland in order to be brought up by their grandmother, Alta-Fruma, and thus represent their late mother in the group of *vilda hayas*.

The religion of this Jewish *shtetl*, which plays an important role in its life, appears to be a sphere where the magic realism of the novel comes to the foreground. The two worlds which existed in the 19th century in Eastern Europe, that of the Christian 'centre' and Jewish 'periphery,' though these two concepts are also questionable, seem to have been mostly separate, which is why certain practices which were real for Jews became magical for Christians. Such a split into two religious realms is not only visible in Europe and within these religious practices. It is a more general phenomenon and is explained extensively by Suzanne Baker in her study of Canadian and Australian aboriginal stories, where she claims that an introduction of "another level of reality, that of suspicion and myth, … is inexplicable according to the logic and reason of Western thought" (Baker 1993). Such an approach can also be applied to other cultures. As a result, according to Rzepa (2009: 19), the "real-magical dichotomy can be sustained only by accepting a non-indigenous, Eurocentric point of view". The strict religious world which governs almost all aspects of the characters' lives is an example of this "irreducible element of magic" which Faris (1995: 168) calls for, as it can always be theoretically explained but creates a mythic sphere unattainable for a non-Jew. This is close to the idea of the creation of a certain mythology or mythic truths which are taken for granted and rarely questioned in such a society.

Such elements of magic do not only stem from religion. As Faris says, "magical things 'really' do happen … and exist symbiotically in a foreign textual culture, a disturbing element, a grain of sand in the oyster of that realism" (Faris 1995: 167-168). In Nattel's novel this inextricable element of magic appears, for example, when the village is visited by the Golem Players, a group of wandering musicians who perform various tricks, such as playing an invisible violin:

> He draws an imaginary bow across an even more imaginary violin that nevertheless plays the opening notes to Tchaikovsky's violin concerto. Tchaikovsky has recently died of cholera. The Traveler looks from his notebook to the absent violin. He is impressed. "It's nothing, my friend," the Director says. "Anyone can do it. Even you." "What's the trick?" the Traveler asks, looking around for a hidden music box. "Nothing at all. Just a bit of magic." "Magic," the Traveler says thoughtfully, studying his notebook again. "Don't get any ideas. Let me tell you the facts. What's magic? A piece of chocolate. An almond torte. Delicious, and then it melts away. But all of this," the Director says waving his hand grandly, "is something else entirely. Open your eyes and look … You've got to look closely and pay attention"
>
> (*RM*, 18).

The closeness of the real world and the world of magic is taken for granted. Even if some characters, such as the Traveller watching the Golem Players, doubt at first, they sooner or later come to the conclusion that the magic realm exists.

Moreover, the visit of the Golem Players introduces an element of the carnivalesque, which has certain affinities with magic realism. Hanna-Leah, who suffers from infertility, her mother-in law's criticism, and her husband's lack of interest in her, "knew that demons came in the night to women who were awake and hungry. Demons with curved horns, a cleft foot, and a red bigness that ruined a woman for any ordinary man, filling her and driving wild. That would be her fate if she didn't take care" (*RM*, 31). This magic dimension is further developed in the book through the idea of storytelling, a convention widely used by Nattel, joining thus the elements of orature, a necessary repetitiveness and metafictional intrusions. Sentences such as: "Listen. You can hear the excitement of the village square" (*RM*, 13), or, "But shh, we can't talk, now. The story is about to start" (*RM*, 19), are juxtaposed with many stories and fables usually told to children: "You see the doll on the shelf? ... That isn't any doll. She tells stories. It's true. And not any stories. Just my Grandmother Rivka's" (*RM*, 57), and, "'Just remember what I'm telling you ... Words do more than miracles'. 'More than magic?' 'Yes'" (*RM*, 140). This storytelling originates to some extent from the Jewish tradition of Haggadah, a type of storytelling rooted in the Torah, traditions and laws which are passed down from generation to generation, unchanged and everlasting.

These elements suggesting the constant intertwining of the real with the magical are also found in the definition of magic realism proposed by William Spindler,[11] who claims that there are two different ways of viewing the term:

> (i) the original one, which refers to a type of literary or artistic work which presents reality from an unusual perspective without transcending the limits of the natural, but which induces in the reader or viewer a sense of unreality;
> (ii) the current usage, which describes texts where two contrasting views of the world (one 'rational' and one 'magical') are presented as if they were not contradictory, by resorting to the myths and beliefs of ethno-cultural groups for whom this contradiction does not arise.
>
> (Spindler in Klonowska 2006: 12).

Though Spindler calls these two modes 'contrasting,' it may be asserted that Nattel's novel joins them and mixes these varying concepts through her unusual portrayal of the Jewish community with a multiplicity of physical and spiritual aspects of its life. In the light of this, the 'sense of unreality' is achieved through the immersion into a 19th century Jewish *shtetl*, which for a 21st century reader becomes both realistic in description and unreal, since such places no longer exist, and contemporary Jewish communities are totally different and inhabit dramatically different lands than Eastern Europe. Moreover, Nattel resorts to the other type of magic realism defined by Spindler by presenting the division of the

---

11   Barbara Klonowska also uses Spindler's mode of understanding magic realism and finds it very useful (Klonowska 2006: 12-13).

Jewish world into the 'rational' and 'magical.' In Nattel's world those who believe in God and strictly follow the doctrine as well as those who turn to the mythical knowledge do not see any contradiction in the co-existence of the two dimensions. Even if such mysticism is not available to everybody, it still has become a common practice to many. This ability to perceive and take part in the two dimensions, in the otherwise hidden and secret world, is especially visible in the case of Misha, the midwife and healer, who is immersed in the magical realm but, through her active participation in the everyday life of the community by visiting the sick, pregnant and dying, has close contact with the real, and remains a rational woman. For Klonowska, such a stance is a combination of "mystery and witchcraft existing without contradictions together with the everyday and mundane" (Klonowska 2006: 12). The importance of mythology is also seen in Mircea Eliade's texts. In his discussion of myths in the cosmic dimension, he views a human being as real only in the religious aspect, since only a human being in his or her transhuman layer becomes immersed in myths. Such a person is created through the sacred history realized through myths, therefore his *imitatio dei* is a consequence and aim of his life according to myths and to the spirituality of one's ancestors (Eliade 1993: 109-115).[12]

Metafictional elements that are scattered throughout the book are closely linked with other postmodern elements such as lack of chronology, repetition, intertextual remarks, and a certain insight into the future of the characters which is given at some points of the text. Nattel introduces a feeling of a lack of chronology in the readers through a blending of plots representing the four main characters, as well as through the disruption of chronology in the description of two important events in the lives of the families – Emma's illness, the visions she has during her fever, her recovery, and the imprisonment of her close friend, Ruthie, Faygela's daughter. These stories are cut into pieces and scattered throughout the novel, leaving the reader to form a chronology out of the fragments. At the end of some chapters, even though the reader is still left with a lack of knowledge about some of the characters, certain codas are provided with various information about the future. It is a way for the narrator to mention the upcoming events of the 20th century, such as the two world wars, pogroms, the Holocaust and the dispersal of the Jews:

---

12   Mircea Eliade analyzed various communities from ancient Jewish through North American Indians and published numerous books and articles in the field. For the sake of this text, as I only briefly refer to his concept of a 'true man', I am using a volume published in Polish as *Sacrum Mit historia* (1993), which is a selection of his texts from a number of sources: *Images et symbols. Essais sur le symbolisme magico-religieux* published by Galimard in 1952, *Le mythe de l'éternel retour. Archétypes et repetition* published by Galimard in 1949, *das Heilige und das profane (Le sacré et le profane)* published by Rowohlt Taschenbuch-Verlag in 1957, *Mythes, rêves et mystères* from 1957 and *Méphistophélès et l'androgyne* from 1962.

> In a hundred years, five thousand miles from Blaszka, Misha's great-granddaughter will
> stand in the synagogue among the men and the women, listening to Kol Nidrei, her
> shawl draped over the child in her arms ... And she will know that her great-
> grandmother at that very moment, in the house above the River Północna, is listening to
> her lover sing the prayer that opens the door beyond time, her babies resting after their
> long swim
>
> (*RM*, 396).

or, "When there is a resurgence of pogroms in Russia ten years from now, Hershel will institute self-defense groups. In fifteen years, he will organize the building of a school in Blaszka. During the First World War it will be used as a hospital..." (*RM*, 220). This recurrent insight into the future becomes a "narrative principle" (Faris 1995: 177) together with the repetition of Jewish celebrations and holy days according to which the members of this community live. All chapters are divided into subsections entitled with the names of various prayers, festivals and celebrations. The events are organized according to the Jewish calendar, such as *Shabbas*, Yom Kippur, Purim, and other holidays and rituals which refer to the continuity of Jewish traditions as well as represent an everlasting cycle of life, which will be destroyed in the following century. The destruction is alluded to by the appearance of words and names such as the Łódź ghetto, Buchenwald, and Theresienstadt (*RM*, 181). These recurrent motifs "situated between the two worlds of life and death ... serve to enlarge that space of intersection where magically real fictions exist", to use Faris's words (1995: 178). Indeed, *The River Midnight* becomes a text about the struggle to "juggle fire" between life and death. This dichotomy is constantly present in the story of a poor village where disease, hunger, and weakness frequently bring about death. Also, symbolically it is the story of the Polish Jewish community destroyed in the Holocaust. This time frame is implied sporadically in the story, but even without its explicit introduction one may feel the coming disintegration of this world.

The communal experience of Jews is only one dimension of this "collective relatedness" (Faris 1995: 183), which is developed also through the community of women portrayed in the book and linked to yet another element, that of the separation of women from men in Judaism. This separation is an innate feature of Jewish tradition: women pray in a separate part of the synagogue, bathe in a separate *mikva* and lead quite different lives than their fathers, husbands and brothers. The world of their religious initiation is based on the status they bear, and all the women of a given community are led by a leader, called *zogerin*, "who knows how to pray. When she opens her mouth, the angels above listen" (*RM*, 28). This communal experience of Jewish women is strengthened by their own rituals:

> Before dawn, when the souls of the dead hovered in the graying sky, the women
> gathered in the synagogue courtyard. They carried candles, the white shawls they wore
> over head and shoulders floating in the misty dawn like the souls of their grandmothers.

> The young *zogerin* didn't carry her double case watch or her silver prayer book, and no pearls swung against her flat chest. Unadorned, she led the women into the graveyard between the synagogue and the woods. They circled the cemetery seven times, soundlessly, stopping at Manya's grave. Once a year the women prayed at Manya's grave. During the days of awe, at the moment of judgment, all the women of Blaszka gathered at Manya's grave and prayed that their mothers and granddaughters and great-granddaughters would intercede for them with the Holy Court
>
> (*RM*, 177).

Such communal experiences unite the group of women and emphasize their separation from the world of men, which underlines the whole story and paradoxically shows their power as their own rituals, and their furtive knowledge to which men have no insight. This superiority gives them power over men. Men are seen as those who in the eyes of the world preserve and exercise force, since they can become rabbis, educate themselves, and possess money. But they seem not to have the 'real' or 'magical' power over life and death. The men of the story mostly come to realize this, especially when their comprehension comes after a seminal experience, such as in the case of one of Faygela's childbirths:

> My Faygela swears by Misha's remedies. And I'll tell you … after five girls, I had a son, and it was Misha who pulled him out. The big doctor from Plotsk told me that Faygela was too tired. He was ready to cut her open, but she begged me to get Misha. Could I deny her? I ran as fast as I could, and Misha came back with me. I told her what the doctor said. So what does Misha do? She marches into the house and to the doctor she says, "And your wife, she cuts off a piece of your *shmeckel* when you get too tired? A little man like you, you'd have nothing left. Get out of here before I cut it off myself." I pleaded with her, "Misha, please. The doctor knows." But he was shaking already, and she pushed him out the door. My boy is three years old, strong as a bull … I heard that the same doctor cut open a woman in Plotsk and made a mess of her … She died and the baby, too. … I heard that Misha cursed him, the next day it turned black at the tip, and it just fell off
>
> (*RM*, 190).

This superstitious atmosphere and "local lore," which Faris (1995: 182) lists among the features of magic realist prose, feature throughout the whole text. It is again Faygela who takes up storytelling and writing. Taught at home by her father, Faygela knows Hebrew and German and is aware of many famous texts written in the 19th century, such as by Goethe and Darwin, because of her father's education at a *yeshiva* and the Rabbinical Seminary, and especially due to his belief that "'Knowledge is freedom' … There's nothing I want more than for my daughter to be free" (*RM*, 69-70). Despite her grandmother's protests, Faygela learns to read and write, and her own writing becomes not only an escape from her duties at home, but also her bastion of freedom and power. Misha, the midwife, also has a similar sphere of liberty in the world of her herbs, recipes known and used by her in her healing practices.

Faygela's experiences are also extremely telling. Her education as well as her immersion in her everyday life as a mother and a bakery worker merge and testify to her rich and multi-dimensional character. She has not attained an initiation like Misha's, as a healer, but she is always eager to learn more about the world of magic, and uses every opportunity to come closer to it. She complains to Misha about her frequent encounters with the ghost of her father, who has been dead for eighteen years. Although she tries to convince herself that ghosts do not exist, at the same time she acknowledges: "I see him like that every few months. Each time I tell myself it's just my imagination playing tricks because I miss him ... But I can't help myself" (*RM*, 68). Faygela's intense spiritual life and her sensitivity to the world of ghosts is realized through her writing which also verges on magic realism and fairytale, visible in the following example: "Here in my village, as small as a yawn, angels grow from pearls thrown into the mud. The pearls sprout into strange and beautiful trees, which then turn into angles when you least expect it. This secret was revealed through the great benevolence of our Little Father in Moscow and the justice of his prisons..." (*RM*, 106). Hanna-Leah, on the other hand, often turns to her long-dead ancestor to prophesy about the future, like when she gives support to Faygela after the arrest of her daughter: "My grandmother came to me in a dream, ... Your Ruthie will be safe" (*RM*, 95). Other instances of women being considered witches also appear in the novel (cf. *RM*, 146). This combination of superstitions and rural 19th century reality recedes to the background, but also enriches the atmosphere of the magic realist text.

Another group of similar motifs is to be found in the instances where the community, or at least selected members of it, are shown as believing in the sacred texts and traditional stories, and interpret them literally. This gives way to gossip and speculations based on such literal interpretations. The history of Hayim, Misha's ex-husband proves to be one of these. She divorced him for reasons unknown to the general public. He was a man with a rare talent for drawing portraits, but was crippled by a speech impediment. However, he was said to be protected from any corruption, for "some said that the insatiable demon Lilith had come to Hayim in the night and had left, worn out and satisfied. Even though he was already forty-four, there wasn't a single grey hair in his beard. There you had proof that the demons protected him from the Evil Eye" (*RM*, 159). In another conversation, Hayim listens to Alta-Fruma's serious explanation of the story of the hardened heart of the Pharaoh's: "The water turned into blood. So what? The frogs fell from the sky. What is that? Magic ..." (*RM*, 167). Although this time magic is compared only to a trick, and tricks are real because they do happen in the natural world ("a tadpole becomes a frog" (*RM*, 169), "magic rock" (*RM*, 264)) and are even planned by God; they stem from the real sphere and offer a bit of magic to the people. Angels also appear in the book, furnishing the dark, muddy village of Blaszka with another magical dimension. The orature and storytelling are subverted by a mocking statement, "In heaven the angels will turn to one another and whisper maybe. Maybe" (*RM*, 181), as if questioning the credibility of the presented story. At other moments their existence is recounted as a hard fact: "Oh yes, they said in Blaszka, angels. My brother-in law saw one in the factory in Łodz. It's true. Right before the saw cut off his hand" (*RM*, 213).

One of the most important climactic moments is Misha's labour near the end of the novel, which is accompanied by a series of non-realistic or magic realist phenomena. The Rabbi who is supposed to lead the prayer in the synagogue during Yom Kippur is unable to make any sound, as if he is being punished for his cowardice in refusing to support Misha. Instead of his voice, visions come to him and "he sees in the distance sparks flying toward Blaszka. Is it the Holy Fire or the Angel of Death?" (*RM*, 327). At the same time, Misha experiences visions of "the walls of her house falling away" (*RM*, 390) and "her bed ... riding the sea" (*RM*, 391). Misha's wailing, heard from a distant part of the village square, brings women from the synagogue to help their midwife deliver the child. It seems impossible to hear anything else except for the wind, but "in the synagogue the women and men look at one another, whispering. Did you hear? That moaning. There it is again. It must be Misha. ... Even though what they really hear is just the wind pushing its way into the walls of the old synagogue. But on the eve of Yom Kippur, when the gates of Eternity swing open, even the wind can speak to an open heart" (*RM*, 392). Thus Misha is not left alone, but is attended by her female friends who, by leaving the synagogue during a very important celebration, testify to the unwritten laws of friendship (as opposed to the written laws of Judaism). In such a way, in the denouement of the novel, the solidarity of females becomes an important message in this patriarchal society.

Situated in a rural area, in a relatively distant past, especially if one takes into consideration a metaphoric perception of the era that was irrevocably lost due to 20th-century events, Blaszka in Nattel's novel is a magical place where, on the one hand, harsh reality imposes a simple, uncomfortable life devoid of almost any entertainment, but on the other hand life is permeated by "verbal magic," to use Faris's term (Faris 1995: 176); and where magic has as much right to exist as reality and merges with reality in an unquestionable way. Despite the story taking place in a historical period that is marked clearly by Nattel, ending in the year 5,655 according to the Jewish calendar (AD 1895), the *shtetl* she depicts is mythical through its folk wisdom and religious practices, as well as by virtue of the fact that such villages no longer exist. The *fin de siècle* perspective brings about the appearance of magic, angels and demons. A fear of change makes them justifiable, but simultaneously foreshadows the tragic fate of Jewish communities in the century to come.

References

Baker, Suzanne. 1993. "Binarism and duality: magic realism and postcolonialism". *SPAN Journal of the South Pacific Association for Commonwealth Literature and Language Studies* 39. (http://www.mcc. murdoch. edu.au /ReadingRoom/ litserv/SPAN/36/Baker.html) (date of access: February 22, 2011).

Buchowski, Michał. 1986. *Magia. Jej funkcje i struktura.* [Magic. Its function and structure]. Poznań: Wydawnictwo Naukowe Uniwersytetu im. Adama Mickiewicza.

Delbaere-Garant, Jeanne. 1995. "Psychic realism, mythic realism, grotesque realism: Variations on magic realism in contemporary literature in English", in: Lois Parkinson Zamora – Wendy B. Faris (eds.), 249-263.

D'haen, Theo L. 1995. "Magical realism and postmodernism", in: Lois Parkinson Zamora – Wendy B. Faris (eds.), 191-208.

Eliade, Mircea. 1993. *Sacrum. Mit. Historia.* [Sacrum. Myth. History] (Translated by Anna Tatarkiewicz.) Warszawa: Państwowy Instytut Wydawniczy.

Faris, Wendy B. 1995. "Scheherazade's children: Magical realism and postmodern fiction", in: Lois Parkinson Zamora – Wendy B. Faris (eds.), 163-190.

Guenther, Irene. 1995. "Magic realism and the Weimar Republic", in: Lois Parkinson Zamora – Wendy B. Faris (eds.), 33-73.

Klonowska, Barbara. 2006. *Contaminations. Magic realism in contemporary British fiction.* Lublin: Maria Curie-Skłodowska University Press.

Nattel, Lilian. 1999. *The River Midnight.* New York: Scribner.

Roh, Franz. 1995. "Magic realism: Post-expressionism", in: Lois Parkinson Zamora – Wendy B. Faris (eds.), 15-31.

Rzepa, Agnieszka. 2009. *Feats and defeats of memory: Exploring spaces of Canadian magic realism.* Poznań: Wydawnictwo Naukowe UAM.

Windling, Terri. 2000. "Summation 1999: Fantasy". (http://www.powells.com /biblio? show=TRADE%20PAPER:USED:9780312264161:7.95&page=excerpt#page) (date of access: February 29, 2012).

Zamora, Lois Parkinson – Wendy B. Faris (eds.). 1995. *Magical realism: Theory, history, community.* Durham and London: Duke University Press.

Subversion of rationalism through feminine excess in Susan Swan's *The biggest modern woman of the world* and Angela Carter's *Nights at the circus*

Nelly Strehlau, Nicolaus Copernicus University, Toruń

ABSTRACT

If realism is a genre intertwined with rationalism, then through contesting the former, magic realism can be seen to attempt to dismantle the codes of the latter. The present article discusses two novels by contemporary women writers, the British author Angela Carter's *Nights at the circus* and the Canadian author Susan Swan's *The biggest modern woman of the world*, analyzing the manner in which magic realism is therein used in order to attempt reallocation of knowledge and power to the irrational subjects of the novels, namely: the women protagonists. The essay argues that the novels subvert the binarism of masculine reason and feminine unreason, which prioritizes the former. Although they traditionally associate masculinity with a wide variety of epistemological discourses, exemplified in particular by investigative journalism and medicine combined with ethnography, respectively, and simultaneously aligning femininity with monstrosity, deformity and carnivalesque excess, nevertheless, their use of magic realism allows for the mockery arising from the grotesque mode to be directed at the former, whose claims to the truth are placed under suspicion. Notably, it is the abject female bodies of the protagonists which become the sources of spatial and temporal distortions, enabling the women to escape the oppressive regimes of power which attempt to enclose them.

In its final part the article poses the question whether the attempted subversion of realism achieves its attributed aim, or merely reinforces the binary opposition which situates women outside the discourses of power.

A number of texts have been written addressing in a detailed manner the ways in which magic realism may subvert realist principles, connected to colonialist discourses of science and reason. As Wendy Faris (1995: 165) notes, it is far from accidental that the origins of this genre may be traced to the colonized Latin America, where through "dismantling the imported codes of realism 'proper'" the mode provided an oppositional voice to national literatures. My aim in the present article is to show that such a subversive shift can also be connected to the manner in which magic realist novels selected for discussion portray gender relations. By conducting a comparative analysis of two novels by contemporary women writers, namely the British author Angela Carter's *Nights at the circus* (1984) and the Canadian author Susan Swan's *The biggest modern woman of the world* (1983), I analyze the manner in which magic realism is therein used in order to attempt reallocation of knowledge and power to the subjects arguably attributed with irrationality, that is: the women protagonists. As follows, the novels may be perceived to subvert the binary opposition of masculine reason and feminine unreason, which prioritizes the former.

While defining magic realism as such lies beyond the scope of this essay, it may be useful to preface the following analysis by briefly reflecting upon possible reasons why this mode can be viewed as particularly suitable for the presentation of the subject matter of the two discussed novels. Firstly, the realist element present in the term may well be attributed to the temporal settings of the two novels. Susan Swan's *The biggest modern woman of the world* begins in 1846 and ends in 1887, whereas Angela Carter's *Nights at the circus* has a more limited time span, as the primary action is "firmly grounded in the historical reality of the [late] 1890s" (King 2005: 133), although a number of flashbacks allow further insight into the characters' lives in the previous two or three decades. The second half of the nineteenth century is not only a time of the dominance of the realist novel, but also that of the rising importance of the emergent scientific domain, which contributed to the discourse of female pathology (cf. King 2005: 12-37), as evidenced for instance in medical, biological or anthropological writings. The connection between the construction of these domains as masculine-gendered and the subjection of (Victorian) women constitutes an issue the two novels seem to emphasise, as the following sections of the essay aim to illustrate. Moreover, even though, as Marshall McLuhan argues, the clock had begun to "[drag] man [sic] out of the world of seasonal rhythms" (McLuhan 1994: 155) well before the latter half of the nineteenth century, it was only then that the railways and, in particular, train schedules enforced unification of time across countries, imposing a certain form of universalization of the sensory experience of the world. This standardized temporal engagement with the world, and the related notion of stable and measured passage of time, may be seen to parallel the expected commonsense linearity of the realist mode. The novels in question, particularly Angela Carter's *Nights at the circus*, appear to undermine these notions through the structure of narrative as well as through the unfolding events themselves.

A number of functions may be attributed to the use of magic in order to disturb the principles of realist fiction. This essay connects its use in the two novels predominantly to the cultural positioning of women as irrational subjects (if subjects at all). Luce Irigaray, in her criticism of myth, has argued that women are denied claims to truth in general and access to the practice and discourse of science in particular (Irigaray 2001: 7), which can be seen as connected to the body / mind split reinforced by the aforementioned changes in scientific discourse of the Victorian age. This issue is portrayed as well as conspicuously problematized in both novels. Narrowly, one may translate this into the terms of narrative unreliability of female narrators or protagonists, but more broadly, Angela Carter's and Susan Swan's respective novels appear to undermine the very notions of epistemological, or perhaps even ontological certainties. The world and the subjects both seem to escape easy definitions, deferring the production of meaning. Although, in a Foucauldian vein, the author function is closer to the purposes of this essay than is the authorial authority, it might be at least of interest, if not enlightening, to refer to the writers here. Angela Carter, while famously and depreciatingly describing myths as dangerous "consolatory nonsenses [sic]" (Sellers 2001: 108), in her writing often utilized and emphasised the subversive potential of the corporeal as well as that of fairy tales. Susan Swan, in turn, in the preface to her novel, directly addresses the question of her novel's problematic fictiveness in relation to the fact of Anna Swan's historical existence. Swan states there that she wanted her novel to be "true" rather than factual, and that to this end, "facts [had to] be in the service of the marvellous;" moreover, she describes her effort in the novel as "subversive" towards "a culture that reveres realistic fiction". In the present essay I argue that the magic realist mode, by disrupting the control of laws of natural science over the worlds of the novels, can be seen to destabilize gender hierarchy as well.

Susan Swan's *The biggest modern woman of the world* and Angela Carter's *Nights at the circus*, to which the present essay is devoted, were first published in 1983 and 1984, respectively; however, correspondences between the two are much more profound than merely their contemporaneousness. To begin with, both novels are considered significant on their respective literary scenes: although *The biggest modern woman of the world* constitutes Susan Swan's debut novel, it is nevertheless considered a major work of Canadian postmodernism (e.g. Hutcheon 1990: 28). Angela Carter's literary position, in turn, had been already established at the time of the publication of *Nights at the circus*; the novel, however, is seen by some as the pinnacle of her career (Waters quoted in Patterson 2006), as well as a work ahead of its time (King 2005: 133). Furthermore, apart from the aforementioned locating of the time of action in the latter half of the nineteenth century, the novels are likewise remarkably similar in terms of the subject matter relating to the early modern show business. *The biggest modern woman of the world* is devoted to the Canadian giantess Anna Swan, and constitutes in part a chronicle of her career as an entertainer, employed by the famous historical figure, show business entrepreneur under the name of Phineas Taylor Barnum. *Nights at the circus*, in turn, presents the life of a trapeze artist and circus attraction, a winged woman called Sophie, and known predominantly under the artistic pseudonym 'Fevvers'. Furthermore, the two novels foreground similar themes, notably including (to name only those pertaining to this essay) constricting gender roles, women being assigned mythical/symbolic functions in fiction and by society, as well as the toll related to being thus perceived, narrative unreliability, and the woman, as well as her abject body, as the object of scientific discourse. Finally, both novels, apart from the device of (auto-)biographical writing, utilize a variety of narrative viewpoints.

The analytical part of the present essay commences by elaborating on the connection between the marvellous within the novels and corporeality (and, in particular, femaleness) as the source of the collapse of the realist mode, before proceeding to describe the manner in which the two novels under discussion blend various literary and extra-literary discourses. The essay concludes with a brief reflection on the differences between the ultimate fates of the two protagonists, and what these differences may be attributed to, or perceived to signify.

In her monograph dedicated to magic realism, Maggie Ann Bowers (Bowers 2004: 9), while discussing the origins of the mode, references the connection noticed by "[t]he art historian Irene Guenther," between the inherent paradox of the magic realist mode and the Freudian notion of "*Unheimlichkeit*," or "uncanniness" (Guenther quoted in Bowers 2004: 9). The uncanny that Freud invokes can in turn be traced in his writings to the womb, the home (*heim*) which is both "monstrous and marvellous" (Bowers 2004: 10), familiar and strange. As Rosi Braidotti (1997: 65) argues in her essay "Mothers, monsters, and machines", drawing upon Julia Kristeva's notions of the abject, elaborated upon in her *Powers of horror: An essay on abjection* (1982), this uncanniness is particularly frequently connected with the repulsion which the female (reproductive) body is supposed to evoke. At this point it might be useful to recall the linguistic connection between the concept of monstrosity and demonstration, meaning showing. The monstrous nature of womanhood, as perceived by patriarchal cultures, of which the two novels are undoubtedly depictions, is located in its corporeal aspect. Whether it is to be signified directly by the Freudian wound, or more generally, by the female body's openness, "borderlessness" and, therefore, vulnerability, the notion of femininity, as Katarzyna Więckowska (2008: 93) puts it in her analysis of Carter's novel, serves to "reaffirm the solidity of the masculine standardized body". This can be conflated with the function of the monster, that is, to signify the border of what is human. Thus, despite the fact that pages of the novels are populated by so-called 'freaks' also of masculine or, in some cases, non-binary gender, woman may be seen to "represent transgression" in herself (Więckowska 2008: 93). Significantly, the magic realism in the novels is usually directly related to the body, often precisely in its gendered aspect, as the following section aims to illustrate.

In *The biggest modern woman of the world*,[1] the events which most directly disturb the presupposed realism of a first-person autobiographical account are related to instances of corporeality asserting itself strongly in the narrative. This occurs, for instance, at the occasion of the protagonist's birth, which, as Marlene Goldman (1997: 90) notes, coincides with an unusual crop. What is more, the subsequent instances of what Goldman (1997: 89) describes as the form of magic realism referred to as "grotesque realism" are directly associated with Anna's puberty. Susan Swan describes its effects as "convert[ing Anna's] physique into a turbulent mass" (*BW*, 27) with "[t]empests rag[ing] above and below [her] chin," as well as "[her] central regions leak[ing] unwanted milk" and, in particular, her menstrual flow "evok[ing] a weatherless condition which caused [her] to sleep for several days" (*BW*, 27). Furthermore, with her growth spurt, Anna's belief in her own magical nature and responsibility for (or at least ability to cause) growth in

---

1   Henceforth indicated as *BW* followed by page number. All quotations are from Swan, Susan. 2001 [1983]. *The biggest modern woman of the world*. Toronto: L&OD.

others (*BW*, 27) is reinforced. While the events themselves might not require full suspension of disbelief and may be partly explained as exaggeration on the part of the young protagonist from whose point of view they are described, they are nevertheless presented in excessive metaphorical terms, suggesting perhaps that the language of realism constitutes an insufficient tool to convey a subjective truth of the corporeal experience.

What is more, Anna is not the only character whose experience of the body is described in such terms: others likewise use excessive language in reference to (her) corporeality. For instance, in a later part of the novel, the sexual intercourse in which Anna engages with Ingalls is, as the narrative provided from his point of view suggests, perceived by him in terms of geology: he describes the encounter as being "sucked into a volcano ... about to go off" (*BW*, 220).

Another instance of the marvellous as connected with physical bodies, particularly in their abject aspect, occurs in the scene where Anna describes her own tears and urine, as well as those of her fellow (women) entertainers (*BW*, 144-146). According to her description, these 'waters' flood the burnt-down New American Museum to the point of people being able to swim in them; in fact, Anna regrets not having wept earlier, during the actual fire, since that "woman-made sea" of bodily fluids "could have quenched" the fire which had occurred (*BW*, 145). Finally, although the description of Anna's supposed hallucination of shrinking New York may not directly connect the magical element with the physiological aspect, Anna affects the change through her body, namely, by singing, which action she then follows with throwing the miniature city into the sea with her hands. This metafictional device of metaphor made literal emphasises the contrast between the literary and the corporeal, as well as the instability of the boundary between the two.

In turn, the oeuvre of Angela Carter is perhaps most frequently described as drawing upon the Gothic tradition. However, she is also often counted among major British writers of magic realism, in its feminist, "transgressive and subversive" form (Bowers 2004: 63), influenced by the Bakhtinian notions of heteroglossia and the "carnivalesque" (King 2005: 133). All these descriptors appear most appropriate when discussing *Nights at the circus*.

A list including all of the numerous instances of fantastical corporeal events of *Nights at the circus*[2] would likely be impossible to provide due to space constraints; however, it deserves to be mentioned that the primary sources of the marvellous in the novel are the monstrous bodies of secondary characters as well as that of the protagonist. Fevvers, whose profession is usually given as that of an "*aerialiste*" (*NC*, 7), is a winged woman (perhaps half-swan) capable of flight,

---

2   Henceforth indicated as *NC* followed by page number. All quotations are from Carter, Angela. 1993 [1984]. *Nights at the circus*. New York-Toronto-London-Camberwell, Victoria-New Delhi-Auckland-Johannesburg: Penguin Books.

whose very existence defies common sense as well as the principles of science. Moreover, throughout her career she has encountered a number of other, similarly fantastically embodied characters, including, to name but a few, Fanny, a woman with a second pair of eyes in place of nipples, Touissant, a mouthless man employed as a servant, or a miniature, Thumbellina-like woman called the Wiltshire Wonder. Although their improbable bodies may be seen to serve as embodiments of metaphors and theoretical notions, this metafictional device which could relegate them to the status of allegories is parodied through the employment of almost naturalistic language to describe their place of employment, which is a peculiar brothel, catering to the more unusual desires of the wealthiest. This contrast in *Nights at the circus* could perhaps be interpreted as somewhat contrary to that of *The biggest modern woman of the world*: whereas in the latter realism is disturbed by the excessive grotesque of corporeality, in the former, while the framing narrative of a journalistic account is essentially realist, within the story of Fevvers' life it is the excessive naturalism that creates a fissure in the fantastical world. Fevvers herself describes her body as "the abode of limitless freedom" (*NC*, 41), due to her wings, which liberate her from the constraints of gravity. However, equally important seems to be the domain of what Jeannette King describes as, "Fevvers' gross physicality which is an affront to the ideal of femininity as delicate, ethereal and spiritual" (*NC*, 133). This excessive corporeality prevents the efforts to contain Fevvers as an embodiment of any notion, situates her on the fringes of society and makes her an unsolved contradiction of a successful artist, an attractive woman, an object of desire, and at the same time the abject inducing revulsion.

Although prostitution constitutes an important theme in *Nights at the circus*, and while repression of sexuality can be seen to constitute a major theme in novels set in the Victorian era, it seems significant that sexuality is not primarily a tool of patriarchal oppression in either novel: contrarily, desire is portrayed as a disruptive, subversive force. Even though both Fevvers and Anna Swan face the dangers of reification due to men treating them as (often simultaneously) sexual and scientific objects, their own desire serves as a counterforce to the efforts to reduce them to the status of stable signifiers of lack, reinforcing masculinity. This process is made explicit in *The biggest modern woman of the world* and can be described using the term coined by the protagonist's lover and fellow Canadian giant, Angus McAskill, namely, "emblem fatigue" (*BW*, 139). He uses this notion in order to refer to the burden of constituting (and being construed as) a symbol for others (*BW*, 139), a process he ascribes to giants, but which may be understood more widely, in reference to any Othered individual. Similarly, in *Nights at the circus* the protagonist at one point experiences mortal danger upon "feeling herself turning, willy-nilly, from a woman into an idea" (*NC*, 289). However, the two women can find freedom from being reduced to the stability of signification precisely through the aforementioned excessive nature of their bodily desires: they cannot be contained by oppressive gaze, even though, as Carter puts it, "to look is to coerce" (*NC*, 222). Fevvers, despite her wings, is neither Azrael, angel of death, as one of the characters would have it (*NC*, 70), nor an angel in the house. She hungers for (primarily common) food (*NC*, 51), experiences sexual desire for Walser (*NC*, 282) and, despite her Marxist upbringing, exhibits considerable greed for financial gain: in fact, according to her business partner and foster mother, the radical Marxist Lizzie, "[t]hink[ing] of [her] bank account … always cheers [her] up" (*NC*, 200). Anna likewise possesses "a healthy sexual appetite" (Goldman 1997: 76), as well as requires significant amounts of food to sustain herself, especially while she is "still growing" (*BW*, 27). In fact, upon moving to New York, she participates in an eating contest with her colleagues, and it is only the corset, representing societal expectations placed on women, that prevents her from unconstrained consumption and from eventual success in the competition (*BW*, 76-77). Even while proving her supposed failure in living up to the ideal of Victorian womanhood, her participation in the contest constitutes a space of freedom from being an idealized and therefore reified embodiment whether of Canadianness, femininity or object of science. If, as Teresa Heffernan (1992: 30) asserts, "[t]he silencing and control of female identity is analogous to the repression of the female body in the Victorian aesthetic of the demure, petite, asexual maiden," then Anna's body, uncontrollable for others—but at times, for instance during her puberty, even for herself—constitutes a protest against identity policing.

The second analytical section of the present essay is devoted to the presentation of the discourses to which the subjective account of the world enabled by grotesque realism of excessive corporeality as well as by magic realism is presented as a counterpoint in the novels. The present section constitutes an analysis of the conflicting elements, aiming to tentatively resolve the question whether the discourses activated by the female characters in their struggle against containment seem to be successful or ultimately fail in establishing a degree of freedom and empowerment for the characters.

Although the variety of discourses and voices is arguably more pronounced in Angela Carter's novel, *The biggest modern woman of the world*, despite being focused on a single character and seldom deviating to introduce stories devoted to secondary characters, utilizes a notably wide range of textual forms. As Ewa Bodal (2010: 115-117) notes, the protagonist herself speaks in more than one voice, taking on stage personas and fictionalizing the account of her life to suit her own purposes, or simply stylizing her diary to resemble various kinds of texts. Marlene Goldman argues, in turn, that the novel can be seen to invoke both a number of literary and near-literary discourses, from "mock-travel narratives", *künstlerroman*, epistolary novel and autobiography, to "pamphlets" and "spiels" connected to "freak-show perform[ances]" of the nineteenth century (Goldman 1997: 63). Perhaps more importantly, however, the novel is likewise abundant in episodes relating to the emergent scientific discourse which position Anna as the object of study. Significantly, this scientific discourse is largely related to Anna's reproductive function, emphasising the gendered character of the inquiry into her body. Within the narrative Anna undergoes physical examination twice. The first one, performed by the dwarf Hubert Belcourt, consists in part in her vagina being measured with an inserted icicle. The episode culminates in Anna's hymen being ruptured, which in turn "puncture[s her] belief in [her]self as a magic being." As a result, Anna realises that "[she is] human and vulnerable--*a female*" (*BW*, 35; emphasis mine, NS), and the violation, which is both sexual and scientific in nature, leaves her deeply troubled, as well as newly self-conscious of her gender identity, to which this event has interpellated her.

The second exploration into her body (*BW*, 172) is performed in order to establish whether she is capable of bearing children, and occurs before her marriage to Martin Bates, a fellow giant, who wants her to be "his mate" as well as to "share [his] scientific objectives" (*BW*, 174), consisting in them bringing forth "the great *Americanus* species" (*BW*, 173)—a race of giants, in whose natural superiority he believes. Both the examination, described (in part) from Bates's point of view, and the poem Anna receives from him contain comparisons drawn by Bates between Anna's body and a land rich in resources, underscoring the connection between gendered scientific and colonial discourses as similarly preoccupied with exploration and exploitation.

The scientific discourse is also present in the very form of teratology, that is the study of monstrosity. Although this subject may appear less central in contemporary science, at the time of the narrative there existed an exceedingly close relationship between the show business aspect of teratology and the development of natural science. As Goldman argues, this is evident for instance "in the use of the word 'museum' in the title of many freak shows, including P. T. Barnum's" (Goldman 1997: 77).

Goldman offers folk discourse of Anna's Scottish ancestry as an antidote to the constraining discourse of Victorian femininity, claiming that "Anna can resist the pressure to conform to Victorian notions of what it means to be a Woman because she can tap into a specific unofficial discourse" within which she "remains acceptable" to herself (Goldman 1997: 89); however, it can be argued that at least part of her belief in this "Celtic folk tradition" is lost to her following the icicle incident described earlier in the essay. Furthermore, while Goldman adds that Anna at times successfully appropriates the discourses used by others to subjugate her, for instance, the spiel of a sideshow announcer (Goldman 1997: 67), the empowerment of performance is put in doubt considering the fact that Anna's femininity or even her life itself constitute a performance in which she is always expected to engage (*BW*, 332). As follows from this, it can be argued that performativity, while providing opportunities for subversion, can also be experienced as oppressive. In fact, the protagonist faces the oppressiveness of performance as part of her professional life—she is not allowed to incorporate her own work, "Giant Etiquette," into her act (*BW*, 109-11), but is expected to take part in a staging of *Macbeth* (*BW*, 102) against her preferences. Furthermore, even though Anna can fictionalize her account of her life to gain a degree of control over her experience thereof, for instance when she modulates her speech perhaps in order to cope with the loss of her first child (*BW*, 239-240), fictionalization is also something she undergoes as a result of others' actions, to her own detriment—for instance in the case of her marriage to Bates, which is essentially a marketing strategy for her employer, but which causes her misery (*BW*, 168, 203). Furthermore, the grotesque or magical elements which granted her a degree of freedom from being imprisoned in signification ultimately prove insufficient in the face of social stigmatization and personal tragedy. Estranged from family, with the exception of her husband, whose behaviour is often a source of suffering to Anna, as well as bereaved of her lover and child, the protagonist dies, writing that "[she] was born to be measured" and that she failed to "fit" in the world (*BW*, 332).

Angela Carter's *Nights at the circus*, in turn, as it has already been mentioned, is conspicuously influenced by the Bakhtinian notions of heteroglossia and the carnivalesque, and has in fact been considered a "critique of carnival's masculinist values" (King 2005: 133). Therefore, it is far from surprising that the novel likewise contains a wide variety of discourses and narrative voices. Moving from the first to the third-person narrative and from one character's story to another, *Nights at the circus* proves extremely difficult to delineate; therefore, the following analysis must necessarily be but partial.

The unexplainable existence of the protagonist, Fevvers, as well as her life story are from the initial pages contrasted with the notions of verifiability and realism, since her Scheherazade-like autobiographical account is given to a journalist whose aim is to establish the answer to the question she herself poses in advertisements dedicated to her act, namely: "is she fact or is she fiction?" (*NC*, 7). Jack Walser, the journalist who has been tasked with conducting an interview with the woman he considers to be a "[h]umbug" (*NC*, 11) as well as his "quarry" (*NC*, 9), represents the New World scepticism in face of Fevvers' show-business fibbing. His masculine journalistic rationalism and professional search for epistemological certainty is contrasted with Fevvers' feminine oral storytelling, which disturbs his sense of time (*NC*, 42), as well as with her profession, which depends on evoking and maintaining ontological uncertainty in her audience. Her claims about her supernatural origins as well as her unusual biography are deemed exaggerated by Walser; however, he finds himself unable, or perhaps unwilling, to ascertain the truth before the end of the tale. Like in the case of the original Scheherazade, he is seduced into becoming a character in the story, even though the shift requires that he forego his own supposedly stable masculine identity to join the carnivalesque institution of the circus, becoming a figure of mockery, namely, a masked clown (*NC*, 90-91).

However, other discourses apart from that of masculine journalism are also invoked as elements of a number of attempts to imprison or exploit the protagonist. Among the most prominent there can be listed those of sexual economy, social class and science, albeit through way of alchemy. As pertains to the discourse of commodified sexuality, Fevvers is not only raised by a group of prostitutes, but also on a number of occasions invited to extend sexual favours in return for material gain (e.g., *NC*, 71). However, while prostitution itself appears not to be inherently oppressive in the novel, or at least, not any more than other social institutions such as marriage, Fevvers is at times sold and bought without her consent as well as imprisoned by those who wish to possess her. This danger is most explicit in two similar episodes of her encounters with aristocracy. The first of them occurs when Fevvers is sold by Madam Schreck, her employer in the curiosities show / house of prostitution, to an alchemist and secret society member Christian Rosencreutz, who believes that if he were to sacrifice Fevvers, he would be granted eternal life (*NC*, 82-83). Alchemy, as the spiritually-influenced precursor of natural science, is shown here to be based on the reification of women, situated as its objects of study, whose ultimate sacrifice will grant the alchemist his desires. Furthermore, not unlike in the case of Anna Swan's measuring incident, sexuality and science are inseparably linked, since the woman is construed as an object of intellectual as well as sexual desire, and the alchemical ritual in which Fevvers is to be sacrificed is in fact based on misogynistic phallic ceremony. Her death is to protect Rosencreutz from death, symbolized by "the female part, or absence, or the atrocious hole, or dreadful chasm, the Abyss" (*NC*, 77), according to a belief that literalizes the aforementioned connection seen in the (psychoanalytic) discourse of Western culture by Rosi Braidotti (after Julia Kristeva and Mary Douglas) between female body and mortality, due to the fact that the "maternal body [constitutes] the site of the origin of life and consequently also of insertion into mortality and death" (Braidotti 1997: 65). In what Więckowska describes as "eroticised epistemology" (2008: 103), the sexual and the scientific acts are united through their violent outcome, as the woman, who "exists for the men only as the veil behind which knowledge resides" cannot survive the inquiry (Więckowska 2008: 103-104): only in death is she a stable signifier.

The second episode of sexual trade occurs in Russia and invokes in an even more direct manner the notion of class struggle. The event in question involves Fevvers entertaining a Duke, who, rather than merely planning to have intercourse with her, as their unwritten contract would imply, aims also to shrink and, subsequently, imprison her in a small egg (*NC*, 192). The danger of objectification and belittlement is made literal here; however, Fevvers manages to escape due to a fissure in reality caused by the corporeal. Having brought the Grand Duke to climax with her hand, she uses his temporary weakness to escape when a toy train turns into the real, life-sized Trans-Siberian Express (*NC*, 192-193).

As has already been demonstrated, unlike Anna, for whom folk discourse proved insufficient for ultimate liberation, Fevvers appears to be largely successful in using to her advantage her unruly femininity, active sexuality and her status as a 'freak,' a combination situating her firmly outside societal norm. Nevertheless, it may be argued that her power seems at times to be dependent on the approving gaze of her audience, to the extent that, once she is deprived of the attention of the public, Fevvers breaks one of her wings, at least temporarily losing the ability to fly (*NC*, 206). Moreover, the masquerade of femininity fails her when she is estranged from the city culture: the loss of hair dye affects not only her colouring, but even her overall posture seems to diminish (*NC*, 280). Nevertheless, the novel ends on a hopeful note. With Lizzie's help, as well as due to finding a new audience and regaining her faith in herself, Fevvers survives the final struggle against the Shaman who, much like Rosencreutz and the Grand Duke, would like to reduce her to a mythic figure (*NC*, 289). She is then reunited with the rescued Walser in a parodist gender reversal of a fairy tale narrative, wherein "the trapeze artiste ... rescues the clown" (*NC*, 281); however, no marriage is planned. What is more, also unlike Anna, Fevvers seemingly rejects the traditional social structure instead of seeking conditional inclusion within its framework: she gives no indication of any intention of starting a family with Walser, instead aiming to mould him to be her lover and "amanuensis" (*NC*, 285), performing the labour of writing her story. This desire of hers to transform her lover into "the New Man" (*NC*, 281) could perhaps be compared to Bates aiming to start a new human race descending from giants;[3] however, while the fate of Fevvers' utopian subversive project remains unrevealed, and Walser eventually appears to become her willing accomplice, Bates' failed scheme to raise giant progeny disregards Anna's own desires and wishes as well as reduces her own role to her function as a prospective mother.

By the end of the novel, some of Walser's questions concerning the factual status of Fevvers find answers, while others remain shrouded in mystery. Fevvers' parentage, for instance, is never explained, leaving unspecified – and therefore, freed of stable meaning – the origins of her abnormality. Whether she was, in fact, "hatched" from an egg is neither confirmed, nor disproven. At the same time, however, the very quest for verification is ultimately ridiculed. The final surprise that Jack Walser experiences is at his discovery of Fevvers' lack of virginity in which he was made to believe. This success of a confidence trick may be attributed to it being based on the man's ultimate willingness to be deceived: while Walser remained doubtful regarding Fevvers' wings and flight, he believed her assertion of being "the only fully-feathered intacta in the history of the world" (*NC*, 294). In this final reveal, the quest for uncovering the mystery of the

---

3   I would like to extend my gratitude to Professor Agnieszka Rzepa for bringing this issue to my attention.

woman's body in the name of knowledge is shown to be reducible to patriarchal interests, which Fevvers managed to incorporate into her (successful) marketing strategy: as she informs Walser, "[he] mustn't believe what [is written] in the papers" (NC, 294).

As I have aimed to demonstrate in this section of the essay, both Nights at the circus and The biggest modern woman of the world mobilize a wide variety of discourses, some of which operate as oppressive, and some as empowering for the female protagonists. Notably, within both texts the discourses of science, journalism and (biographical) realism, as well as the discourse of Victorian femininity, take on an oppressive role, aiming towards the containment of the woman protagonist through supposedly impartial practices such as measuring and examination, which are in the novels revealed to be distinctly gendered and sexualized.

The present essay constitutes an attempt to showcase the connection drawn within the novels between the mode of realism and oppressive discursive practices. Within both texts the gendered, excessive body can be seen to constitute a primary locus of subversion, which is underscored by the Rabelaisian descriptions of the physical and physiological aspects of the abject feminine body, which draw upon the mode of magic realism, particularly in its grotesque form. What remains to be investigated further is the question whether by presenting the excessive femininity of the protagonists the novels posit corporeal femininity itself as transgressive. The analysis has tentatively suggested that the protagonists are situated outside the norm not only because of their difference in regard to size and shape, but also due to their gender characteristics, since the attempts to subdue difference are typically gendered and sexualized, allowing for the interpretation that the difference they are ultimately seeking to discipline is that of fearsome femininity.

What is more, both of the novels problematize the efforts to stabilize the female body as a signifier, demonstrating that such an attempt can be constraining. Due to the usage of the mode of magic realism rooted in the marvellous, uncontrolled and uncontrollable body, irrational corporeality may seem to be portrayed as possessing a degree of superiority over the parodied range of discourses aiming to discipline the body into an intelligible social construct, including not only the discourses of gender roles or natural science, but also, to an extent, literary discourses, the coherence of which seems dependent on assigning the gendered body a stable signification.

Nevertheless, the two novels can be seen to differ in their ultimate outlook regarding the subversive potential of unruly femininity enabled and prioritized by magic realism which disproves the superiority of reason. While Fevvers manages to achieve freedom from signification through sexuality and femininity, the same is not true for Anna Swan, who not only loses her family and lover, but eventually dies feeling unable to adjust to the world surrounding her. One reason for the difference in the fates of the protagonists appears to be related to their respective social surroundings. Anna cannot fit in within the community of a small Ohio town (*BW*, 273) despite her temporal bonding with the local women over the common issue of (excessive) menstruation (*BW*, 272) and she does not manage to regain her erstwhile fame, whereas Fevvers retains close relations with her adoptive parent, Lizzie, and manages to regain her audience's approval due to her self-confidence. While Anna expresses the idea that she "do[es] not fit in" (*BW*, 339), Fevvers wants to change her mate "into ...[a] fitting mate for the New Woman" that she herself is (*NC*, 281), together with whom she will "give the world a little turn into the new era" of the upcoming twentieth century. Thus, although Fevvers' optimism may well be perceived as naïve from the twenty-first century reader's perspective, the same should not perhaps be stated about the subversive potential of desire which she proclaims (to which, however, she cannot be reduced).

References

Bodal, Ewa. 2010. "The metaphorical feminisation of Canada in selected novels by contemporary Canadian women writers". Unpublished MA thesis. Poznań: Adam Mickiewicz University, 2010.

Bowers, Maggie Ann. 2004. *Magic(al) realism*. Abingdon, Oxon-New York: Routledge.

Braidotti, Rosi. 1997. "Mothers, monsters, and machines", in: Katie Conboy – Nadia Medina – Sarah Stanbury (eds.), 59-79.

Carter, Angela. 1993 [1984]. *Nights at the circus*. New York: Penguin Books.

Conboy, Katie – Nadia Medina – Sarah Stanbury (eds.). 1997. *Writing on the body: Female embodiment and feminist theory*. New York – Chichester, Columbia University Press.

Davidson, Arnold E. (ed.). 1990. *Studies on Canadian literature: Introductory and critical essays*. New York: MLA of America.

Faris, Wendy B. 1995. "Scheherezade's children: Magical realism and postmodern fiction", in: Lois Parkinson Zamora – Wendy B. Faris (eds.), 165-190.

Goldman, Marlene. 1997. *Paths of desire: Images of exploration and mapping in Canadian women's writing*. Toronto: University of Toronto Press, 1997.

Heffernan, Teresa. 1992. "Tracing the travesty: Constructing the female subject in Susan Swan's *The biggest modern woman of the world*", *Canadian Literature*, 133: 24-37.

Hutcheon, Linda. 1990. "The Canadian postmodern: Fiction in English since 1960", in: Arnold E. Davidson (ed.), 18-33.

Irigaray, Luce. 2001. *Ciało-w-ciało z matką* [Le corps-a-corps avec la mere]. (Translated by Agata Araszkiewicz.) Kraków: Wydawnictwo „eFKa".

King, Jeannette. 2005. *The Victorian woman question in contemporary feminist fiction.* Houndmills, Basingstoke – New York: Palgrave Macmillan.

McLuhan, Marshall. 1994. *Understanding media: The extensions of man.* Cambridge, Massachussetts-London: MIT Press.

Patterson, Christina. 2006. "Angela Carter: Beauty and the beasts." *The Independent* January 2006. (http://www.independent.co.uk/arts-entertainment/books/ features/ angela-carter-beauty-and-the-beasts-523499.html) (date of access: July 10, 2011).

Sellers, Susan. 2001. *Myth and fairy tale in contemporary women's fiction.* Houndmills, Basingstoke – New York: Palgrave Macmillan.

Swan, Susan. 2001 [1983]. *The biggest modern woman of the world.* Toronto: L&OD.

Więckowska, Katarzyna. 2008. *On alterity: A study of monstrosity and otherness.* Toruń: Wydawnictwo Naukowe Uniwersytetu Mikołaja Kopernika.

Zamora, Lois Parkinson – Wendy B. Faris (eds.). 1995. *Magical realism: Theory, history, community.* Durham, NC: Duke University Press.

Pain overflowing boundaries: Magic realism and US theatre

Jacob Juntunen, Ohio University, Athens, OH

ABSTRACT

By tracing the development of "serious drama" in the United States, this paper argues that US. playwrights from marginal subject positions in the late-twentieth century deployed magic realism's subversive hybridity and self-reflection, its exploration of memory for the recovery of repressed texts, and its ability to revise the concept of nation to challenge the dominant ideology conveyed by realism onstage. While early twentieth-century playwrights in the U.S., such as Susan Glaspell and Eugene O'Neill, wrote strict realism in their early plays, later authors, such as Clifford Odets, Arthur Miller, Tennessee Williams, and Edward Albee combined various forms of drama into hybrid plays. Since magic realism is centered on hybridity, these authors created crucial steps towards the magic realist plays that emerged in the US in the 1990s and 2000s. Each of the magic realist plays examined—*Angels in America*, *The piano lesson*, and *How I learned to drive*—challenges nation, ideology, and memory. They all employ the visual, aural, and formal aspects of the stage to disrupt the empirical universe. Magic realism, though created by playwrights in marginal subject positions, holds a powerful place in US mainstream theatre, and US playwrights use the mode to create concrete representations of emergent ideologies when realism is insufficient.

In 1915, US drama took a remarkable turn when a group of bitter intellectuals built a stage utilizing a run-down wharf in a small fishing village outside of Boston. Two writers in particular began experimenting with realism, for them an avant-garde European form. Those writers, Susan Glaspell and Eugene O'Neill, along with the rest of the Provincetown Players, eventually turned the tide of US theatre from minstrel shows and melodrama towards realism and expressionism. This native drama took root, though, not as an imitation of European schools or as a set of artistic dogma but instead as a pragmatic use of the tools at hand to create political statements about US culture. This formal pragmatism became and remains the norm for US playwrights; rather than utilizing a style as a vessel in which to hold a play's content, playwrights use conflicting methods from different styles as tools to create a hybrid whole. Thus, magic realism is but one tool used by US playwrights at the end of the twentieth century. A concise method of demonstrating the lineage and function of magic realism in US drama is to trace a brief genealogy between the Provincetown Players and current US playwrights, particularly noting the connection between realism and journalism, and then to elucidate the use of magic realism in three Pulitzer Prize-winning plays and their use of more abstract, "painterly" techniques. In the late-twentieth century playwrights from marginal subject positions deployed magic realism's subversive hybridity and self-reflection, its exploration of memory for the recovery of repressed texts, and its ability to revise the concept of nation to challenge the dominant ideology conveyed by realism onstage.

It is sometimes difficult for European audiences to understand the extent to which US drama may be based on strict adherence to realism. Take, for instance, the recent play *Memory house* which was produced across the US between 2005 and 2010. In it, a real pie is baked onstage from its basic ingredients; the script demands it, and the symbolism hinges on it. Why this dramatic need for ovens that bake and sinks that spurt water on the US stage? It is in part because early twentieth-century playwrights in the US, such as those in the Provincetown Players, were journalists, not trained theatre professionals or visual artists. They wanted to document life onstage, generally for activist purposes. While some late-twentieth century US playwrights continue in the realist tradition, others, particularly from marginal positions, began to utilize the visual elements of the stage. When they did so, it stands to reason that magic realism was invoked. After all, as Agnieszka Rzepa reminds us, "magic realism's roots [are] in visual arts criticism," and the US playwrights utilizing magic realist techniques create visuals which "disrupt the European, post-Enlightenment, empirical universe" (Rzepa 2009: 12). But before US playwrights could fully take advantage of magic realism on stage, the Provincetown Players needed to wrench US theatre away from the formulaic melodramas of the nineteenth century and introduce realism to the American stage.

The shift towards serious drama in the US had many facets, of course, but one could do worse than looking towards the Provincetown Players as the theatre company that set the change in motion. This group began in 1915 as a clique of New York City intellectuals, mainly journalists and labor activists, who were frustrated with politics and, particularly, their inability to change labor laws or keep the US from entering World War I. So these people rented beach cabins that summer in the fishing village of Provincetown and started making theatre to amuse themselves. Its major players included journalists Susan Glaspell, Hutchins Hapgood, Mary Heaton Vorse, John Reed, and Louise Bryant. Susan Glaspell's husband, George Cook, stirred up interest in the group in the fall and winter, and in summer of 1916 more people came to Provincetown to take part in theatre, including Eugene O'Neill. After rejecting several of his initial plays, Glaspell set up an opportunity for O'Neill to read his play *Bound east for Cardiff* to the group. It was after that reading that, as she put it, they then "knew what they were for" (*Road to Temple*, 254). The group became O'Neill's champion and also propelled Glaspell's work into the popular mainstream.

That 1916 season included O'Neill's play along with Glaspell's most famous work, *Trifles*, a feminist play based on a murder case she covered as a journalist in the Midwest. *Bound east for Cardiff* is a play set at sea about a dying sailor inspired by O'Neill's own time at sea. These two most successful plays in the early Provincetown Players repertoire are famous for their strict adherence to realism: they each unfold in real time; they are both set in one location; and the original Provincetown productions strove to create the most realistic sets possible, including opening a door in the wharf so audiences could view the ocean at night during O'Neill's sea play. This became the norm for "serious" US drama.

Examples of this desire for extreme realism extend especially into the agit prop theatre in the 1930s, particularly in the work of the Group Theatre. The Group Theatre is the dominant ensemble in the generation immediately following the Provincetown Players, and it is impossible to understand the US theatre that follows—both realism and magic realism—without first understanding the centrality of the Group Theatre. In fact, its most famous director, Elia Kazan, co-created much of the most highly regarded art in both the theatre and cinema over the next twenty years. Kazan worked not only with the Group, but, later, with both the playwrights Arthur Miller and Tennessee Williams, and he "discovered" actor Marlon Brando and directed him in the canonical film *On the waterfront*. With movies like *On the waterfront* and *A tree grows in Brooklyn*, Kazan created a gritty, realist style of drama that spoke to the desire of the poor to climb the social strata. However, it was not the same type of "journalistic" drama that the Provincetown Players created.

The Group Theatre was comprised of theatre professionals, not journalists, and early in the economic depression of the US they wanted to create a new form of theatre to address social concerns and to change them. To do so they also mainly relied on realism, but they turned to Russia for their models, both Stanislavski's directing and acting theories and the USS.R.'s agit prop theatre techniques. From their particular reading of Stanislavski, the Group was based on the idea of ensemble acting. Instead of stars, the focus was on a believable whole. With a permanent "group" of actors, the theory went, they would become more familiar with each other both on and off the stage, thus their onstage relations would be more "real." They took from Soviet agit prop techniques the idea of using cinematic techniques to create theatre that would appeal to the masses.

Perhaps their most remembered play, 1935's *Waiting for Lefty* by Clifford Odets, put the audience in the middle of a union meeting of taxi drivers. While Odets was no journalist, he took inspiration from real events of New York City's 1934 taxi strike. He also broke the strict rules of realism that *Trifles* and *Bound east for Cardiff* established in US drama. While portions of his play were extremely realistic portrayals of a union meeting debating whether to strike, there were also a series of vignettes portraying the private lives of the various taxi drivers who spoke about pros and cons of the strike. This hybrid drama, utilizing cinematic techniques of flashback and montage, was so effective that, legend has it, the opening night audience left the auditorium and marched into the street chanting, "Strike! Strike! Strike!" along with the actors. This is an early example of a US playwright experimenting with hybridity of form, a first step towards magic realism. Because hybridity is a fundamental feature of magic realism (Rzepa 2009: 11), this was a crucial step towards its creation onstage.

Though Glaspell and O'Neill would eventually write plays in both the realist and expressionist traditions, they never combined the two. While *Waiting for*

Lefty was not technically realism since it moved from location to location and utilized flashbacks, each vignette in itself was realism. The post-WWII generation immediately following the Group Theatre, embodied by Tennessee Williams and Arthur Miller—both of whom would collaborate with the Group's director Kazan and many of its actors—utilized realism and expressionism simultaneously in their early successes, such as *The glass menagerie* and *Death of a salesman*.

The early hybridity of Miller and Williams was often concerned with memory and focused on making the protagonist's internal state apparent onstage, but no magical elements disrupted the realism of universe. For instance, while Williams' stage directions in *The glass menagerie* call for screen projections, off-stage music, and other devices that would disrupt the realism and make this memory play more abstract, they were dropped in the 1944 Chicago and New York premieres. Never one to argue with success, Williams did not insist on reincorporating his original ideas in future productions. So, while the play begins with Tom, its protagonist, addressing the audience from the future after he's abandoned his mother and sister (Williams 2001: 1068), the play's soliloquies and scenes as performed in the 1940s remained rooted in realism. If the character Tom could inhabit two chronological moments simultaneously and speak directly to the audience, it was not seen as magical; in fact, it may have felt retrogressive since the narrator and soliloquy were both tried and true devices of US nineteenth-century melodramas.

Miller's 1949 memory play, *Death of a salesman*, premiered in New York under the direction of Kazan. The set design for the premiere of *Death of a salesman* was expressionistic in order to accommodate Miller's stage directions suggesting "whenever the action is in the present the actors observe the imaginary wall-lines, entering the house only through its door at the left. But in the scenes of the past these boundaries are broken, and characters enter or leave a room by stepping 'through' a wall" (Miller 2001: 1164), but the action, again, was based in realism. The scenes in the "present" were depicted with utmost care and utilized the Group Theatre's method of acting that strove for as much emotional verisimilitude as possible. The scenes in the "past" were on-stage representations of the protagonist's memories, and, hence, were not magical. Instead these scenes had, like memories, the ability to penetrate and affect the present, to shift, to arrive unbidden, and to contradict themselves. Thus, like Williams' *The glass menagerie*, Miller's *Death of a salesman* was a hybrid of realism and expressionism, but the playwrights used these techniques to depict the interior lives of their protagonists, not to deploy a hybridity "that disrupts the post-Enlightenment, empirically-based Western concept of what constitutes reality" (Rzepa 2009: 12). The use of hybrid theatre modes on the US stage, however, continued and would eventually lead to magic realism.

In the 1960s and 70s Edward Albee combined realism and absurdism in plays such as *A delicate balance*, creating a new form of experiment on the US stage and taking another step closer to magic realism. In Albee's 1966 drama directed originally by Alan Schneider, the director of the US premiere of Samuel Beckett's *Waiting for Godot*, the married protagonists, Tobias and Agnes, are having a quiet evening at home when their friends Edna and Harry arrive unexpectedly and announce that they need to stay with Tobias and Agnes because they were home alone and they "were scared... It was like being lost: very young again, with the dark, and lost. There was no... thing... to be... frightened of, but... WE WERE FRIGHTENED... AND THERE WAS NOTHING" (Albee 1966: 46-48; ellipses and emphasis in original, JJ). Into what had, prior to this entrance, been a rather normal domestic drama was inserted an absurd element: two friends, demanding to stay in the house, afraid of "nothing." This is a different type of hybridity than what was seen in *The glass menagerie* or *Death of a salesman*. In those plays, the expressionist aspects could be explained away as the protagonists' memories, but in *A delicate balance* the absurd, almost Beckett-like despair over "nothing" invades the typical US realist form. In the end, however, it is not magical. Nothing disturbs the "empirical universe" of the play's living-room setting. But in the progression from the journalistic realism of the Provincetown Players to the US magic realism that begins in the 1990s, Albee's plays stand out as an important moment when on-stage modes collided head-on.

Each of these plays and playwrights provided new and innovative hybrid forms, but they did not explode the empirical universe. Also, critically, they created their hybrid forms concentrating on text rather than focusing on the subversive potential of theatre's visual aspects. None of them explored the visual components of the stage that would truly allow magic realism to flourish on the stage. Thus, while these playwrights contributed mightily to the hybrid forms that flowed towards the popularization of magic realism on the US stage, it was in the early 1990s that the material embodiment of magic alongside a mundane realism occurred onstage. And, beside these experiments in hybridity and the more recent excursions into magic realism is a simultaneous tradition of strict realism in which an actual pie must be produced by the end of the play if a pie is baked in the plot. This shows the ways in which popular plays in the US have a schizoid quality of style, with no one mode which one could call distinctly "American," and how US magic realism developed out of US realism and twentieth-century playwrights' experiments with hybrid forms.

Between 1990 and 2010, the Pulitzer judges split the prizes almost equally between realism dramas such as Tracy Lett's *August: Osage County* and John Patrick Shanley's *Doubt* and magic realism scripts like Tony Kushner's *Angels in America*, August Wilson's *The piano lesson*, and Paula Vogel's *How I learned to drive*. Accepting the Pulitzer Prize as a mark of prominence and mainstream acumen endows these three magic realism plays as notable case studies of US drama; examining these playwrights, all of whom occupy marginal subject positions within the US, demonstrates that their use of magical realism allows them to make emergent ideologies into stage pictures by breaking realism's strictures. These stage pictures are utilized "for examining the formation and deployment of the narrative of the nation and revising it" (Rzepa 2009: 23).

Though there are examples that pre-date *Angels in America*, Tony Kushner's 1993 magic realism "Gay fantasia on national themes" is surely the most well-known, and its immediate success with audiences, prize committees, and critics marks a turning point for magic realism's US viability. Writing of the Broadway premiere, one New York newspaper critic gushes: "For some time, possibly a lifetime, I have been searching in vain for the new American drama of imaginative ideas, a form of magic realism transcending the bourgeois or the naturalism of movies. *Angels in America* is that landmark drama. It is, on the one hand, painfully concrete; on the other hand, it delights in the theater of magic images (Heilpern 1993: 26). Notice that the reviewer describes the formalism of *Angels in America* as a hybrid of the "concrete" and "magic images." The use of non-realistic images, while painting a clear ideological argument, do so by necessarily utilizing magic realism as a "mode [which] provides a space for voicing marginalized perspectives" (Rzepa 2009: 11). This is the goal of all US magic realism onstage. It is as if the painful aspects of the play's topic overflow the boundaries realism sets in drama, and in so doing creates sculptural images and self-conscious uses of theatricality that concretize the play's ideology.

The plot of *Angels in America* is long, convoluted, and well-known, but, briefly, it follows two couples and the dissolution of their romantic relationships in 1985 New York City. Prior and Louis, a homosexual male couple, live together. Their relationship falters under the strain of Prior's illness with AIDS. Meanwhile, Joe and Harper, a heterosexual Mormon couple, endure an unhappy marriage. Their relationship finally disintegrates because of Joe's closeted homosexuality. One day, Joe and Louis meet, and over time, they begin a romantic relationship. This relationship ends, however, when Louis discovers that Joe is mentored by the ultra-conservative Roy Cohn, whose own struggle with HIV is a major part of the play. Prior, in the meantime, begins either to hallucinate or to see angels. As part of this experience, he is eventually led to heaven where angels tell him that God has left and that humanity's "movement" (which is not exactly defined) is destroying heaven. In a few of Prior's hallucinations, he meets a drugged Harper, and, in their altered states, they reveal secrets to each other, which causes Harper to confront Joe about his sexuality. Because of this confrontation, Harper leaves Joe, and the audience last sees her on an airplane heading west and waxing poetic about angels and ozone. Prior refuses to be the angels' prophet of stasis and instead asks for more life, which he is granted. He survives with the AIDS virus past 1990 when the epilogue is set. In this epilogue, a ragtag group of friends is seen arguing politics: Prior and Louis (who are now platonic friends), Belize (an African American drag queen), and Joe's Mormon mother, Hannah. Prior speaks directly to the audience, declaring, "We will be citizens" and blesses them with the phrase "More life." He ends with the benediction, "The Great Work Begins" (Kushner 1993: 146). Considering all these characters were in some way outside the dominant ideology of the US when the play premiered—gay, black, female, and Mormon—the final declaration that they "will be citizens" defiantly revises the concept of nation and challenges the dominant ideology conveyed by more realistic US drama.

Though there is ambiguity about whether Prior hallucinates or receives visitations from an angel and ghosts, and that ambiguity is intentional, spectators are forced to recognize that magic disrupts this play's empirical universe through a number of incidents. One involves the impossible meeting of Prior and Harper, the wife of the man for whom his lover left and its depiction through a magic, visual moment. The meeting is impossible because both are hallucinating. Throughout the play there have been dual scenes onstage, like a split screen film, so spectators have seen Prior and Harper onstage simultaneously, but always with the convention that they cannot see one another. During a moment when Prior and Harper are both hallucinating due to drugs, Kushner allows them to notice one another, breaking the visual rules he's established and disrupting the empirical universe. The interruption of visual rules is a painterly moment, one in which the visual elements of the theatre are harnessed in order to create a magical picture of two characters who have never met having a conversation. In this moment, each character gives the other a "revelation": Harper tells Prior he will survive his illness, and Prior tells Harper that her husband is gay. These revelations will eventually lead to each character's freedom. Harper is able to leave her husband, and Prior is able to use this faith to demand health and a place in US society. Given that magic realism originates in visual art criticism, it makes sense that Kushner would deploy a visual trope in order to create a magic moment that ultimately allows his characters' freedom. This moment also utilizes the type of "memory" defined by Edward Casey when he writes, "remembering can be said to be gong on *between* the embodied human rememberer and the place he or she is *in* as well as *with* the others he or she is in the presence *of*" (Casey 2000: 312, Casey's emphasis, JJ). The picture Kushner paints onstage is literally of two characters remembering hidden facts about the other's life that they could not possibly know; this type of metanarrative embodied onstage visually overflows realism's possibilities and identifies the pain hidden in each of these characters' lives.

A second scene which upends the reading that Prior's angels are mere hallucinations comes when Hannah, the conservative mother of the man for whom Prior's lover left him, sits with Prior in the hospital and tells him: "An angel is just a belief, with wings and arms that can carry you. It's naught to be afraid of. If it lets you down, reject it. Seek for something new" (Kushner 1993: 103). This may be, but then a stage direction reads: "There is the sound of a silvery trumpet in the dark, and a tattoo of faraway drums. Silence. Thunder. Then all over the walls, Hebrew letters appear, writhing in flames. The scene is lit by their light. The Angel is there, suddenly. She is dressed in black and looks terrifying. Hannah screams and buries her face in her hands" (Kushner 1993: 115). Notice that this visitation is first described purely in visual terms, in a stage direction. The magic of the moment is, again, painterly, before any dialogue, and it is the very visual, very tactile presence of the Angel that Hannah cannot deny. She says,

> Hannah (trying to shut it all out): I don't, I don't, this is a dream it's a dream it's a...
> Prior: I don't think that's really the point right at this particular moment.
> Hannah: I don't know what to...
> Prior (overlap): Well it was your idea, reject the vision you said and...
> Hannah (overlap): Yes but I thought it was more a... metaphorical... I...
> Prior (overlap): You said scriptural precedent, you said... WHAT AM I SUPPOSED TO...
> Hannah (overlap): You... you... wrestle her.
> Prior: SAY *WHAT*?
> Hannah: It's an angel, you... just... grab hold and say... oh what was it, wait, wait, umm... OH! Grab her, say "I will not let thee go except thou bless me!" Then wrestle with her till she gives in.
> Prior: YOU wrestle her, I don't know how to wrestle, I...
> (The Angel flies up into the air and lands right in front of Prior. Prior grabs her—she emits a terrible, impossibly loud, shuddering eagle-screech. Prior and the Angel wrestle)
>   (Kushner 1993: 116).

Just as Hannah cannot deny the physical presence of the Angel, the audience can no longer believe that the Angel is merely Prior's hallucination since Hannah, too, can see her. This is not proven simply with dialogue, but more dramatically through visuals—the Angel's entrance, her flight and landing in front of Prior, and the wrestling match between them. Prior successfully overcomes the Angel and demands "more life." Hannah, based on this vision, is forced to reject her previous beliefs and incorporate this new Angel who visits a gay man and calls him a prophet. Once again, two characters are transformed during a shared vision that is not possible if one believes Prior is simply hallucinating creating a magical moment onstage that shatters the post-Enlightenment view of the universe.

But to what end is magic realism utilized in *Angels in America*? In a moving epilogue delivered directly to the audience by Prior, he paraphrases Hannah's words that beliefs can be changed; he insists that he and the other gay men of the play "will be citizens". Kushner, a gay man himself, employs magic realism to visually represent his outsider status and the emergent ideology of gay civil rights in the US. In Wendy B. Faris' words, readers, or spectators, of magical realism "may experience some unsettling doubts in the effort to reconcile two contradictory understandings of events" (Faris 2004: 7). Throughout *Angels in America*, and particularly in the scenes discussed here, self-reflexive visuals alongside its text utilize the tools of magical realism to create two contradictory modes: the first, a realist telling of the history of AIDS and gay civil rights in the US during the 1980s. The second, a magical, quasi-religious depiction of the same events. The two, combined, create a new narrative of the decade demanding a revision of who is included in the US nation, using the subversive potential of magical realism.

Whereas *Angels in America* posits a revolutionary concept of gay men's position within the nation, August Wilson uses magic realism in *The piano lesson* to heal a divided African American family. Wilson's characters stand in for the African American community, and his use of magical realism challenges the popular assimilationist ideology held by many US citizens and suggests that African Americans must heal themselves by acknowledging their history and roots. *The piano lesson* won the Pulitzer Prize in 1990 and its magical elements allow a depiction of memory which, as Rzepa suggests, "in magical realism is... often used as a tool that allows for the recovery of the hidden 'text' of pre-colonial past and mythology and validate it in the contemporary context" (Rzepa 2009: 22). The traumatic communal memory of an African American family in this play is pre-Emancipation, and their slave-era past, through Wilson's use of magic realist tools, is reassessed, revitalized, and, ultimately, reconciled in the character's contemporaneous moment. It also speaks to the 1990 debate within the US African American community between assimilation and multiculturalism.

The piano lesson is set in 1936 Pittsburgh and mainly follows the conflict between the Charles siblings, Boy Willie and Berniece. Boy Willie unexpectedly arrives from the South and parks a truck of watermelons in front of Berniece's house. He informs her that Sutter, the grandson of the man who owned the Charles's ancestors as slaves, fell in a well and died. Boy Willie hopes to sell the watermelons in order to return south and buy the land his family was once forced to work. But, easier than selling watermelons, would be selling the family heirloom piano which is ornately carved with African masks and scenes of the Charles family history. Over the course of the play, the piano's complicated story comes out: in slavery times, Sutter's grandfather wanted to give his wife a piano for a present but could not afford one. Instead, he traded two slaves for the piano. The slaves were the grandfather of Boy Willie and Berniece and their father as a boy. At first, the wife is very happy with the piano, but she comes to miss her slaves. So Sutter's grandfather hires the grandfather of Boy Willie and Berniece to come carve their faces in the piano and to keep his wife company. But the slave does far more than that. He carves the entire family history onto the piano, including their time in Africa before the Middle Passage when their ancestors were captured and forced to come to the US After slavery ends, the Sutters still have the piano and the now-adult father of Boy Willie and Berniece obsesses over it, stating that as long as the Sutter family owns the piano, they are not entirely free. The father of Boy Willie and Berniece successfully steals the piano, but Sutter and a gang of white men burn him alive along with some other black men in a boxcar as he tries to escape. Boy Willie and Berniece's mother polishes the piano endlessly and forces Berniece to learn to play it, and, when Berniece moves north to Pittsburgh, she brings the piano with her. Berniece refuses to let Boy Willie sell the piano because of this history, but neither will she play it. To do so, she says, would bring up bad memories, perhaps even evil ghosts. Willie could care less about the family history and would even sell it to a white man who collects African art.

The play is also populated with a host of African Americans representing many aspects of the community during the Great Depression, but the magic of the play inserts itself as the unseen ghost of Sutter who first appears upstairs to Berniece's young child. Over the course of the play, the ghost appears more and more, though never to the audience, and Berniece questions whether Boy Willie killed Sutter by pushing him in a well. Boy Willie denies this, stating that the ghosts of those Sutter's grandfather burned alive in the boxcar killed Sutter. The ghost continues its visitations, until, in a climactic scene the ghost throws the house into disarray: the piano plays by itself, pictures fly from the walls, and lights turn on and off. Again, as in *Angels in America*, the magic that disrupts the empirical universe here is visual and aural; it is not in language, but in pictures and sounds onstage. The local Christian priest attempts an exorcism, but his efforts are useless. Boy Willie rushes upstairs to fight with the ghost, and spectators view him grappling with an invisible foe and losing the battle until Berniece sits at the piano and plays, calling on the spirits of her ancestors. The sound of a train approaching floods the theatre and Sutter's ghost is defeated. Boy Willie, now in a rush to leave the house and understanding the importance of the piano, yells that if Berniece and her daughter "don't keep playing on that piano ain't no telling; me and Sutter both liable to be back" (Wilson 2007: 107). After Boy Willie leaves, Berniece, still sitting at the piano, whispers, "Thank you" and the play ends (Wilson 2007: 107).

The pain of this family's traumatic past overflows realism's bounds in the form of a ghost, African song, and the sound of a phantom train. While that may not sound as abstract or painterly as much contemporary mainstream European theatre, one must remember that in the US realism eschews abstraction to the point where a pie must be baked onstage. In *The piano lesson*, spectators experience the haunting of this upwardly-mobile African American family by their past slavery not in the plot or dialogue, but in visual and auditory signs of Sutter's ghost. The African heritage of these characters is not simply a mark on their skin, but carved ornately on a magical piano which dominates the set. Finally, we see the failure of Christian spirituality for these characters; what is necessary to drive away the white man's ghost is for Berniece to play her own music, to call on her own mystical strength, which is represented as a song her mother taught her and the sound of a train in which black people were burned alive. This finally drives away the white owner that still haunts them. August

Wilson uses magic realism to suggest that, no matter how far from their African and slave histories, African Americans must reconcile these aspect with their present situation in the United States. This play suggests that the only way to represent this spiritual struggle is by breaking the bounds of realism set by a white tradition. In other words, buying the land on which these African Americans were originally enslaved will not free these characters from their history, nor will the European tradition of Christianity. Only when these African American characters accept the veracity of Sutter's ghost—in other words, understand the fact that their history literally lives and haunts them—and embark on physical combat with him employing the songs of their African Ancestors can they move forward. This is the "hidden 'text,'" as Rzepa calls it, that Wilson reveals through magic invading a realist piece of theatre "as a tool allowing for the reestablishment of severed community links, a renewal of community" and which creates the "possibility of both retribution and reconciliation" for these African American characters (Rzepa 2009: 22-23).

How I learned to drive, by Paula Vogel, wins the Pulitzer Prize in 1998 and explores a hidden memory of a more personal kind: childhood sexual abuse. It does so using a number of magic realist techniques, including a self-reflexive narrator who speaks directly to the audience, a structure based on non-chronological memory fragments, three actors who function as a chorus, and, finally, a ghost.

Though not told in chronological order, the plot is relatively simple. In rural Maryland in the 1960s and 70s, Li'l Bit, nicknamed by her inappropriate family for the nub between her legs at birth, is molested by her Uncle Peck, who is also nicknamed for what is between his legs. This incestuous relationship begins when Li'l Bit is cloven and ends when she is eighteen and in her first year of college. The first of her family to attend higher education, her Uncle Peck's emotional support through adolescence is largely the force that allows her to break free from her rural upbringing and reach higher education. However, she is kicked out of college for drinking, and Uncle Peck drinks himself to death. Li'l Bit's father is gone for unknown reasons, and actors who also play the chorus who enter chanting platitudes from driver's manuals play her Grandfather, Mother, and Uncle Peck's wife. The chorus, too, plays a significant part in the play's climactic scene, which happens near the end of the script but is the earliest presented memory of Li'l Bit. The importance of this lack of chronology in narration cannot be overstated.

The play begins with a monologue from Li'l Bit as an adult in an ambiguous present; she asserts, "Sometimes to tell a secret, you first have to teach a lesson" (Vogel 1997: 9). The secret and the lesson are revealed in fragments of memory that refuse linearity, teleology, or even reverse chronology. After the initial monologue the script jumps forward and backward, from year to year between 1962 and 1979, before returning to a final monologue. The play's lack of linearity refuses the possibility that Li'l Bit is simply a victim of trauma. The play does not shrink from her wounds, but it avoids a typical realism structure that would define a character based on earlier events. In other words, victimhood is not the defining mark of Li'l Bit's life.

Negotiating this ambiguous chronology creates a self-reflexive view of Li'l Bit's memories and allows a more complex view of the "secret" and "lesson" she promises in her opening monologue. Since self-reflexivity in a text is a hallmark of magic realism (Rzepa 2009: 16), the play's mode is clear from its first moments. The play begins with Li'l Bit telling the audience, "It's 1969 and I am very old, very cynical of the world, and I know it all. In short, I am seventeen years old, parking off a dark lane with a married man on an early summer night" (Vogel 1997: 9). The actor then enters a relatively realistic scene, but always subverted by the self-reflexive frame provided by the opening monologue. At the end of the first scene, the audience learns that the married man with whom Li'l Bit has her affair is her Uncle Peck. Therefore the secret of the play is not incest; the incest is revealed before anything else. There is, however, a mystery that will be revealed by the end of the play, not surprisingly given that "memory in magic realism is then often used as a tool that allows for the recovery of the hidden 'text'" (Rzepa 2009: 22).

Midway through the play there is a clue to the real enigma. In a scene set in 1968, during a celebration of Li'l Bit's new driver's license, her drunken family behaves completely inappropriately. Her grandfather comments on her large breasts, her mother tells her how to drink appropriately around boys to keep them from raping her since, in her mother's view, that is ultimately the goal of all boys, and the presence of Uncle Peck and his wife are unsettling simply due to the audience's knowledge of the incest. In comparison with her family's dinner behavior, however, Uncle Peck is downright charming and supportive. He saw some of the world during his army stint in Vietnam, and he and Li'l Bit are both outsiders in the family, slightly more sensitive, more intellectual, and more ambitious. Though Uncle Peck never escapes his rural surroundings, he encourages Li'l Bit to do so, and, it seems, she ultimately does. The secret, then, that begins its slow reveal in this scene is that, though predatory, and damaging, their relationship may also contain aspects Li'l Bit values.

Furthering this reading, the play then jumps to 1979 and Li'l Bit, as a twenty-seven year old, relates in a monologue directly to the audience the experience of picking up a high school senior and being his first sexual partner. She addresses the spirit of her then-dead Uncle Peck relating the allure of being the teacher, the one in control. This suggests that the secret is not incest, but her own active desire mixed with the abuse, hatred, and identification with Peck. In the play's penultimate scene, Uncle Peck visits Li'l Bit in college on her eighteenth birthday hoping for sex. She has been struggling with the relationship, and the audience expects her to throw him out in anger, but she does not. Instead, she gives in to his suggestion that they lie down together, clothes on, and hold each other, regardless of their familial relations, because, as he says, "Sometimes the body knows things the mind doesn't" (Vogel 1997: 52). Her agreement implies that some part of her at least is curious to see what will happen lying down with her uncle, if not actually desiring to do so. After lying in bed together, she moves so their faces are inches apart, as if about to kiss, but then she sends him away. It is the last time they see each other. She drinks her way out of college; he drinks his way out of life. The secret is exposed here: not only were there aspects of her incestuous relationship that she valued but, in fact, there were moments in which she experienced desire for her abuser. The next scene, however, and its magic realism, undercuts any idea that this desire is healthy.

The subsequent scene jumps back in time to 1962 when Li'l Bit is 11 and receiving Uncle Peck's first driving lesson. In a scene that is truly uncomfortable to watch Uncle Peck takes the eleven-year-old Li'l Bit onto his lap in the car and molests her as a Chorus Member standing to the side of the stage says Li'l Bit's lines, such as "please don't," and ends with, "This isn't happening" (Vogel 1997: 57). The actor playing Li'l Bit then gets off Uncle Peck's lap and says to the audience, "That was the last day I lived in my body" (Vogel 1997: 57). By having two actors play Li'l Bit—that is, utilizing the visual aspects of theatre to create a painterly image—the spectators have literally seen Li'l Bit leave her body. Magic realism has made material the experience of abuse.

But, again, belying total victimhood, Li'l Bit gives the final monologue, back in the ambiguous present, saying the only time she feels free is when driving, an odd statement given the location of her trauma. And, in the play's most magical moment, she describes entering the car, checking the side mirrors as taught, and, as she adjusts the rearview mirror, she sees Peck's ghost sitting in the backseat—and so does the audience as the actor playing Peck enters and sits. He smiles and nods and her, and she smiles back. The stage direction reads that they are happy to be going for a long drive together. And the final thing Li'l Bit says is that she floors the gas pedal. Thus, by breaking chronological storytelling with a self-reflexive narrator and providing this literally haunting final image, the play is able to circumvent the all-too-familiar trauma/victim path of realist abuse narratives. Similarly, by utilizing two actors for Li'l Bit's climactic moment, and a ghost of Peck in the final monologue, Li'l Bit's pain overflows the boundaries of realism and the magic realism onstage more directly represents the character's experience.

These are but three examples of magic realism in US theatre, all of which pragmatically use the form when what is being expressed cannot be contained within the strictures of realism. Since the birth of "serious" US drama in 1915 by the Provincetown Players' use of the then avant garde European form realism, each subsequent generation of US playwrights has found their way utilizing modes of narrative as tools in a toolbox, any combination acceptable as long as the play is built securely. While some US playwrights—perhaps, even, the majority—follow realism's strictures, some of the most recognized US playwrights, particularly those in marginal subject positions, find that magical realism is a mode or a tool necessary to express their point of view. Magic realism, then, on the US stage in the late twentieth century expresses a challenge to the dominant ideology. Each of the three plays identified here—*Angels in America*, *The piano lesson*, and *How I learned to drive*—in its own way, challenges nation, ideology, and memory. And, while each is individual in its concerns and methods, they all utilize the visual, aural, and formal aspects of the stage to disrupt the empirical universe; the magic goes beyond the spoken text. Magic realism, though created by playwrights in marginal subject positions, holds a powerful place in US mainstream theatre, as the Pulitzer Committee recognizes approximately every other year, and US playwrights use its form to create concrete representations of emergent ideologies when realism simply will not do and pain overflows its boundaries.

References

Albee, Edward. 1966. *A delicate balance*. New York: Atheneum.
Casey, Edward. 2000. *Remembering: A phenomenological study*. Bloomington and Indianapolis: Indiana University Press.
Faris, Wendy B. 2004. *Ordinary enchantments: Magical realism and the remystification of narrative*. Nashville, Tennessee: Vanderbilt University Press.
Glaspell, Susan. 1927. *The road to the temple*. New York: Frederick A. Stokes.
Glaspell, Susan. 2001. "Trifles", in: Michael Greenwald – Roger Schultz – Roberto Pomo (eds.), 1056-1063.
Greenwald, Michael – Roger Schultz – Roberto Pomo (eds.). 2001. *The Longman anthology of drama and theater: A global perspective*. (Revised first edition.) New York: Pearson, 2001.
Heilpern, John. 1993. "Angels in America: Indeed, the millennium approaches", in: Peter W. Kaplan (ed.), 86-87.
Kaplan, Peter. W. (ed.). 2009. *The kingdom of New York. Knights, knaves, billionaires, and beauties in the city of big shots as seen by The New York Observer*. New York: HarperCollins.
Kushner, Tony. 1993. *Angels in America: A gay fantasia on national themes, part two: Perestroika*. New York: Theatre Communications Group.
Miller, Arthur. 2001. "Death of a salesman", in: Michael Greenwald – Roger Schultz – Roberto Pomo (eds.), 1159-1199.
Odets, Clifford. 1994. *Waiting for Lefty*. New York: Grove Press.
O'Neill, Eugene. 1954 [1914]. "Bound east for Cardiff", in: *The plays of Eugene O'Neill*. New York: Random House.

Rzepa, Agnieszka. 2009. *Feats and defeats of memory: Exploring spaces of Canadian magic realism.* Poznań: Wydawnictwo Naukowe UAM.

Tolan, Kathleen. 2005. *Memory house.* New York: Playscripts, Inc.

Vogel, Paula. 1997. *How I learned to drive.* New York: Dramatists Play Service.

Williams, Tennessee. 2001. "The glass menagerie", in: Michael Greenwald – Roger Schultz – Roberto Pomo (eds.), 1064-1091.

Wilson, August. 2007. *The piano lesson.* New York: Theatre Communications Group.

Pak's Britannica[1]: An Interview with David Dabydeen

Liliana Sikorska, Adam Mickiewicz University, Poznań / University of Social Sciences, Warsaw

David Dabydeen, a professor of literature, a literary critic, a novelist and a poet, for a number of years juggling his career as the Director of the Centre for Caribbean Studies at the University of Warwick (Coventry), United Kingdom. He was a member of UNESCO Executive Board, and Ambassador to UNESCO since 1997. His first collection of poems *Slave song* (1984) won the Commonwealth Poetry Prize and the Quiller-Couch Prize. *Coolie Odyssey* was published in 1988. The volume entitled *Turner: New and selected poems*, was published in 1994, and reissued in 2002, was inspired by the painting by J.W.M. Turner "Slavers throwing overboard the dead and the dying" (1840). His novels such as *The intended* (1991), *Disappearance* (1993), *The counting house* (1996), *A harlot's progress* (1999), *Our lady of Demerara* (2004) and *Molly and the Muslim stick* (2008) all show the (post/anti) postcolonial links between Britain, Guyana, India and Africa. His novel were awarded a number of prizes including 1991 Guyana Prize for Literature – *The intended*; *A harlot's progress* was shortlisted for 1999 James Tait Black Memorial Prize; in 2004, the Raja Rao Award for Literature (India) Dabydeen has been awarded the title of fellow of the Royal Society of Literature. He is the third West Indian writer (V.S. Naipaul was the first) and, until 2007, the only Guyanese writer to receive the title. His critical works include *Hogarth's Blacks: Images of Blacks in 18th-century English art* (1987), and *Pak's Britannica* (2011). Dabydeen edited and co-edited a number of critical works such as *The Oxford companion to Black British History* (2007) with John Gilmore and Cecily Jones. Among his most notable edited works are *The Black presence in English literature* (1985), *A reader's guide to West Indian and Black British literature* (1987, with Nana Wilson-Tagoe), *India in the Caribbean* (1987, with Brinsley Samaroo), *Black writers in Britain 1760-1890* (1991, with Paul Edwards), and *Across the dark waters: Ethnicity and Indian identity in the Caribbean* (1996). In 2001 Dabydeen wrote and presented *The forgotten colony*, a BBC *Radio 4* programme exploring the history of Guyana. His one-hour documentary *Painting the people* was broadcast by BBC television in 2004. In 2010 David Dabydeen was a guest of honour of Literature in English Symposium organized by the School of English, Adam Mickiewicz University, Poznań, Poland. The same year he accepted the position of the Guyanese Ambassador to China.

Liliana Sikorska: A politician turned writer is quite a common sight, but a writer turning into a politician is an interesting development of one's career. What made you decide to leave the university and become a diplomat?

David Dabydeen: All writing is political in some sense. I am not a Party Politics person, but I have overwhelming respect and reverence for Cheddi and Janet Jagan, leaders of the People's Progressive Party in Guyana. They were both Presidents of Guyana, and close friends. The Jagans lived a modest, even frugal, lifestyle, and were completely committed to the goal

---

1   The title is borrowed from a book of David Dabydeen's articles and interview edited by Lynne Macedo (Jamaica, Barbados, Trinidad and Tobago: University of the West Indies Press, 2011).

of poverty alleviation. They were also incorruptible. Cheddi Jagan, attacking the luxuries of the elite, once declared that "you cannot have a Cadillac lifestyle in a donkey-cart economy". When he died in 1997 it was my privilege to address the UNESCO Executive Board, and I quoted him on cadillacs and donkey carts, and stated that he was one of the few leaders of the developing world who never stole from the national treasury (the Ambassadors of Nigeria and other developing countries, sitting around the UNESCO table, squirmed at that!). I am almost completely opposite the Jagans, in terms of a lewd and lavish lifestyle (of late, anyway), but I try to fulfil their response to poor people. My being in China would have pleased them, since they were admirers of Chinese Communism. I have a different outlook: the colossal efforts made by the Communist Party to lift hundreds of millions of people out of poverty, deserves universal praise, but there needs to be some 'truth and reconciliation' process to acknowledge the inhumane bloodshed and starvation in the past. All jailed dissidents should also be released: China is a mature and powerful enough nation to allow for dissident voices. Having said that, China is on the road to reform and renewal, and it's an exciting place to be if you want to witness the promise of the future. As to why I left academia, it's simply because I spent 26 years teaching at Warwick, and ten years before that in university environments. Also, theory and ideology was taking over literary studies. A literary text was put under the scrutiny of race, class and gender issues. A necessary corrective to earlier literary criticism, but appreciation of the beauty of language and other aesthetic aspects were being neglected. So, a badly written novel, if it said the 'right' things about race, class and gender, was being placed on reading lists instead of being tossed to the recycling bin.

LS: How is China? How different/strange is it? Any interesting stories?

DD: China is impossible to understand deeply unless you master the language, which I have not, so China remains an enigma. So many things get lost in translation that it becomes a bewildering and frustrating experience being here. The architecture, traditional and modern, is spectacular, and some of the parks too. What really moves me is the kindness and helpfulness of people. People will go out of their way to help you as a foreigner, if you are lost on the streets for instance. I find people courteous and exemplary in their good behaviour (unlike parts of Coventry…). I've been stuck in the office so I've not yet had a chance of discovering peculiar and memorable incidents. India was different, something bizarre, picturesque, carnivalesque happening every day, with the rush and tumult of people. China is more 'mannered'. Some compare China to Germany in this respect, and India to Spain.

LS: The stories about travelling are part of our peripatetic existence as scholars, what is it in case of an itinerant writer?

DD: Travel is crucial to uplift the spirit and be dazed by newness, but you can write anywhere, really. I found a café in Cochin, in the south of India, where I can smoke and drink coffee and look out unto the street. Some days I see a bevy of nuns eating ice-cream followed by procession of auto-rickshaws, each waving a Communist flag, with a lorry's speakers blaring out propaganda, followed by some wayward goats ,followed by a Hindu holy man with dyes on his forehead and ankle bracelets and an elaborately carved staff. What are the connections? Probably nothing, probably quantum.

LS: Writing as much as reading is said to open out horizons. Has your literary/academic career prepared you for the encounters with China?

DD: Although my great aunt is Guyanese Chinese, and my cousins and my sister-in-law, China is a completely novel experience for me, and I came deliberately unprepared. The Guyanese Chinese are wholly creolized and would be as perplexed by China as I am. The longer I stay in China the more I come to appreciate how gracious and kindly the Chinese Guyanese are, and how much they have achieved. The first Chinese arrived in 1853 as indentured labourers in the sugar plantations. Within a generation, some of them bought over sugar plantations! A man called Ho Shau arrived in Guyana in 1874, aged 20 or 21, as a worker. Ten years later he had saved up enough money to send his daughter to study at Cambridge and Edinburgh universities. Both she and her sister (also an Edinburgh University student) became medical doctors. His story is not unusual. A woman called Martha Fung Kee Fung (the Chinese converted to Christianity, to better integrate into colonial life, and took on Biblical names but kept their family names), from very modest beginnings, ended up owning a grocery, cake shop, liquor shop, a rice mill and two sugar estates. The first President of Guyana, 1970-1980, was a Chinese Guyanese, Arthur Chung, a distinguished Judge. So from field labourer to President...astonishing courage and resilience on the part of the Guyanese Chinese. Having said that, as a boy in Guyana, I hated Dr Fung-a-Fat, the only dentist in New Amsterdam. He'd slap you if you wriggled in the dentist's chair or expressed pain. His hand trembled from the after-effects of alcohol, so the needle to numb your gums was inserted in the wrong part of your mouth. His surgery had phlegm and blood everywhere, and there was nowhere to spit after he had butchered you except in a gutter outside. He was murdered a few years back by some black men dressed in Rasta wigs, a victim of a robbery. Shamefully, I felt no pity for him. I do now, now that I am in China.

LS: How is your family adapting to the new home? Did you take your cat with you?

DD: My son, aged 5, and my daughter, aged two are Mandarin speakers. They love Chinese food, Chinese costumes, Chinese everything. My wife too, except for the foul air: the skies are seriously polluted, you can get a 'high' just by breathing in deeply... Clare Short, our cat, was left behind, but in luxury: she has a full-time carer and the run of the house. The Embassy has many stray cats in the yard, they'd kill her in an instant.

LS: When you were in Poznań, you promised us the new (more "laid-back", Caribbean) version of Joseph Conrad's *The secret agent*, are you working on the novel? Or rather do you have time to work on the novel with all your new duties?

DD: I've just finished a novel which I will call A GALLERY OF MADONNAS. It'll be published in England next year. Then I plan to start on the Conrad idea. The trouble is, as always, finding time. I just have to, and plan to leave China this year, once I've helped set up a Confucius Institute at the University of Guyana.

LS: Maybe China would deserve a new volume of poems?

DD: I really would like to write another book of poems, and have made a start. I'd like to spend all the time I have left writing poetry, because it's so difficult and only a few friends read it, i.e. nothing sensational or commercial about the craft of poetry, no hype, no status...just the writing for its own sake, and the beauty of the difficulty of it. I read poets like Graham Mort and John Burnside, and their work is full of marvel.

LS: The present volume of essays is concerned with magic realism. Do you perceive the (new) reality around you as marvellous, magical or entirely mundane?

DD: Everything is carnivalesque and unreal, or as Wilson Harris would say, 'quantum'. The warmest moments I have, when I hug the children or they smother me with kisses, are also the coldest and bleakest, because one day I'll never see them again. A sense of absence is always with me, even when I am full of bounty. So there's marvel there, and magic, and the mundane, all one, all none.

Studies in Literature in English

Edited by Liliana Sikorska

www.peterlang.de

Liliana Sikorska (ed.)

Empty treasure chests dumped from departed ships

Re-Mapping (Post)Colonialism in Art and Literature in English

Frankfurt am Main, Berlin, Bern, Bruxelles, New York, Oxford, Wien, 2011.
110 pp., 1 graph
Studies in Literature in English. Edited by Liliana Sikorska. Vol. 3
ISBN 978-3-631-63555-1 · hb. € 22,80*

Empty treasure chests dumped from departed ships is a quotation taken from David Dabydeen's poem *The Old Map* in which the hope of a new world is green but green symbolizes also the gangrene of the sailors. Such rather unsavory paradoxes can be found in the works of contemporary (post)postcolonial writers, who engage in a dialogue with literary history while actively re-shaping contemporary culture. Far from seeking easy reconciliations, the contemporary (post) postcolonial writers rewrite the colonial experiences in relation to art and literary works. The theme of this volume are the works by and about David Dabydeen, a Guianese British writer, poet and literary scholar, whose efforts have always been directed toward re-creating the lives forever lost; those of nameless slaves and coolies of the West Indies. His inspiration, in turn were, among others, the paintings of William Hogarth and Joseph Mallord William Turner. Accordingly, the papers collected in this book address the question of (post)colonialism in a contemporary (post)postcolonial reality.

*The e-price includes German tax rate. Prices are subject to change without notice

Frankfurt am Main · Berlin · Bern · Bruxelles · New York · Oxford · Wien
Distribution: Verlag Peter Lang AG
Moosstr. 1, CH-2542 Pieterlen
Telefax 00 41 (0) 32 / 376 17 27
E-Mail info@peterlang.com

40 Years of Academic Publishing
Homepage http://www.peterlang.com

Peter Lang · Internationaler Verlag der Wissenschaften